1536 Free Waters and Other Blackjack Endeavors

Finding Profit and Humor in Card-Counting

1536 Free Waters and Other Blackjack Endeavors

Finding Profit and Humor in Card-Counting

Stories and Graphics by
Glen Wiggy

Illustrations by Leif Olson

iUniverse, Inc.
Bloomington

1536 Free Waters and Other Blackjack Endeavors
Finding Profit and Humor in Card-Counting

Copyright © 2012 Glen Wiggy

iUniverse books may be ordered through booksellers or by contacting:

iUniverse
1663 Liberty Drive
Bloomington, IN 47403
www.iuniverse.com
1-800-Authors (1-800-288-4677)

ISBN: 978-1-4759-4564-5 (sc)
ISBN: 978-1-4759-4566-9 (hc)
ISBN: 978-1-4759-4565-2 (e)

Library of Congress Control Number: 2012915870

Printed in the United States of America

iUniverse rev. date: 08/28/2012

ACKNOWLEDGEMENTS

To my wife, Lori, my inspiration for everything that is important: life, love, and family. We have fun, don't we?

To my children, Sarah and Mitchell, you are smarter, funnier, and better looking than me—if that's possible.

To my grandchildren, Hayden, Harper, and Jack, plus any others I am blessed with in the future, one day you will learn blackjack.

To my harshest critic, my dog, Newman, one day you will die, and then a month later, I'll get a new dog.

To my loving mother in heaven, the definitive source of my sense of humor, thanks for my life.

To my father, my inspiration for all things golf and gambling, the contents of this book would fit on a matchbook without you.

And to George Carlin, my comedy idol, who died the same week that I finished my book. I had planned to ask him for an endorsement. I like to think that George would've written, "Buy this book, or don't buy it. Who gives a shit?"

CONTENTS

PREFACE

This book is unlike every other blackjack book on the market. To prove it, take a look at the cover. The vast majority of blackjack books feature the same two cards on the front, an ace and a face card. This, of course, is a "blackjack," also known as a natural, a total of twenty-one. However, you are mathematically more likely to be dealt a two-card hand of twelve when playing the game. No blackjack author in their right mind would put a hand of twelve on the cover. I did. You know why? Because I'm not in my right mind. I'm sure you'll reach that same conclusion after reading a few chapters.

Typical blackjack strategy books are serious and boring; I don't know why. Going to the casino is fun and exciting. Bright lights, loud noises, free food, door prizes, unlimited alcohol—what a concept. While playing blackjack in a casino, you'll witness some of the most interesting people in the world: millionaires, elderly couples, truck-driver college graduates, Japanese businessmen, soldiers, reality TV aficionados, dog owners, surfers, fat guys who are good at racquetball, the nearsighted, newlyweds, vegetarians, hillbillies, movie stars, telephone call center operators from New Delhi, pro bowlers, chain-smokers, worthless co-workers who say, "I can't do anything in the morning until I get my caffeine fix," farmers, weight-watchers, stevedores, tourists, hot dog vendors, people who still like Family Circus, Mark and Brian radio listeners, hookers, Democrats, college students who watch Comedy Central all night instead of studying, jelly-bean addicts, Chris Bloomer, plumbers, fantasy baseball team owners, feminists, dentists, bikers who defend their vehicle choice by saying "I love the freedom of the open road" when in fact all they really mean is, "When I bought a motorcycle, I didn't have enough money for a car," Buddhists, Avon ladies, bloggers, tweeters, loggers, twits, Los Angeles Clippers fans, Rush Limbaugh lovers, ombudsmen, ombudswomen, my Aunt Wilma before she died at bingo, MENSA members, movie directors, horticulturalists, talk-show hosts with a three-person panel of experts, dudes, prudes, broods, Apple Store geniuses, and just plain ugly people. These folks put their differences aside as they sit next to each other at a table with one goal in common: beating the dealer. Sometimes they'll give each other a high-five. Other times, they'll curse one another. When such a diverse group gets together in pursuit of fun and fortune, stories abound. I've documented some of those dramas and comedies for your reading pleasure. I wanted to call the book, *Chicken Soup for the Blackjack Gambler's Soul*, but my teenage son, Mitchell, told me that I might be sued for title infringement. Apparently, someone else has the copyright to that naming scheme. Plus, only a handful of my stories are uplifting or filled with positive life messages. No chicken soup here. Instead, I titled the book, *1536 Free Waters and Other Blackjack Endeavors*.

If you were looking for a more traditional blackjack strategy guide with an emphasis on introductory card-counting strategy, I'll give you that too. My foray into serious blackjack gambling started because I wanted to see if the card-counting advantage was a mathematical myth. It is not. I have the background and experience to support my assertion. I was a Scientific Analyst in the United States Air Force and an associate college professor of probability and statistics at the Air Force Academy. I recorded an enormous amount of empirical data while counting cards at blackjack during more than eight-hundred casino visits from January 2001 until June 2008. My overall winnings during the seven-year experiment were modest, but relatively consistent and statistically noteworthy.

Unlike other strategy texts, I won't promise a way for you to "kill" the dealer or make a living playing blackjack. Instead, I'll give you enough probability and statistics, and enough confidence, to approach your blackjack endeavors with a positive attitude and reasonable expectation of winning. I'll also let you know, in a fun way, what to expect from the cards and the wonderfully strange people that you may encounter. Part how-to book, part memoir, *1536 Free Waters and Other Blackjack Endeavors* should put a smile on your face and casino chips in your pocket. Enjoy.

ILLICIT BLACKJACK TERMINOLOGY

Practically every blackjack strategy book begins with an introduction of the game, including a definition of terms used at the table and around the casino. You can't play the game correctly unless you learn the lingo. Otherwise, you'll stand out at the blackjack table like tourists walking into a lamppost on a New York City street because they were gawking at the tops of skyscrapers. Although knowledge of proper terminology is key to any endeavor, I was reluctant to start my book with a discussion of blackjack terms. I didn't want to offend numerous readers with all the references to drugs and sex. You're probably thinking, "Drugs and sex? What the hell is this guy talking about?"

Consider terms used in the illegal narcotics community. To set the scene, picture a dark trash-filled, back-alley in the slums of a major city. If you have never seen a dark trash-filled, back-alley in the slums of a major city, pretend you're viewing one of the numerous scenes from the following old and new television shows: *The Wire*, *NYPD Blue*, *Law & Order*, *24*, *CSI*, *The District*, *The Shield*, *The Practice*, *The Sopranos*, *Miami Vice*, *Hill Street Blues*, *Starsky & Hutch*, *Adam-12*, or *The Brady Bunch*. Imagine a seedy looking guy in a dirty, oversized trench coat suspiciously looking over his shoulder while muttering to an associate, "I desperately need a good hit. If I get it, I'll give the dealer a toke." This exact quote, albeit in a different context, could be overhead at any blackjack table in any casino. The phrase is loaded with terms used in the game:

> **dealer** = the casino employee who shuffles the cards, distributes the cards to the players, enforces the rules and procedures of the game, maintains the house bank (chips), and manages payouts for each hand.

toke = a tip given to a dealer or waiter/waitress for their services. A toke can be cash or a chip previously purchased in the casino. I suppose you could also write a check for a toke, but I've never seen that happen.

hit = an optional card selected by the player. The value of the card is added to the total of the player's existing hand. The dealer may also take a hit, but the action is involuntary. The dealer's play is dictated by established rules of the house. If you are in a casino or a shady gambling parlor where the dealer can take an optional hit, run for the nearest exit immediately.

Be careful not to confuse another drug reference, "pusher" with the blackjack term, "push":

push = a tie, the total of the player's hand matches the dealer's total. In regular casino blackjack games, the player does not lose on a push. In some special casino games, however, the house wins on a push. If you are in a casino or shady gambling parlor where the house wins on a push, run for the nearest exit immediately.

Now consider some of the potentially appalling blackjack terms used as sexual references or innuendos in other venues. For this mental exercise, you'll have to picture a scene from an adult movie or website. If that is not your cup of tea, pretend you're watching one of the many television shows currently on the FOX network. This time, I won't give you an exact quote that could be heard at a blackjack table. Children might be reading. Instead, I'll defer to you to examine the double entendres in each of the following blackjack terms: bust, stiff, penetration, hard, split, and "in the hole." For those of you with an especially perverted mind like mine, it isn't too far a stretch to associate filth with some more terms used around the casino: shoe (fetish), pit boss (a pimp), Pat (*Saturday Night Live*), the "eye in the sky" (voyeurism), queen (transvestite), "double-down" (twins), and six of diamonds. (Actually, I don't know an illegitimate meaning for this term, but I bet some pervert out there will make one up and dedicate an entire Internet website to it.)

Since I vowed to make this book educational, I suppose I should provide the true definitions of all the terms previously mentioned. Please keep your mind out of the gutter while learning:

bust = to exceed a total of twenty-one on a hand. When a player busts or is "busted," the player automatically loses. When a player stands (stays) on a total of twenty-one or less and the dealer busts, the player wins the hand.

stiff = the dealer's up card when a two, three, four, five, or six is showing. The dealer has a good chance of busting when a stiff card is displayed.

penetration = the depth that the dealer places the reshuffle (or cut) card in a newly shuffled and cut shoe. Card-counters hope for deep penetration, meaning the player sees more cards, and fewer cards return to the house for reshuffle.

hard = a hand containing an ace counting for eleven. When the ace counts as one, the hand is "**soft**." One quick rule to remember: never, ever, stand on a soft seventeen (an ace and six).

split = making two separate hands from an initially dealt pair. Another quick rule: always split eights and aces. Depending on the local table rules, a split pair may be re-split.

"in the hole" = the dealer's down card, as opposed to the up card. Theoretically, if a dealer were to stick his down card into his mouth, you could scream, "Get your hole card outta your hole!"

shoe = the mechanical contraption used by dealers in most casinos to distribute the cards in an organized manner. Shoes may contain one or as many as eight decks of playing cards.

pit boss = the supervisor of one or many dealers in the "pits," a group of table games.

pat = a hand that does not require a hit. A dealer's hand is usually pat when it totals seventeen, eighteen, nineteen, twenty, or twenty-one. The term "pat" is also used to describe a dealer's up card when a seven, eight, nine, face card, or ace is showing. The dealer has a good chance of making a hand without busting when a pat card is displayed.

"eye in the sky" = surveillance cameras above the tables and throughout the casino.

queen = one of the symbols/pictures on a playing card; a deck of cards also includes jacks and kings. If you aren't familiar with what a "queen" is in cards, you might want to consult a few more basic card playing books before reading this one.

double-down = doubling your bet in certain situations. The extra risk is offset by advantageous opportunities for winning on a good hand. Make sure you always know when and when not to double-down.

Not all the slang associated with blackjack gambling is potentially vile and corruptive. Baseball terminology is used to describe seating arrangements at a casino blackjack table:

first base = the seat/player at the table immediately to the left of the dealer; the first player to receive cards in a hand of blackjack.

third base = the seat/player at the table immediately to the right of the dealer; the last player to receive cards, not counting the dealer, in a hand of blackjack.

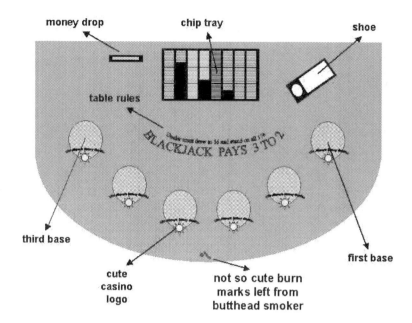

money drop   chip tray   shoe

table rules

BLACKJACK PAYS 3 TO 2

third base

first base

cute
casino
logo

not so cute burn
marks left from
butthead smoker

I've often wondered how these baseball terms found their way into the casino. I don't see the link between the card game and the sport. I've never seen anyone at Wrigley Field playing blackjack. I've also never seen anyone at Harrah's Casino playing baseball, but I bet that Pete Rose has been in a casino at some time or another. I understand that "first base" depicts the first player to be dealt cards, but "third base" doesn't necessarily depict the third player dealt. The player at third base might be the second, third, fourth, fifth, or sixth player to receive cards. In fact, the player sitting at third base could also be the first player. Would a single player at the table be considered sitting at first *and* third base? Derek Jeter isn't even good enough to play two positions at once.

Here is more confusion with the baseball-naming scheme. Runners in baseball proceed around the bases in a counter-clockwise manner. Blackjack dealers distribute the cards and conduct the game in a clockwise manner. Maybe the dealer should start with the player to his or her right. Then, the reference would match baseball. But if that were the case, the player to the dealer's right would be sitting at first base, and the player to the dealer's left would be sitting at third base. Again, if the player was alone, both first and third would be covered. I get the funny feeling that Abbott and Costello should be involved in this explanation.

For the sake of argument, let's accept the seating chart for first base and third base positions as originally defined. There are still more questions to ponder. Where is second base? Some gamblers and casino personnel will tell you that second base is the position directly across the table from the dealer. Oh yeah? Then where the hell is left field, behind the table near the slot machines? Or the third base coach? I don't see anyone giving me signs on what do next. Should there be a designated hitter? Maybe, but it would only be in American League casinos. If I get angry with the dealer and throw a chip at his head, would that be considered a "beanball"? Probably not, but I'm sure I would get ejected from the game.

One final thought: is it possible to combine the sexual innuendo present in casino blackjack terminology with the wholesome goodness of baseball? Certainly. Remember how hot and bothered you became trying to get to first or second base on a date? Did you blush? What about getting to third base? That was always a mystery for me, because my teenage friends and I could never agree on what "third base" was with a girl. If you want to get the third base at the blackjack table, just sit there; no mystery or blushing required.

THE IOU

My hometown is Midwest City, Oklahoma, population 55,000, give or take a few thousand Sooners. In recent years, the city has experienced significant tragedy. Even though the April 1995 bombing at the Murrah Federal Building occurred thirteen miles away in Oklahoma City, the sound of the blast was loud enough for my mom to think someone smashed a car into our garage. My sister's friend's brother was a victim in the blast. The gentleman who cuts my dad's hair lost a grandchild. Practically everyone in my hometown knew someone, or had a link to someone, who was involved in the bombing. If Timothy McVeigh's nearby idiotic work wasn't tragic enough, Midwest City has also been devastated by two major tornadoes since 1995 and a wildfire in 2009.

Things weren't as chaotic when I was growing up in the city. I was familiar with only one bombing, which involved our school's mascot. Midwest City High School's nickname was the "Bombers." From that information, you might easily infer that our town was near an Air Force base. Our mascot was a bomb-laden B-52 aircraft with eight black plumes of smoke streaming from the jet engines, indicating that death and destruction were imminent to any visiting football team. Coincidentally, my junior high school was nicknamed the "Thunderbirds," another military aircraft reference.

The crowd that I hung out with in high school had plenty of opportunities to get into trouble. When I say trouble, I don't mean drugs, heavy crime, or gang violence. That wasn't our style or the city's style. I'm referring to the numerous opportunities for our participation in underage drinking, small-time illegal gambling, and farm animal vandalizing. Despite what you may have heard, cow-tipping is not a myth. On a typical Friday night, my friends and I engaged in one of three activities: 1) drinking illegally purchased beer at Regional Park, 2) drinking illegally purchased beer while watching movies at someone's house, or 3) drinking illegally purchased beer while playing cards. The first two of these activities usually involved the fruitless pursuit of female Bombers. When no girls were in sight, someone would invariably say, "Hey, let's play cards."

The main card game of choice for my circle of friends was gin rummy. We played two-on-two, exactly like I'd seen my father play at the golf course clubhouse. JD Fennell, Bruce LaBrie, Barry Clark, Justin Springer and I would begin the evening by arguing which four of us would play first. Whoever didn't play in the initial game was responsible for placing two frozen Tony's pizzas into the oven. We always gambled at gin, but not for a dime-a-point that my dad was accustomed to playing. Instead, we played for a dollar-a-game. Nobody cared to play for more. The game was merely a setting for average food, good beer, and great humor. Even on the most lopsided of evenings, someone would leave the house down only five bucks. Sometimes, toward the end of the game, when I was the big loser for the evening, I would try to change the game, "Anyone wanna play blackjack?"

My friends didn't bite. "No way, Wig," JD would say, "You cheat."

True. Even as early as junior high, my friends occasionally busted me dealing from the bottom of the deck or sabotaging the shuffle. When those ploys no longer worked, I would change the rules of the game to my advantage. I knew nothing about blackjack card-counting back then, but I was aware that certain rules favored the dealer over the rest of the players. I made it through the entire summer of my freshman year dealing blackjack while claiming, "The official rules say you can't split aces unless the dealer is showing a face card." As the guys grew older and wiser, they learned that I dealt a lot of bullshit along with the cards. As a result, none of my closest friends would play blackjack with me, or anyone in my family.

Fortunately, there were other Midwest City High School students unaware of my blackjack shenanigans. One Friday night, during the fall of my senior year, a large number of us celebrated a Bomber football victory at Rick Ogle's house. Fifty or sixty people filled the residence and spilled into the front yard. Although nobody at the party was twenty-one years old, empty beer cans and Reunite wine bottles were everywhere. Don't judge; we were in the middle of Bumfart, Oklahoma. What else was there to do? As a group of us guys devoured five larges from Pizza Inn, a nickel-dime-quarter poker game broke out on Ogle's rectangular living room table.

I spilled a few drops of pizza sauce on the carpet during the shuffle before the first hand. Should I clean it up or rub it in? Screw it. I rubbed it in. Rick was a friend, but not one of my best friends. If I had been at Barry's or Justin's house, I would retrieve a dishrag from the kitchen to clean up the mess. Instead, I concentrated on the poker game. I surveyed the players to decide whether I should play fair or risk a butt-kicking by cheating. Since there were only a few dollars on the table, I decided to play legitimate. Plus, one of my regular gin rummy buddies, Bruce, was in the game. He would be watching me like a hawk.

After an hour, and some matched-pot stakes in an exciting game of three-card guts, a significant amount of money started to appear on the table. I was down $20. A couple other guys were also losers. Bruce left the game, saying he'd rather spend time with his girlfriend, Samantha. What a degenerate. Rick Ogle, our evening's host, left the game a $30 winner. Enjoy it while you can, Rick. Your mom will have you using that cash tomorrow to rent a carpet steam-cleaner. The only winner remaining at the table was Todd Crites.

Todd was a star baseball player at our school. He and his friends came to Midwest City High School from a different junior high, so I didn't know him as long as my other friends. In my opinion, Todd's group was a little on the crazy side. Instead of getting drunk and tipping cows, some of his friends would get really, really drunk and try shooting cows with a bow-and-arrow. Todd had been especially happy that night at Ogle's; he was up $50 and started giving me crap about it.

"What's the matter, Wiggy? I thought you were supposed to be a good card player."

"You know I am, Todd, but my game is blackjack, not poker or guts."

"Well, let's play some of that," Todd said, falling directly into my trap.

He slid the unshuffled pile of cards in my direction, signifying that I should deal. As the word "blackjack" echoed through the room, JD, Barry, and Justin came by the table to see what I had up my sleeve, maybe literally. I grabbed the cards and initially dropped them, as if by mistake. I wanted to survey where the aces were located. I quickly scanned the deck, and tried arranging the cards to my liking. I didn't have the dexterity to do it—too many Budweisers. I would get busted for sure if I tried stacking the deck or dealing from the bottom. Instead, I modified the rules.

"Okay. I'll deal everyone's cards face-up, except mine. You only get to see one. You can hit as many times as you want, but I have to stay on hard seventeen and above. If I have a soft seventeen, I have the option of taking a hit or not. You can double-down if you have ten or eleven. You can split any pair of cards, but not aces. No doubling down after splitting."

Since I didn't get any apprehensive looks at that point, I tried slipping in one more rule variation, "And, the dealer wins all ties."

"Bullshit, Wiggy!" Todd exclaimed as he stood abruptly, "That's too much of an advantage for you."

"No," I retorted with as straight a face as possible, "it evens out because I pay one-and-a-half times on a player's blackjack."

Todd slowly sat down without responding. He hadn't run for the nearest exit immediately. I took this as a sign to begin the game with the rules as stated. I had shuffled one last time and offered the cut to my right. If I had been stacking the deck, I wouldn't have offered a cut at all. Not many high school kids would have called me on it either.

"Place your bets."

Todd and the two other guys at the table started with $1 or $2 bets. I lost the first three hands, which ended up being a good thing. It wasn't long before Todd started pressing his bets and pressing his luck. Betting $5 after a new shuffle, he hit successfully with a smile, to twenty. However, he pushed, and lost according to the tailored rules, when I uncovered a twenty of my own. He grimaced, but didn't say a word. The next hand, Todd doubled-down and lost. As Todd upped his bet to $20 for the next hand, the other two players quit. One of them said something to the effect, "The game is just Wiggy and Crites now." The number of players was reduced to two, but the crowd of onlookers grew to twenty or so.

Todd won the first $20 hand, but lost the next three in a row at the same stakes. His previous stack of cash and change was gone. He was furious, to say the least. Just when I thought the game was over, Todd asked a few guys at the table to float him a loan. No takers. He then asked to borrow from me.

"Sure," I replied, "Here's forty back, but I need an IOU first."

Todd grabbed a flyer that was attached to the one of the Pizza Inn box tops lying on the end table. He wrote on it, "CRITES OWES WIGGY $40." Todd bet the entire $40 loan on the next hand. He lost when he didn't hit a twelve against my two. I received the beautiful nine he should have taken, giving me twenty-one. Before I had time to gather the cards from the hand, Todd ripped another section of paper from the pizza flyer. A $50 IOU this time. Instead of trading it for cash, I told him to simply bet the IOU. Another push, and subsequent loss for Todd.

"Jesus Christ!" he yelled in frustration.

My best friend, JD, chimed in with impeccable timing, "Don't you mean Jesus Crites?!"

Todd was not thrilled with the obvious word play on his last name. The rest of the room howled with laughter. I wanted to laugh harder than anyone, but I had been resolved to keeping a modest game face.

Todd spent the next few minutes ripping off paper from the pizza flyer to finance his bad run of cards. He finally left the table in disgust, kicking the hell out of one of Rick Ogle's living room chairs. After I tallied the pile of IOUs, Todd owed me $405. As he stormed out the door with a much needed beer, I said, "You owe me four-o-five, but let's make it an even four-hundred."

Todd wasn't impressed with my gratuity. He yelled back, "You ain't getting shit!"

I spent the rest of the evening in pretty good spirits. I followed JD around the party as he told the Jesus Crites story over and over to anyone who would listen. Each time JD blurted the punch line, "Jesus Crites," he would bust his own gut with laughter. Meanwhile, Todd was nowhere in sight. I wondered if he was going home to get my cash. Maybe he would visit one of those new ATMs that had just started popping up around town.

I didn't see Todd until the next week at school. He told me repeatedly that he needed time to get the money. Days turned into weeks. After Christmas, I overheard Todd telling someone that he had received cash as a gift from one of his relatives. I didn't get a cut. Todd always made some excuse to keep from paying me. Classmates told me that I was a sucker, that I would never get paid. Kerri Ives, a friend of mine since fifth grade, said, "You should kick his ass." I had a few problems with her idea. Although I was the baddest dude on the Bomber men's varsity golf team, and sixth meanest guy in the Midwest City High School accelerated math class, I wasn't known for my toughness. I was the class clown for Crites' sake. Also, I hadn't won a fight since elementary school. And the girl who I had beaten way back then still disputes the fact that I won.

Instead of fighting for what was mine, I tried underhanded schemes to embarrass Crites into paying. First, while participating in a Knowledge Bowl competition in front of the entire school body, I flashed a homemade sign that read, "PAY ME TODD." That plan backfired. I spent the rest of the afternoon explaining the sign, and the preceding card game, to two teachers and the principal. They lectured me on the evils of gambling. My second attempt to intimidate Todd also backfired miserably. I asked my older brother, Brian, a Midwest City policeman, to pay a "friendly" visit to Todd in an attempt to strong-arm him. I didn't want Brian to be violent or do anything unethical. I simply wanted him to show up in uniform to scare Crites. Brian agreed to the plan and later informed me that Todd wept like a baby. Maybe I'd finally get paid. Nope. Brian had mistakenly strong-armed a kid named Ted on the street adjacent to Todd's.

I graduated from Midwest City High School in May 1984. I didn't see Todd again until eleven years later when I joined a group of guys in Florida for a Memorial Day weekend trip. Todd was there with a new circle of friends that included Bruce, JD, and others guys from Oklahoma State University. Their group had been partying at Fort Walton Beach, Florida, every spring break since college. As they had grown older, the trip morphed into a Memorial Day tradition of golf, beaches, and alcohol. Since my college education and subsequent career in the Air Force took me on a different path, I didn't join the Florida fun until 1995. Repayment of the $400 IOU was a non-issue at that point. Todd never brought it up. I never brought it up. I suppose there existed some sort of unwritten ten-year statute of limitations that applied to juvenile things that happened in high school. Plus, I now knew that I had cheated Todd considerably back then. I estimate that I had a 10-15% advantage over him with the screwy blackjack rules I enforced that evening at Rick Ogle's house.

As for the "Jesus Crites" catch phrase, it became legendary with the guys on the annual Fort Walton trip. Anytime anyone was pissed or shocked, it was acceptable to yell "Jesus Crites" in disgust. JD took things further one Memorial Day when he stubbed his toe at the beach playing sky ball. During his alcohol and adrenaline induced rage, he uttered the extra emotional phrase, "Jesus Fuckin' Crites." An elderly women lounging on a chaise near us said, "Young man! How dare you take the Lord's name in vain?"

JD, slowly hopping on one foot, responded, "I wasn't, lady, I was taking Todd's name in vain."

The woman didn't understand the obscure reference. Instead, she packed her beach bag and scurried to another portion of the beach. She was one of many beachgoers we offended that day. We continue to offend many others on a yearly basis.

Even when I'm away from the Fort Walton Beach crowd, I find myself uttering "Jesus Crites." The phrase comes in handy at the blackjack table. You know, during those times when the dealer draws a card that seems to put a stake in your heart. Of course, you can't get mad every time that happens. It happens a lot. I use the phrase only in a specific situation. I think *Jesus Crites* or utter it lightly under my breath, on the exact occurrence when the dealer draws to a hard twenty-one against my twenty. I reserve the hardcore phrase, *Jesus Fuckin' Crites*, for the rare occurrence when the dealer draws to a hard twenty-one, beating me after I doubled-down and hit twenty. In my opinion, there is no better time to take Todd's name in vain. Give it a try next time on my behalf. Crites won't care. He owes me.

LEARNING TO COUNT CARDS

In the fall of 1993, I purchased our family's first personal computer. It was a beauty in those days. One megabyte of RAM, ten megabyte hard drive, and a 2400-baud telephone modem quick enough to download a small grainy picture of bikinied Cindy Crawford in just twenty minutes. Shortly after the downloading-girlie-pictures-with-a-computer phase of my life grew old, I purchased the PC's first piece of software, a casino emulation game produced by the Spirit of Discovery company called "Beat the House." The game featured interactive roulette, slot machines, video poker, and blackjack. Spectacular graphics and sound made it one the most realistic and entertaining games of the time. The virtual casino included unique features such as a sign-in book at the front desk and a High Rollers club for players reaching $100,000 in winnings. The game also booted your ass out of the casino if you went broke. *Boy, that always made me mad.* In my opinion, however, the most impressive feature of the game had nothing to do with the software. It was an accompanying player's manual authored by Avery Cardoza entitled, *Beat the House Companion.* I learned basic blackjack strategy and card-counting from that text. I follow the same modified hi-low counting method to this day. I appreciate having the powerful weapon at my disposal when I enter a casino. This book exists because the *Beat the House Companion* motivated me to commence on a card-counting endeavor. I considered dedicating this book to Avery Cardoza, but my wife and kids would have been pissed.

Before reading Cardoza's book, I thought I knew how to play the cards in blackjack for every situation. I was wrong, big time. For example:

- I would stay on a hard twelve against the dealer's upturned two or three. Basic strategy dictates a hit as the correct play.
- I would split eights, but never against a dealers' nine, ten or ace. I now fully comprehend one of the most basic, but misunderstood maxims in Basic Strategy: always split eights, no matter what the dealer is showing.
- I knew a hard sixteen was a lousy hand against a seven, eight, nine, face card, or ace, but I didn't necessarily hit because of the high probability of busting. You should be confident in always hitting during that situation.
- I would never consider doubling down on a hard nine. There are several situations when it is not only advisable, but also quite profitable.
- I would take insurance against the dealer's upturned ace when my hand was strong.

insurance = a side-bet offered at blackjack tables where the player may wager half of the original bet against the house when the dealer's up card is an ace. The player buying insurance is betting that the dealer will have a blackjack. Buying insurance against the dealer's ace is rather tempting for most players when they have a strong hand. However, buying insurance is a terrible move, unless you count cards and know that a significantly large proportion of face cards remain in the deck.

I blame my flubs in previous blackjack strategy on stubbornness and ignorance. My father had dealt me hundreds of hands as a child, and I had played the game with buddies in high school and college, but I never really cared enough about blackjack to pursue every intricacy of the game for significant profit. Why bother? I was well aware that the odds were against me. Everyone knows that. Everyone knows that the dealer has the advantage in blackjack. Everyone knows that casinos make millions of dollars on the game. Everyone knows that you can't change the odds. Everyone is wrong. Cardoza, and several blackjack strategists before him (Ed Thorp, the pioneer of card-counting, among others) had known the truth:

An educated card-counting blackjack player, using Basic Strategy to hit, stay, double-down, or split when appropriate, has a mathematical edge over the dealer.

Math and winnable blackjack. Who knew? Like the inventor of Reese's Peanut Butter Cups, I decided to combine these two dominant concepts from my life into something special—a quest for truth and the almighty dollar. Let the games begin.

In the *Beat the House Companion*, Avery Cardoza asserted that the cards favor the player when there is a proportionately large number of face cards and aces remaining in the deck. Conversely, the deck favors the dealer when a bunch of small cards remain. The theory behind counting cards is simple:

Bet more when a significant number of high cards remain. Bet less, or leave the table, when a significant number of low cards remain.

As a mathematician, I knew I would eventually have to validate the claims made by previous card-counting theorists. For the time being, however, I wanted to begin practicing the running count as described in the *Beat the House Companion*.

My initial practice session started on an especially sour note. I couldn't find a damn deck of cards in the house. I looked in the old El Producto cigar box in the cabinet above our washer and dryer. Two decks of cards should have been there, along with other knick-knacks I've accumulated over the years. I saw the replacement cord for my Weed-Eater trimmer, a brown shoe-horn adorned with the Professional Golfers Association logo, the adapter to plug my obnoxiously large headphones into the small jack on my portable CD player, a 1947 penny, a 1982 penny, assorted golf tees, an AA Duracell battery with corroded tip, a thirteen-cent postage stamp with dust and lint adhering to the back, a Honda key for a car that

I sold nine years ago, and the top hat game piece from a long-gone Monopoly game.

"Honey, where are my playing cards?"

My lovely wife, Lori, didn't answer. Either she didn't hear me or she was pre-occupied with her current task—trying to corral my dirty, naked son, Mitchell, into the bathtub.

I walked into my twelve-year-old daughter's room. "Sarah, where are my cards?"

"You mean the ones with the pictures of dogs and cats on the front?" she replied.

"Yeah, those are the ones. I need them for an experiment."

Sarah reached underneath her bed. More like "dug" underneath. There were at least ten articles of clothing and four towels obstructing her way.

"I lost one deck at school, but here is the other one."

As she handed me the deck, I counted the contents. Forty-eight cards.

"Sarah, there are four cards missing."

"I know," she replied, "Grandma liked the ones with puppies on them. I gave her those to keep." *Great, my first card-count ever was off by four.*

I drove to the 7-11 convenience store about a quarter-mile from our house. The clerk showed me playing cards on the shelf behind the counter, but the only style featured Joe the Camel smiling with a cigarette in his mouth and giving a "thumbs up" gesture with his camel hoof. Lori wasn't fond of smokers. I feared she might discard the box of cards, confusing them with a pack of cigarettes that had been left in the house by my mother. I purchased two decks anyway. I returned home in time to see Mitchell running naked around the house again. This time, however, he was squeaky clean. After both of my kids were asleep for the evening, I began my self-taught instruction on card-counting. I'll walk you through the process, just like Cardoza instructed.

Always start a card-count at zero. Assign a "+1" value to each three, four, five, and six in the deck. You also assign a "−1" value to each ten, jack, queen, and king. The rest of the cards are assigned a

"0," meaning zero value, or no count. They can be disregarded. The card-counting values are summarized as follows:

Card	2	3	4	5	6	7	8	9	10	J	Q	K	A
Value	0	+1	+1	+1	+1	0	0	0	-1	-1	-1	-1	0

While there are numerous other blackjack card-counting strategies, I've never deviated from this basic count description. I eventually learned to employ a separate count for the number of aces remaining. For different strategies, refer to your favorite Internet search engine or the "Gaming" section of bookstores. After learning the point value assigned to each card, it is important to understand the concept of the "running count":

> **running count** = the ongoing count, or numerical value, maintained by the player from the first card dealt to the last card seen, until a deck or shoe is reshuffled. In general, the cards favor the player when the running count is positive.

Do not start practicing the running count by playing hands of blackjack. Instead, start by simply flipping a shuffled deck of cards one at a time. When I did this the first time, I ended the deck with a running count of "–1," meaning that I had missed tallying a low card somewhere. Since the deck contains as many plus-one cards as minus-one cards, the running count for an entire deck should always total zero. I shuffled and counted the deck again. Minus one. *Sunuvabitch.* I counted the cards again to make sure there was not a smiling Joe Camel missing. Fifty-two. I tried again. This time, and the next four times, I flipped through the deck and finished the running count with a perfect zero each time. *Now we're getting somewhere.*

Give it a try yourself. I recommend that you do it perfectly many times in a row before going to the next step in the process. I'll sit back listening to music by Roger Waters, former front man of Pink Floyd, while you practice.

♫ *...the species has amused itself to death...* ♪

Ready? After mastering the count on a full deck with no deviation from zero, you are ready to analyze cards in groups. Calculate the running count for the following series of cards:

If you finished with a running count of +2, you are correct. If you finished with –2, you might be getting the positive card values mixed up with the negative. If you finished the count with +164, you are experiencing some sort of learning difficulty which will make the rest of the card-counting exercises difficult to comprehend. I suggest you try an activity which requires minimal brainpower, like doing word search puzzles or reading *Us Weekly* magazine. Try again.

Before you delve too far into the wizardry of counting cards, be sure to establish good habits. Don't count out loud, don't point, and don't move your lips. Also, you should practice being quick and confident in maintaining the running count. Try counting cards while in front of a television to practice in a noisy environment. Casinos are full of distractions. There are loud bells and beeps, musicians or canned music, dealers and pit bosses yelling transactions, lots of alcohol, and smelly people. Do you think those distractions are there by accident?

If you haven't already discovered the trick on your own, the next step to improving proficiency in the count involves "canceling" cards. Look for high-low pairs (+1 and −1 = 0) that eliminate each other. By canceling pairs of cards, you can quickly and efficiently tabulate the running count when many cards surface at once on the blackjack table. For instance, the queen of diamonds cancels with the five of spades in the following graphic. Remember to disregard the neutral cards:

As a final step, practice counting full hands of blackjack with a pretend dealer and several players receiving their cards in a realistic manner. Also, keep track of the running count from hand to hand. In the following scenario, assume that the running count is −3 before the hand begins:

The count for the hand was +1. Combining that total with the running count before the hand began means the running count is now –2. The running count goes from hand to hand, from the beginning of the shoe until the dealer reshuffles. It "runs" throughout. Get it? For six deck shoes, the running count can fluctuate as high as +25 down to –25. Shoes with such extreme counts are rare, but possible.

If cards are dealt face-down where you play, you must glance at the cards as the dealer collects them at the end of the hand. Don't worry. Dealers must always spread out the cards, face-up, in a manner that allows the eyes in the sky surveillance cameras to monitor the action. Remember to play the cards correctly as you practice the count. Counting cards and playing according to Basic Strategy go hand in hand.

At this point, you should have enough training and foresight to dispel two of the most common myths about card-counting in blackjack:

Myth: Only a person with incredible intelligence, like Raymond "Rain Man" Babbitt can count cards.

Myth: It is impossible to count cards when the casino uses multiple (two, four, six, or eight) decks.

Both myths are untrue. If you have followed my instruction up to this point, you are counting cards successfully. Do your friends or family call you Rain Man? No? They will, soon enough. You also have enough horsepower to debunk the second myth. You can maintain the running count for any number of decks. With one-hundred decks of Joe Camel cards, you could tabulate the running count until all 5200 cards were distributed. Keep in mind, however, that maintaining the running count is only a small part of the challenge. The hardest part of counting cards involves determining the "true count" and adjusting your bet accordingly. We'll get to those drills soon enough.

BASIC STRATEGY – DOING THE RIGHT THING

My wonderful wife of many years, Lori, provided continual support and positive inspiration throughout my first attempt at being a writer, "You aren't going to use any of your dumb analogies in the book, are you?"

"Maybe one," I exaggerated. For her sake, I'll get it out of the way early.

There are numerous blackjack books on the shelves advocating countless strategies and methods for obtaining advantages over the house. Similarly, there are hundreds of weight-loss books on the market promoting one diet over others. However, only one weight loss strategy is needed for most people in life—eat less and exercise. Similarly, only one blackjack strategy is needed—follow Basic Strategy. Sounds simple enough, but in reality, it is far from simple. In dieting and blackjack gambling, most people are too lazy or reluctant to do the right thing. Or, they are too impatient to follow the slow and methodical path, instead opting for quick results. Why diet and exercise when a miracle pill can shed pounds for you? The "miracle pill" in blackjack is luck. Why would anyone in his or her right mind disregard laws of probability and rely strictly on luck at the blackjack table? I'll tell you why. This is where the analogy ends. Unlike the miracle diet pill, luck sometimes works in blackjack.

The aspect of luck in gambling brings a significant amount of excitement to the game. Theoretically, a person could enter the casino with five dollars and leave a millionaire. You're thinking, sure, by hitting the jackpot payoff on one pull of the slot machine. Think harder. If a blackjack player bet five dollars on a hand and won, and continued to double the bet and win for eighteen more hands, the player would accumulate approximately $1,300,000. Talk about excitement. But, if you walk into the joint thinking you'll win the first nineteen hands, you have your head buried deep into the posterior portion of your anatomy. The probability of such a streak is incredibly small, about one chance in 770,000. Impractical, but not improbable. For the record, I won fourteen hands in a row once. I've also lost sixteen in a row. Luck, whether slight or extreme, good or bad, is impossible to predict or model mathematically at the blackjack table, or anywhere else in the casino.

For the rest of this book, I will disregard luck as a determining factor in strategy. Instead, I will approach every blackjack hand from the standpoint of always doing the right thing. Win or lose, a good player does the right thing.

So what exactly constitutes the "right thing" or a "good player" in blackjack? It depends on whom you ask. A pit boss might say, "A good player is one who maximizes winnings while minimizing losses." Thanks a lot, buddy. Did the casino tell you to spout that drivel? If you enter a casino without knowing, "Win money—good, lose money—bad," then reading this book might be too difficult for you. Instead, you may want to try reading Garfield's latest treasury.

A dealer might say, "A good player is one who leaves when the cards go bad." Exactly right, except for one, teensy-weensy problem. God, Superman, and the guy with the x-ray glasses in the movie, *Austin Powers, International Man of Mystery*, are the only folks I know with the ability to see what card is next. A dealer might also say, "Leaving the game when you are ahead is the right thing to do." More superfluous logic. You would be ahead if you won the first hand. Who leaves the casino after one hand?

A casino waiter or waitress might say, "A good player is one who is friendly and tips." Nice try, drink server. By that definition, many frequent customers at Denny's would be considered "good players." Stay out of the conversation and bring me the Diet Coke that I ordered a half-hour ago. Just kidding, you know I love you.

A professional athlete would probably say, "A good player is someone who knows the rules, develops the best strategy, and always sticks with the game plan no matter how bad the other player is beating you." Good advice. I would add, "...and steers clear of steroids."

Non-gamblers, and those who despise the wonderful hobby that you and I so thoroughly enjoy, would say, "The right thing is to not gamble. Period." Give me a break.

Blackjack purists say, "A good player is one who always obeys the rules of Basic Strategy for hitting, staying, doubling down, and splitting. No hunches, no deviations, no superstitions. Play the game with a distinct set of rules, just like the dealer."

I agree with the last definition the most, although I've got to tell you, the comparison of a good blackjack player to a pro athlete deserves honorable mention. In truth, playing blackjack is dirt simple and requires zero skill once you learn the rules of the game and how to use Basic Strategy. Think about that assertion—no skill is required to play blackjack. All other card games require some skill in knowing what your opponent may do next. Texas hold' em, bridge, poker, gin rummy, pinochle, spades, crazy-eights, even old maid, requires a good player to know or consider what cards the other player may be holding and playing next. If you make a wrong play in these games, and your opponent takes advantage of your mistake, the odds of winning decrease. Blackjack is different. Unless you know something about the composition of cards remaining in the deck or shoe, there is absolutely no second-guessing or wondering if you made the correct decision in a hand of blackjack as long as you use Basic Strategy.

The following chart shows Basic Strategy for the most common multi-deck blackjack table rules:

Blackjack Multi-Deck Basic Strategy

S = Stay   SP = Split
H = Hit   D = Double-down

	Dealer's Up Card									
	2	3	4	5	6	7	8	9	10	A
2-2	SP	SP	SP	SP	SP	SP	H	H	H	H
3-3	SP	SP	SP	SP	SP	SP	H	H	H	H
4-4	H	H	H	SP	SP	H	H	H	H	H
5-5	D	D	D	D	D	D	D	D	H	H
6-6	SP	SP	SP	SP	SP	H	H	H	H	H
7-7	SP	SP	SP	SP	SP	SP	H	H	H	H
8-8	Always Split									
9-9	SP	SP	SP	SP	SP	S	SP	SP	S	S
10-10	Always Stay									
Hard 8 or below	Always Hit									
9	H	D	D	D	D	H	H	H	H	H
10	D	D	D	D	D	D	D	D	H	H
11	D	D	D	D	D	D	D	D	D	D
12	H	H	S	S	S	H	H	H	H	H
13	S	S	S	S	S	H	H	H	H	H
14	S	S	S	S	S	H	H	H	H	H
15	S	S	S	S	S	H	H	H	H	H
16	S	S	S	S	S	H	H	H	H	H
Hard 17 or above	Always Stay									
A-A	Always Split									
A-2	H	H	H	D	D	H	H	H	H	H
A-3	H	H	H	D	D	H	H	H	H	H
A-4	H	H	D	D	D	H	H	H	H	H
A-5	H	H	D	D	D	H	H	H	H	H
A-6	H	D	D	D	D	H	H	H	H	H
A-7	D	D	D	D	D	S	S	H	H	H
A-8	S	S	S	S	D	S	S	S	S	S
A-9	Always Stay									
A-10	Blackjack									

Player's Hand

To use the chart, select the exact two-card combination of your hand from the left-most column. You must be precise in selecting the hand, or you may interpret Basic Strategy incorrectly. If you have a 3-4, seven, it is played differently that an A-6, soft seven. Similarly, an 8-8, sixteen, hand is played much differently than a 7-9, sixteen, hand. After selecting the appropriate row, find the column corresponding with the dealer's up card. Then follow the instructions on the interior of the chart by staying, hitting, splitting or doubling-down.

Unless you are a card-counter, never deviate from Basic Strategy. Some deviations are permissible if you know the ratio of high to low cards remaining in the deck/shoe. These are sometimes called "index" plays. Also, never let another player tell you, or persuade you, to play other than Basic Strategy dictates. The phrase, "Don't hit a twelve against the dealer's three. You don't want to take his bust card" is heard at many a casino. Horseshit. Also, you might hear, "I never hit a sixteen. I can't win if I bust." More horse caca. If a player stays on a sixteen against a dealer's seven, eight, nine, ten or ace, it is the same as staying on a thirteen, or a ten, or an eight, or a four. The only way a player can win with sixteen is if the dealer busts. Don't believe any of the superstition or faulty logic. Follow Basic Strategy. I coined a term long ago to describe individuals who refuse to follow Basic Strategy. It is crude and demeaning to call these people dumb or silly. Instead, I opt for a less offensive term:

blackjackally challenged = term used to describe blackjack players who regularly deviate from Basic Strategy during the course of play.

I make it a rule to never offer unsolicited advice in the casino. That maxim works well in the world outside the casino as well. Offering unsolicited advice is routinely successful for only one person: Oprah. If I am asked for help or my opinion at the blackjack table, however, I do my best to convey the right message. I once had the following conversation at the casino with a blackjackally challenged couple:

LADY: [asking her husband] I have a thirteen. Should I hit? [the dealer was showing a five.]

HUSBAND: I'm not sure. [turning to me] What do you think?

ME: You shouldn't hit. According to Basic Strategy, you should stay in this situation.

LADY: I feel lucky. [hits, and gets an eight.] Wheeee! I guess it was the right thing to do.

ME: No, it wasn't.

LADY: How can you say that? I got twenty-one. I played it right.

ME: No. You played it wrong. The results were good.

HUSBAND: The way I see it, she played it right all the way.

ME: [no response]

A few hands later, the dealer distributed similar cards. The lady had a fourteen against the dealer's five.

LADY: Should I hit again?

HUSBAND: [pointing at me] He'd say "No," but I think you should.

LADY: [hits and gets a six, for twenty. I stay with twelve. The dealer draws to a nineteen. The lady wins. I lose.] "I did it again! I guess we know the right way to play."

ME: No, you still played it wrong.

LADY AND HUSBAND: [almost in unison] Why do you keep saying that?

ME: In blackjack, or any game of chance, there are probabilities of winning and losing in every situation. You can defy the odds by making the wrong move, but it isn't the right way to play.

HUSBAND: It's all luck. You can play any way you want if you are lucky.

ME: Okay, I won't argue. Except, you can't claim you are playing right.

HUSBAND: Sure we can.

ME: No, you can't. Suppose you and the missus were like Bonnie and Clyde, making a fortune robbing banks and shooting up lots of people on the way. If you did the wrong thing, but never got caught, would you say it was the right thing to do?

HUSBAND: No!

LADY: That's the stupidest analogy I've ever heard!

ME: Never mind. What is it with wives not liking my analogies?

I should be perfectly clear on one issue. Using blackjack Basic Strategy is not guaranteed to win every hand. You don't even win or tie 50% of the hands using Basic Strategy in the long run. Why do you think the casino makes so much money? But, the strategy gets you as close to 50% as possible. Quitting at the right time during normal fluctuations in highs and lows can often allow the regular player to emerge a winner. If you deviate from Basic Strategy, regardless of playing just a few hands or a thousand hands, the probability of experiencing a high fluctuation decreases. You have less chance of being a winner.

Let's go back to the Basic Strategy chart. This time, so you don't think I'm a self-serving, broken record, I've asked some everyday casino blackjack players to provide their testimonial on certain strategic moves:

Blackjack Multi-Deck Basic Strategy

S = Stay   SP = Split
H = Hit   D = Double-down

Splitting eights does not increase your chances of winning, but it decreases your chances of losing. Always split eights.

Always double-down with eleven against an ace, unless the dealer stays on soft seventeen. In that case, take a hit.

Other players may go nuts if you hit a twelve against a dealer's two or three. But it is the right way to play. I promise!

Never stay on a soft seventeen.

Player's Hand	Dealer's Up Card									
	2	3	4	5	6	7	8	9	10	A
2-2	SP	SP	SP	SP	SP	SP	H	H	H	H
3-3	SP	SP	SP	SP	SP	SP	H	H	H	H
4-4	H	H	H	SP	SP	H	H	H	H	H
5-5	D	D	D	D	D	D	D	D	H	H
6-6	SP	SP	SP	SP	SP	H	H	H	H	H
7-7	SP	SP	SP	SP	SP	SP	H	H	H	H
8-8	Always Split (This is a no-brainer)									
9-9	SP	SP	SP	SP	SP	S	SP	SP	S	S
10-10	Always Stay (Unless card-count is HUGE)									
Hard 8 or below	Always Hit									
9	H	D	D	D	D	H	H	H	H	H
10	D	D	D	D	D	D	D	D	H	H
11	D	D	D	D	D	D	D	D	D	D
12	H	H	S	S	S	H	H	H	H	H
13	S	S	S	S	S	H	H	H	H	H
14	S	S	S	S	S	H	H	H	H	H
15	S	S	S	S	S	H	H	H	H	H
16	S	S	S	S	S	H	H	H	H	H
Hard 17 or above	Always Stay									
A-A	Always Split (Easiest decision ever)									
A-2	H	H	H	D	D	H	H	H	H	H
A-3	H	H	H	D	D	H	H	H	H	H
A-4	H	H	D	D	D	H	H	H	H	H
A-5	H	H	D	D	D	H	H	H	H	H
A-6	H	D	D	D	D	H	H	H	H	H
A-7	D	D	D	D	D	S	S	H	H	H
A-8	S	S	S	S	D	S	S	S	S	S
A-9	Always Stay									
A-10	This is a beautiful blackjack!									

Splitting eights against a strong dealer's card can be one of the most difficult situations to play correctly for most blackjack gamblers. Granted, everyone will agree that sixteen is a crappy starting hand. By splitting eights, you turn one lousy hand into two slightly less than average hands. Despite my wife's chagrin, I have another famous analogy to describe this phenomenon.

Getting dealt a pair of eights in blackjack is like making a grade of "F" on a paper or assignment in school. Splitting the eights is like replacing the "F" grade with two "C minuses." Would you rather have one failing grade, or two slightly mediocre, passing grades? Also, you may get dealt a two or three on the split eights. Now the teacher (dealer) has given you the opportunity to change one or both "C–" to a "B" or an "A." By staying with a sixteen instead of splitting, your only hope is that the teacher throws out the assignment on which you made the "F" grade (dealer busts).

Another difficult decision in blackjack involves playing a hand where you have a twelve against the dealer's two or three. No analogies here. Just take my word that you have a better chance of winning the hand by taking a hit. How many times have you seen the dealer make a good hand out of twelve? That could be you. Michael Shackleford, the "Wizard" from wizardofodds.com, will attest with great mathematical precision that the player who never hits a twelve against the dealer's two or three gives the house an extra 3.91% edge in the long run. Anyone who quotes statistics or probabilities with two decimal points sounds like a formidable expert to me.

Okay. Let's suppose at this point that I've convinced you. You firmly and fully agree with me—Basic Strategy is the bomb. For you geriatric readers, that means "Basic Strategy is the bee's knees." Your next concern might regard the difficulty in memorizing all the possible variations and combinations displayed on the Basic Strategy chart. No problem. A casino will almost always let you use a card or slip of paper annotated with Basic Strategy to aid in your decision-making. Some casino gift shops sell the learning aids. Don't be embarrassed to use a card. Even with my extensive experience at the game, I keep a laminated card in my wallet for reference. I always forget what to do with an A-4 against a three (hit) or against a four (double-down).

If you use a Basic Strategy chart or reference card, be sure to select the correct strategy based on the specific rules of the blackjack table where you gamble. There are slight deviations in Basic Strategy depending on the number of decks used, whether the dealer hits or stays on a soft seventeen, or whether you can double-down after splitting. Also, there are different strategies dependent upon whether or not the casino offers a "surrender" option. The Basic Strategy chart depicted in this book is one of many. I recommend you surf the WWW to get the right chart for your gig. Again, for the older crowd, that last sentence means "Consult another source to obtain the most appropriate reference for your precise gambling needs, Granny!"

Don't get wise with me, sonny! I may be 87 years old, but I'll drop-kick your analogy-spoutin' carcass across the room!

THE GAMBLING FAMILY

There is concrete scientific evidence that the DNA of my entire family contains "gambling" alongside the usual chromosomes found in a human being. I think the rare phenomenon was first discovered in the mid-1950s shortly after my father officially changed his last name to "Wiggy." My dad was born Thomas Walter Wielgoleski, in Pittsburgh, Pennsylvania, in 1930. My grandmother and grandfather Wielgoleski immigrated to the United States a generation earlier. Before they journeyed across the Atlantic Ocean, my grandparent's spelled their Polish name, "WyćźlhśłezęŹszczćhąckóźlhśłezęŹszczć zźżzźźsky." Be sure not to confuse the name with another acceptable spelling variation, "WyćźlhśłezęŹszczćhąckóźlhśłezęŹszczćzźźźzźźs ki." The immigration officials did my lineage, and the entire country, a favor by transcribing the spelling of the name into the easier-to-manage "Wielgoleski" on all legal documents. My father grew up working at a golf course country club with several of his brothers. My Uncle Stanley became a golf professional in Pennsylvania around the same time as Arnold Palmer—they competed against each other in high school. My father joined the profession a few years later. Apparently, when Dad and Uncle Stan played in the same golf tournaments, there was often confusion on the tee-time pairings sheet and on the official scoreboard because two different Wielgoleski's had been listed. As a result, Dad changed his name to his childhood nickname, "Wiggy," in 1955. That's the story he tells me. Personally, I think my father changed last names to win a bet.

My father was a huge gambler. While growing up, I watched my dad bet on anything and everything: pro football, cards, college football, dice, high school football, the numbers, Pop Warner football, soccer, Australian-Rules football, horses, dogs, chickens, cockroaches—you name it. And golf. He was a big, big gambler at golf. My dad was the only person I knew who could lose $20 a hole to his opponent on the first seventeen holes of a golf match, but birdie the last hole with a "Hawaiian Press" and somehow end up winning $100 for the day. He was that good at golf and gambling. Dad once told me the time he let a guy win a weekly $10 golf bet each and every week for several months until the guy got cocky and bet his Buick Skylark on a round. My mom loved driving that car afterwards.

As the youngest of six children, I also watched the influence of gambling on my mother, Helen, as well as my brothers and sisters. Mom loved bingo and slot-machines. She helped keep the local Knights of Columbus in business by participating in Saturday night bingo all throughout the 1970s. When Helen had the rare chance to face-off against a slot-machine in a casino, the machine usually had better odds of winning, but Mom always won the battle because she could sit in one place longer than the actual slot-machine. Have you ever seen a slot-machine give up and break down from being overplayed?

My older brother and sister, Kirk and Kara, are twins. In addition to sharing the same Wiggy gambling DNA, they also shared a womb. Kirk and Kara hit the casino whenever they get the chance, but they satisfy their daily gambling fix a different way than the rest of the family. Both are expert prize-winners on the radio. Together, they have won tens of thousands of dollars worth of trips, restaurant gift certificates, concert tickets, movie passes, hotel stays, and every other possible prize offered on the radio. They don't have favorite radio stations—both listen to whatever broadcast is offering the best prize or contest at the time. The station could be plugging its format, *"Playing all your favorite Ernest Borgnine, Yoko Ono and William Shatner hits from the 60s and 70s, as well as hourly crop reports from Somalia and the Sudan, this is K-R-A-P, Crap radio,"* and Kirk and Kara would care less, as long as the station promised to give away a free, Sonic 20-ounce cherry limeade during the nine o'clock hour. They often competed in the same on-the-air treasure-hunt style games and promotions when they both worked desk jobs in Oklahoma City, like the "Guess the Location of the 7-Up" contest. Kirk won a trip to Disneyworld for four, including hotel and round-trip airfare, plus a year's supply of 7-Up in a promotion that was scheduled to last a few weeks. Due to superb, pre-Internet era investigative skills and the help of a local Orlando, Florida, phone operator, Kirk won the contest on day two. The marketing and promotions staffs at the radio station were not happy. After the free family vacation, Kirk, in true Wiggy make-a-quick-buck fashion, sold the year's supply of 7-Up to a local supermarket for $200.

It is rumored that Kirk later moved to Colorado so he and Kara would have separate turf. A few months after the move, local CBS radio affiliates in Denver enacted the "Wiggy Rule" to keep Kirk from winning too often. It didn't matter. Kirk has dozens of fake radio voices coupled with fake phone numbers and addresses to skirt the rules.

Besides being a radio junkie, Kara also fills out every possible sweepstake entry form in supermarket aisles, on cereal boxes and in magazines. She won a Super Bowl commemorative ring and $40,000 during a promotion conducted by Miller Beer. When a private investigator visited Kara to ensure she had met sweepstake eligibility requirements before the grand prize was awarded, Kara had no idea which one of the hundreds of entered contests she won.

My older brothers, Brian and Scott, weren't twins, but they might as well have been because they worked precisely and fluidly as a two-person team when beating me to a pulp or playing a practical joke to make me look ridiculous. Ask anyone in our hometown about the time Glen Wiggy was tricked into eating pizza that had been found face-down on the middle of a busy intersection. The "Street Pizza" story is legendary. Brian and Scott, and their friends, Mike Evans, Rick Simon, and Brian Barnett, as well as my older cousin Johnny introduced me to the joys of card gambling when I was young. The guys played poker on a weekly basis, and never let me play. I would watch the game over their shoulders, until I eventually became a pest to someone, then I'd somehow end up with my upturned T-shirt hanging on the back of a door on a closet hook while my feet wildly kicked inches above the floor.

The only time my brothers and their friends let me play cards is when I showed up at the table one night with $20 in birthday money, which had been recently given to me by my Aunt Jenny. All of a sudden, fifth-grader Glen was sitting at the playing table with the high school guys instead of dangling on a hook. Imagine that—what a great bunch of fellas. I won money, too. I might have been in fifth grade, but my math and memory skills were already better than the lot of them, especially since I hadn't been drinking beer. However, the winnings were only temporary. I suspect that I developed a bad poker face, like the time I got a pair of kings in three-card guts, but nobody stayed in to match the pot because I was grinning and hopping around the table like an idiot. Later, I lost all my money in guts when I had a pair of aces, but was beat by Brian holding three jacks. To this day, I think there was something fishy about that hand because Scott was dealing. That's okay. I stole enough quarters from both my brothers' rooms in those days to play hours and hours of video games. That made up for all of the gambling losses or practical jokes.

I didn't notice the gambling-DNA influence on my older sister, Kim, until she moved to New Orleans after high school. Anytime our family visits Kim in the South, we are hoisted away on a day-trip to the casinos of Gulf Port, Biloxi or Bay St. Louis. Kim definitely has the gambling gene like the rest of us, except she is five times louder when screaming for joy on a lucky play or cursing the dealer on a bad stroke of luck. Of all my siblings, Kim gets special credit because she was the only one who invested cash in the early goings of my blackjack card-counting venture. I returned Kim a nice profit on her initial investment, plus I gave her one of the first DVD players that I received as a frequent player comp.

Growing up in a gambling family, I thought it was normal to stop at horse races, dog races, harness races, or some other gambling locale in the middle of long road trips. Other kids went to amusement parks, swam at lakes or stopped to see roadside attractions, like the World's Largest Moose Turd. My siblings and I learned how to pick daily-double winners and beat carnival games because we had known the gaff. When I told other kids about my gambling adventures, they would reply, "Wow, you got to bet on jai-alai! All I did for the summer was vacation in the crappy Bahamas."

The full extent of the Wiggy gambling DNA on my children is unknown. The fact that my wife, Lori, has never gambled, and will never gamble, has discombobulated the composition of the gambling genes in my kids. For instance, my daughter, Sarah, would never play cards for money or make a friendly wager on anything, but she will accompany me to the casino or submit football pool picks via email for her betting husband. I think she might be a compulsive gambler enabler, a rare genetic offshoot stemming from the normal generative gambling DNA.

My son definitely possesses the gambling gene, but like a young Spiderman, Mitchell has yet to harness the full power of his gambling super-abilities. I taught him how to count cards in blackjack at age twelve, but he has yet to play on a real table. Soon, Mitchell will reach legal gambling age. When he and I visit Las Vegas for the first time, day one will be spent playing every other game in the casino for fun. Craps, poker, slots, pai-gow, roulette, whatever—I'll let Mitchell lose a few bucks to see how the normal casino patrons live. He and I will even have a few drinks. On day two, Mitchell and I will camp out together, alcohol-free, on the blackjack tables to count cards for the first time as father and son. What a Hallmark moment it will be.

My granddaughter, Hayden Grace, is not yet three years old. However, she may have the gambling gene more than anyone. We have a quarter slot-machine in the basement of our home. Hayden is on the machine constantly. As an infant, her first words were "ma-ma," then "da-da," then "sot-maceen." Nobody has won the grand prize on the one-armed bandit, but Hayden has hit the next highest jackpot. She is well on her way. In May 2009, I was blessed with another granddaughter, Harper Madeline. I suspect she will be a gambler; the obstetrician said Harper popped out of the womb holding a deck of cards.

Now that you understand the genetic make-up of the rest of my family, let's examine the full extent of my father's gambling lifestyle on yours truly. While there were six kids in the Wiggy household, I was the only one to pursue the game of golf seriously like my father. I think it was the summer between fourth and fifth grade when Dad began to let me tag along to the 18-hole golf course on Tinker Air Force Base, near Oklahoma City. My father was the Head Golf Professional and Manager at Tinker for over thirty years. Don't think for a minute that the life of a golf pro and manager was easy. Dad typically worked six days a week, anywhere from ten to fourteen hours a day, to ensure active and retired Air Force personnel had a place to unwind when duty no longer called. My father was especially known for taking care of the interests of the enlisted men and women first, before the high-ranking generals and colonels. "I don't like officers," he told me, as I was about to graduate from the United States Air Force Academy as an officer.

In the summertime, I spent almost every day at Tinker. In the early mornings, I'd help bring up golf carts from the storage shed with Bevo Russell and Andy Nagurny. Nobody complained that a ten-year-old kid was driving golf carts on federal government property. They all knew the carts would be ready for use much quicker with my help. I also picked up golf balls at the driving range. I was too young to drive the automated ball picker-upper-thingy, so my job was to retrieve the balls, by hand, that were under bushes or next to tree trunks where the automatic picker-upper-thingy couldn't maneuver. After I labored in the morning, Dad usually made me practice golf before I could play the course. I had a killer short-game when I was young. It wouldn't be long before I played golf for money.

In fifth and sixth grade, I played with the retired geriatric crowd of golfers who gambled for 25¢ skins. These were the same guys who calmly and peacefully told me horrific, blood-and-guts war stories from World War II and Korea, then complained and cursed loudly like the devil when they lost a quarter to someone on the golf course. I never had any money when I played with the older men, so Dad was my banker.

"Dad, can I borrow 75¢? I didn't win any skins today." I had always "borrowed" when I lost, but never paid the banker when I won. I remember borrowing a lot in the beginning. Each and every time before a round, my dad would tell me not to gamble unless I had the money. Each and every time at the end of a round, however, he would lend me the cash if I had lost while gambling.

After eighteen holes of golf, sometimes thirty-six holes or more, I helped Dad and his friends in a much different way at the clubhouse. At the end of a long, hot day for everyone, card-games broke out in the lounge. Most of the card players were the same retired military guys who had played golf during the day. Other men, like Dan Gutilla, Paul "Ho-Ho" Smith, Jim Dixon or John Cassup would just show up for the card games wearing a coat and tie or other work clothes. My dad would join them after the golf course pro shop was closed for the day. The men usually played pitch or pinochle. I watched and learned all of the games. I had three important jobs during the card games: picking up trash, emptying ash trays and bringing drinks from the snack bar. The drinks were not always Coke or Dr Pepper—I'm talking mixed alcohol and beer. I knew all the drink names and combinations. My dad drank a VO-press. Other guys ordered a seven-and-seven or a whiskey sour. Ahh, the good ole days, when a ten year old could order alcohol at an Air Force base and deliver the elixir to gentlemen who sometimes tipped a quarter or fifty cents. Try sending your fifth-grader to retrieve alcohol now. You'll wind up in jail for child abuse. If I wasn't playing waiter or barkeep, I would diligently watch the card games. It didn't take long to learn the strategies. One time, I was looking over the shoulder of a guy named Warren Bachelor when he failed to play a trump suit from his hand in a game of pitch. I loudly yelled, "You reneged!" While everyone had laughed, except Warren, I was sternly counseled by my father to not make any comments while watching the games. Later in the car going home, Dad told me it was one of the funniest things he had ever seen in a card game. He gave me a high-five.

In seventh and eighth grade, when my golf game picked up to the point where I was close to breaking eighty, the old retired guys quit letting me play in their golf groups.

"Get the hell outta here, little Wiggy!" Joe McGowan once told me after he had lost $1.25 in skins. "You need to play with the guys on the blue tees."

So I started gambling with the better golfers. These were the guys further from death. Most had been recently retired or were active-duty Air Force personnel who played only on the weekends. They played $1 skins and $1 a-nine side bets. Since the level of play had been harder, it was typical for me to say, "Dad, can I borrow $4? I lost bets to Clyde Reese and Rex Lierman."

Dad would pull ones out of his wallet while saying, "I told you not to gamble."

Around the same time I played with the intermediate golfers, my role at the card tables in the lounge changed. My father would permit me to keep score during the gin rummy and pinochle games. Sometimes the men would let me play their hand while they went to the bathroom. During a dark day filled with lightning, thunderstorms, and a tornado watch, when the otherwise busy golf course had been deserted and few card players ventured to the clubhouse, my dad and two of his friends were aching to play pinochle, but didn't have a fourth player. Dad suggested that I play as his partner. I was extremely nervous, but proud as hell. It was a father-son moment that I will never forget. To be asked by my dad, my golf and gambling idol, to join him at the green felt table was an honor. I tear up thinking about it now. We didn't win, but the game was close. In the end, Dan Gutilla told me while pocketing his winnings, "You're still better at Pinochle than Colonel Dailey."

In ninth and tenth grade, after my dad had coached me and pushed me to the practice tee at every opportunity, I was regularly shooting golf in the seventies. Funny thing—many of the golfers who previously made me borrow from Dad were no longer willing to play me for money. I was forced to move up again in the golf course strata of players. Now, I was playing with the chiselers. These were guys like Russ Moody and David Dover. They were not only great golfers, but also great gamblers. I remember times when I had scored better than Russ and Dave, but I lost money in the end.

"Okay, Little Wig," Russ explained, "Our team lost the front-side but won the back and the Nassau. I pressed you individually, when I was two-down after the sixth hole, then won the next three. You won the back side, but I won the automatic press on eighteen on the partner bets with me and Ralph and me and Bill against you and Carl and you and Lou. I also won the rabbit with two legs. You owe me $19."

"Just a second. I need to get change."

I then went to the ATM in the clubhouse. Not the automatic teller machine—those things didn't exist yet. The "ATM" in this case was "All Tom's Money."

"Dad, can I borrow $19? Moody won a bunny rabbit or something like that."

"Don't gamble with those guys. They'll take all your money," Dad explained as he forked over a twenty. "Go practice."

Sometimes I practiced, but other times I headed straight up the stairs to the player's lounge after golf. Guess what I did at this age? You remember those old geezers who quit letting me play in the 25¢ skin game on the golf course? They had their own card game afterwards in the lounge, knock-poker. Dad would have never let me play in the pitch game along with his buddies for $5-and-2 or $10-and-4, but he would let me play in the 50¢ poker game with the Veterans of Foreign War crowd. Sometimes I'd win, sometimes I'd lose.

"Dad, can I borrow $5? I knocked with a flush but Bill Wooten had a full house."

"I told you not to gamble with those guys unless you had money. Maybe you should get a job."

"I know, I know."

My final ascension into the golf and gambling world occurred during senior year when I was one of the top high school golfers in Oklahoma. I won a qualifying tournament that earned me the chance to represent the state in the All-American High School tournament in Lexington, Kentucky. My proud father, who previously shied me away from the hustlers at the Tinker Air Force Base golf course, now embraced my golfing and gambling abilities. He fully took me under his wing as a gambling protégé outside of Tinker. I was now playing with Dad and his professional golf acquaintances at Twin Hills Golf and Country Club and other courses around the Greater Oklahoma City area. The first time I played with the big-time gamblers at Twin Hills, Dad filled me with advice that I had never heard.

"Don't shoot well today. I don't want you breaking eighty."

I didn't know how to suck on purpose. "Dad, why not? I've been waiting to play this course forever!"

"Do as I say. If you beat the pants off everyone today, we'll never get another game. They already think I'm a seven handicap. You need to be worse than me. Plus, whatever we lose on the golf course, I'll make up when they play gin after the round in the clubhouse."

"Can I play in the gin game?"

"No," Dad said emphatically "I don't want you gambling with these guys."

He meant "...gambling with these guys on the card table."

Dad had been perfectly fine with me gambling on the golf course, especially as his partner. The first day I had played golf at Twin Hills, I shot an eighty-five. I wasn't good at missing shots on purpose, so I selected the wrong clubs all day. On some holes, my approach shot was well short. On other holes, my club selection put me over the green. On the eighteenth hole, when all the bets had been doubled, and I normally played with ice in my veins, I flew my second shot forty yards over the green and out of bounds. The ball bounced off Doc Randall's Cadillac Seville in the parking lot and almost hit the widow Hayes walking into the clubhouse.

"Christ, Tom, you gotta stop feeding that kid!" Don Davidson commented happily. He and his partner doubled up on us when my dad uncommonly missed a two-footer for par on the hole. As we were cleaning up in the clubhouse, Dad gave me $50 to hold.

When they tallied the bets, Dad and I lost $45 each. I had never lost that much on a bet. In front of ten other men, my father asked if I had the money to cover my share of the losses. I was embarrassed as I reached into my pockets and pulled out the fifty. Later, Dad told me that it was important to look like I had my own money. Then, as he had prognosticated earlier, my father won a couple hundred dollars at the gin table. He gave me a cut of the winnings.

The next time we gambled with Don Davidson on the golf course, he had a different partner, Robert something-or-other. Robert was in the oil business. He and three of his buddies were in town just for the day. The other three guys would be playing in the group ahead of us with one of the regular players. Before the round started, I heard Don say that he'd take Robert versus me and Dad best-ball. Plus, Davidson said he'd take each of the three visiting guys in the front group against Tom and me. The bet was $50 Nassau for each two-man partnership, meaning $50 bet on the front nine, $50 on the back nine, and $50 for the total eighteen holes. I watched as the three other oil guys teed off ahead of us. All of them hit decent shots down the center of the fairway. In our group, Robert smacked one down the center as well. Dad told me, "Don't hold back, today."

At this point in the story, I don't feel it is necessary to bother you with the details of how that golf match ended at Twin Hills Country Club on that sunny day in June 1984. It is more important to stress the unbelievably strong bond that was built between father and son during the four-and-a-half-hour journey. A bond between two men, two gamblers, one of them, who started to turn gray as he approached retirement as a golf pro, which meant he would now be unencumbered to play golf for fun instead of playing golf for a career, and another, younger man, about to graduate high school a top-notch golfer, but headed to the United States Air Force Academy, where the golf season was only five months long each year because of the weather, and where golf would criminally take a backseat to the pursuits of professional officership and academia, which meant, the younger golfer would never, ever, play golf to the caliber he did in the summer before going to college. That is not important. It is the *bond*, the *love*, between two men sharing the same gambling DNA that is important in this story. It is the *memories* that each would have of each other, and the day they shared on the green grass and cool breeze in perfect 75-degree weather, that is key in this story.

It isn't important, for example, to know that the father-and-son team of Thomas Walter "Wielgoleski" Wiggy and Glen "Little Wig" Wiggy shot an impressive six-under par best-ball, that glorious spring day. No, no, that is not important. It is also not worth mentioning that Dad and I scored no worse than par on every single hole as a team on the difficult Twin Hills layout that glorious spring day. And, for example, it would be spitefully trivial to point out that bets had been doubled, and even tripled at one point during the round because Don Davidson's oily friends were in trees, bunkers, creeks and other natural and man-made pitfalls the entire glorious spring day. That means nothing. It is also meaningless to mention that my father birdied the ninth hole, and I birdied the eighteenth, sealing all possibilities for last-minute try-to-get-even-on-the-final-hole heroics on the part of the opposing teams on that glorious spring day.

Finally, it is not even worth the paper this book is printed on to know that Don and his friends tried winning back their massive losses on the gin table later in the day, but proved terribly unsuccessful. My father, the wonderful man who never let me play cards with the big fish, the man who always told me "No" when I wanted to gamble for the big bucks on the card table, the man who just won a small fortune on the golf course, do you think he considered letting me play cards with Don Davidson and the oil men that day in the Twin Hills clubhouse? *Hell no!* Oh well, I still have the bond.

Epilogue:

As you might imagine, my father's gambling was not always a positive influence on the family. Growing up, I remember a few late-night arguments between my parents about "losses" and "bills to pay." Dad didn't win every time. Nobody does. If a gambler, especially a blackjack card-counter, tells you he wins every time, he is completely and utterly full of bullshit. Don't listen. In fact, walk away. My father was never like that. He took the good with the bad, the wins with the losses. While he didn't win every time, he was certainly creative in under-emphasizing losses and over-embellishing wins. For instance, two days before my sister, Kim, married Brad the Cajun in 1981, my father won approximately $2000 on a trifecta at the New Orleans Fair Grounds racetrack. I was there. It was a most joyous occasion. Funny thing, at the wedding reception, Dad told everyone that he won $3000. Ten years later, when Dad recounted the story, the trifecta at the horse track before Kim's wedding paid $5000. A few years ago, while in great spirits at my parent's 50th wedding anniversary celebration, Dad asked me, "Remember when I won $10,000 at the track before Kim got married?" *Priceless.* I look forward to the day when my DNA causes me to exaggerate to my great-grandkids about the millions of dollars I won while counting cards at blackjack at the turn of the twenty-first century.

THE WARNING SIGNS

When all blackjack tables are the same (number of decks, bet limit, rules, etc.,) it doesn't matter where you play the game in the casino. Mathematically, this is a simple concept. Psychologically, however, where you sit may be a huge decision. After all, nobody wants to share the table with an unfriendly dealer or a blackjackally challenged player. In order to maximize your playing experience, try to avoid the following people:

- The elderly couple who refer to the game as "twenty-one."
- The dealer whose stomach is so large, it hangs over the entire chip tray.
- The thirty-something guy who claims to win every time. Meanwhile, he's sporting a $3 K-Mart shirt and betting the table minimum.
- The waitress who jokingly says, "If you don't tip me, I'll spit in your coffee."
- The tiny old lady who buys in the game for $10 by giving the dealer quarters, dimes, and nickels.
- The new twenty-one year old who proclaims, "Don't worry, I know how to play. I watch Texas hold'em on TV all the time."
- Players who bet weird amounts every hand, like one green chip, one red, one pink, and one silver. Count how much time is wasted on each deal and payout.
- The ninety-seven-year-old man who brings an oxygen tank to the table—and two packs of Salem cigarettes.
- Anyone who doubles down with a hard seven then gets genuinely excited after drawing a face card.
- The casino that gives you $95 in chips for every $100 buy-in.

Seriously, I saw this once at an Indian reservation casino in Oklahoma. If you are in a casino or shady gambling parlor where the house charges you to play, run for the nearest exit immediately.

- The female dealer with pictures of her kids or pets attached to her ID card. She will eventually start talking about them.

- The businessman who sits next to you and discusses his recent bout with swine flu.

- Anyone who loudly claims, "I don't care if I win or lose. I just wanna have fun!" These people should be banned from the casino. People who whistle or sing at the table should also be banned.

- The elderly gentleman who takes seven minutes to place a bet. He may also refer to the game as "twenty-one."

- The man who slaps you on the back each time your first card is an ace, saying, "Good luck on that ace." Sometimes, a woman will do this, but she'll usually touch your hand or shoulder gently.

- The homeless looking guy who hasn't showered since the Reagan administration.

- The dealer who smiles or laughs each time you bust.

- The 450-pound man eyeing the chair in the 15-inch space between you and the nearest player.

- Any player who says, "The deuce is the dealer's ace." Clearly, as any second grader can tell you, the ace is the dealer's ace, and the deuce is the dealer's deuce. If you hear someone say, "The deuce is the dealer's ace," be sure to point out how stupid they are.

- Anyone who is drunk. Although, it is fun to watch them lose.

- The woman who says, "You know, they gambled for Christ's clothes before he was crucified." I sat on a table where this happened. Later in the game, the woman didn't know whether to hit a hand or not. I asked her, "What would Jesus do?"

- The southern guy who disregards any Basic Strategy advice and claims, "The people that wrote them books is in cahoots with the casino."

- The guy who seems to be bragging when he says, "I lost three-thousand yesterday."
- The woman who proclaims to everyone at the table, "I won't be here long. My newborn will be waking up soon."
- The mild-mannered man in the NRA hat who, after losing, tells the dealer, "What comes around, goes around."
- The old woman who asks the dealer, "How much do I have?" *every* hand. She might also refer to the game as "twenty-one."
- Any player who kisses the cut card, for luck.
- Any player who refuses to hit on a thirteen, for luck.
- Any player who sits out the first hand, for luck.
- Any player who arranges the chips a distinct way each time before placing the bet on the table, for luck. One of my Air Force co-workers, Casey Sere, was guilty of this foolishness.
- Any player who places something on the table—a rabbit's foot, horseshoe, four-leaf clover, mood ring, yin/yang symbol, hot wheel car, rose stone, rosary, miniature Buddha, or fake dog poop—and constantly rubs it, for luck. Sometimes the casino will give trinkets or beads to each player, for luck. I throw them into the urinal for target practice.

LEARNING TO COUNT CARDS, TRULY

To review, the running count is the numerical value maintained by the player from the first card dealt to the last card seen until a deck or shoe is reshuffled. In theory, the deck or shoe favors the card-counter when the running count is high. How high does high need to be before "high" is "HIGH"? While this question may sound like a presidential response from the impeachment investigation of Bill Clinton—you know, the same proceedings in which he testified to using Monica Lewinsky as a humidor—the correct answer is, "high" must be "relatively high." The running count is not a good enough indicator on its own to judge the relative number of high cards remaining to be played. For instance, suppose the first ten cards dealt from the top of a six-deck shoe are all low cards (three, four, five, or six). The running count would be +10. Toward the end of a shoe, a +10 running count is a heavy heartbeat, "Omigosh" moment which might require the player to bet as much as nine times the original unit bet. At the beginning of a six-deck shoe, however, a +10 ten running count is only a mild fluctuation. Think about it. With only ten cards played from a six-deck shoe, there are 302 cards remaining to be seen—way too many to start betting the bank.

To accurately gauge the running count against the number of cards remaining, you must use the "true count":

> **true count =** the running count divided by the number of half-decks remaining in the deck or shoe. The true count stabilizes the running count based on the number of cards remaining. Note: many other card-counting strategies tabulate the true count using full-decks instead of half-decks.

You might be wondering, "What the livin' heck is a half-deck?" A half-deck is twenty-six cards, or half a deck. Duh. Pardon my sarcasm. Some concepts in gambling, as in life, are dirt simple. Since I don't want you bad-mouthing my instructional methods this early in the book, let me show you some graphical aids. A normal deck of fifty-two playing cards is approximately the same height as a U.S. dime:

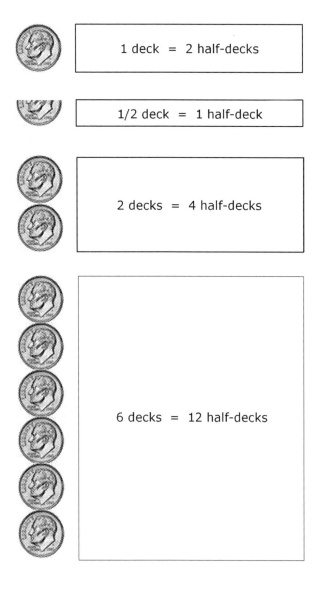

1 deck = 2 half-decks

1/2 deck = 1 half-deck

2 decks = 4 half-decks

6 decks = 12 half-decks

It does not take long to visualize a deck of cards using the dime method. If necessary, keep Roosevelt's little head next to the cards while you practice. When I teach probability and statistics in the classroom, I make it a point to offer students more than one frame of reference to reinforce key concepts. Therefore, I offer the following graphic aids just in case the dime visualization isn't working for you.

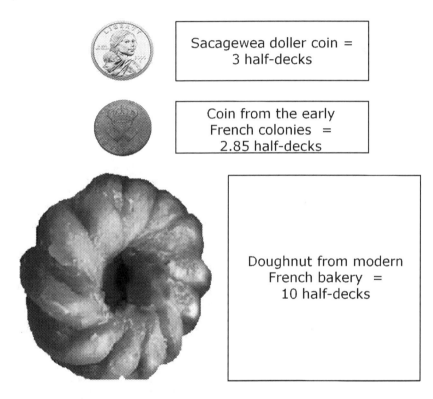

Sacagewea doller coin =
3 half-decks

Coin from the early
French colonies =
2.85 half-decks

Doughnut from modern
French bakery =
10 half-decks

While the running count is maintained from hand to hand, the true count must be calculated or approximated before each hand, by dividing the running count by the number of half-decks. If the running count is +8 and four half-decks remain in a multi-deck shoe, the true count is +2. If the running count is −2, and two half-decks remain, the true count is −1. If the running count is +14, and five half-decks remain, the true count is actually 14 ÷ 5 = +2.8, but an approximation of +3 can be used. If the running count is −3 immediately after the start of six-deck shoe, the true count is $-3 \div 12$ = -0.25, so you should consider the true count to be zero.

At this point, you should practice, practice, practice. In the beginning of your practice sessions, use pencil and paper if necessary to do the math. Of course, you must eventually be able to convert the running count to the true count in your head. I suspect it would be easy for a pit boss to spot a card-counter if he or she was doing long division on a cocktail napkin before each hand.

Hang in there. I estimate that we are more than halfway done with the most difficult part of card-counting. If you can fully grasp the following three important points regarding true card-count computation, you'll be ready to continue:

(1) If you visit a casino where the cards are dealt from a multiple-deck shoe, it is sometimes difficult to see or determine how many cards remain in the shoe. In that case, it might be necessary to look at the stack of discarded cards to approximately how many half-decks remain in the game. For instance, if two half-decks have been played in a six-deck shoe, then ten half-decks remain. If half a deck has been dealt from a double-deck shoe, three half-decks remain.

(2) You do not have to determine the true count *exactly* from the running count. For instance, if you determine the true count is +2.85, you are being too precise. Personally, I round the true count to the nearest whole number. If you determine the true count is somewhere between +2 and +3, but you don't know which value to use for the final approximation, use the smaller value (+2) to be safe.

(3) Once you decide on the true count, and adjust your next bet accordingly, don't forget to resume the running count after the cards are played. There is absolutely no need to recall the true count once your bet is made—a new true count calculation will be required for the next hand. However, the running count must be tracked from hand to hand until the next shuffle.

So far, you've learned how to tally the cards using the running count. You've also been shown how to approximate the number of half-decks remaining in a deck or shoe. Using the running count divided by the number of half-decks, you were able to calculate the true count. Soon, you will learn the final steps in the blackjack card-counting process—how to adjust your unit bet to capitalize on the strength of the true count and the number of cards remaining. Now is the time for more practice. While you do that, I'm going out for a snack. For some strange reason, I have a craving for Krispy Kreme doughnuts.

BETTING ON THE COUNT

In February 1998, a cadet in my probability and statistics course at the United States Air Force Academy approached me after class to discuss concepts covered that day. Practically every probability and stats instructor uses coin flips, dice rolls, lottery drawings, and playing cards to demonstrate basic probability concepts. That day in class, I used numerous gaming examples.

"Using combinatorics, you can answer a question such as: what is the probability of being dealt a royal flush in spades? If the deck is thoroughly shuffled, and the cards are randomly dealt, the odds are approximately one in 2.6 million." I emphasized the importance of randomness to the class, "Of course, if the cards are shuffled by my father, the odds can be as low as one in three." Most of the cadets got the joke, and laughed. The ones who hadn't would eventually join the ranks of many Air Force officers that I've met throughout the years who have absolutely no sense of humor.

"Do you gamble, sir?" Cadet Second Class Reese Williams asked, once the other students departed the classroom on their way to the noon lunch formation and parade.

I thought about my response to the question carefully, trying to find the delicate balance between answering truthfully, but also remaining a good role model for the officer candidate. I remember the cadet lifestyle—I was in USAFA Class of '88, first class with refrigerators. Back then, I gambled all the time, breaking several cadet wing regulations. I did not want to reveal that fact in the conversation with Cadet Williams.

I replied, "I play golf or cards for a few bucks now and then with my friends."

"No, sir. I mean, do you gamble at casinos? You seem to know a lot about games of chance. I'm from Las Vegas and will be old enough to legally gamble this summer."

Wow, he was from Vegas. It has always been my secret dream to live in Nevada. Too bad my mother wasn't a showgirl. I could have been born and raised under the flashing neon lights of Las Vegas Boulevard instead of the Oklahoma heartland.

"Wow, you're from Vegas? It has always been my secret dream to live in Nevada. Too bad my father wasn't a croupier. I could have been born and raised in the desert oasis instead of smack dab in the middle of tornado country."

"I know, I know. I feel the same way, sir," Cadet Williams beamed. "I can't wait to card-count in blackjack. Do you know anything about counting?"

"Certainly, but you need to get to the lunch formation. Come back and see me after last period."

During my lunch hour, I quickly drove home and dug through a couple boxes of books to find my copy of the *Beat the House Companion* by Avery Cardoza. I wanted to brush up on the details of counting before the young, inexperienced cadet came to my office. I would obviously take the lead in discussing the finer aspects of card-counting. Cadet Williams would learn a few new tricks from the master.

He arrived in my office at 1600 hours (4:00 p.m. for you civilians.)

"Here is what I've been studying," Cadet Williams announced as he arranged no less than seven blackjack references on my desk. I forget most of the titles and authors, but the stack contained *Beat the Dealer* by Edward Thorpe, and I believe there was a text in the collection by Stanford Wong, plus one book that was over an inch thick. The texts contained numerous charts, graphs, probability distributions, and card-counting algorithms. There were numerous insightful notes and calculations penciled in the texts. I recognized Williams' handwriting.

"I've modeled most of the High-Lo options as well as the All-Sevens variation used in Europe. I'm toying with my own card-counting strategy by assigning non-parametric, tiered values for groups of aces as they appear geometrically within post-shuffled, non-repeating Boolean sequences."

I was shocked by the cadet's knowledge on the subject. The only reference I had on blackjack card-counting was 8-12 pages from a book that had been packaged with a casino software game.

My response, as I pointed to the *Beat the House Companion* booklet, "If you lose all your money in this computer game, you get kicked outta the casino. Neato, huh?"

In the two hours that Cadet Williams spent in my office, I did little speaking and a whole lot of listening. He taught me a lot that chilly February day. I hadn't been able to "learn him" anything about card-counting, but I did shed some light on lesser-known probability distributions that could be used for math modeling. The next weekend, I did some modeling of my own on blackjack. I didn't have any fancy-schmancy reference books like Williams, but I did possess six decks of cards. I reviewed the basic Hi-Lo counting option that I had learned from Avery Cardoza's book a few years earlier. I hadn't practiced counting in awhile, but the technique came back in no time at all. Just like riding a bike.

As I mentioned earlier in this book, a card-counter in blackjack gains the advantage by betting more when a significant number of high cards remain, and betting less, or leaving the table, when a significant number of low cards remain. Most popular blackjack card-counting strategies are similar. Using the half-deck method, start with a unit bet, say $10, at the beginning of the deck or shoe. While maintaining the running count from hand to hand, adjust the bet for each successive hand using the true count as follows:

True count	-1 or less	0	+1	+2	+3	+4	+5	...	+x
Bet (units)	1	1	2	3	5	7	9	...	2x - 1

Is that a little taste of algebra at the end of the chart? Wow, I never thought I'd use algebra again after 11th grade. Thanks, blackjack!

For instance, if the true count is zero, continue betting $10 a hand. If the true count becomes +1, you would bet two times, or double, the unit bet. The wager for the hand would be $20. If the true count was +3, your wager would be five times the unit bet, or $50. If the true count is −1 or lower, wager the unit bet or consider leaving the game. Note: Some betting strategies require the player to also adjust the unit bet based on a side-count of aces remaining in the deck. That type of supplemental strategy is beyond the scope of this book. Feel free to explore it on your own once you have mastered basic card-counting.

For my rudimentary math model on card-counting, I recorded the results of five-hundred hands of blackjack dealt from a six-deck shoe. I constructed a spreadsheet that tallied the running count throughout each sequence of hands. I simulated a game with three players and a dealer, but only tallied the results for one player's hand. For simplicity, I assumed that everyone at the simulated table played according to Basic Strategy. I adjusted the unit bet before each hand according to the guidelines in the above chart. The results for the five-hundred simulated hands:

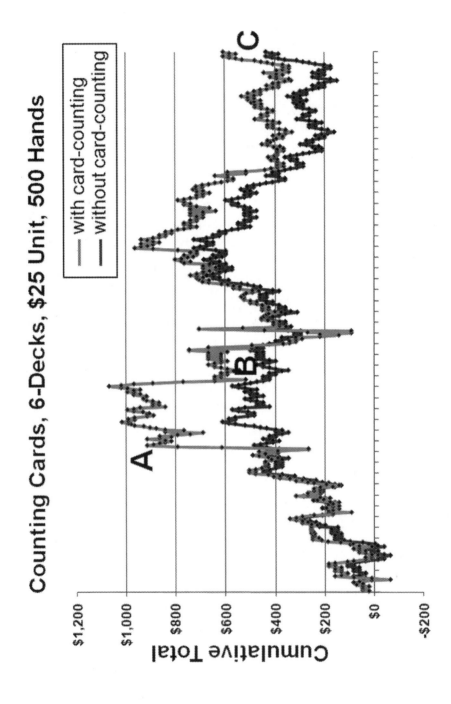

Counting Cards, 6-Decks, $25 Unit, 500 Hands

The bottom line on the graph represents the results for a player who did not card-count. The top line represents the exact same results for each of the five-hundred hands, except the bet was adjusted according to the true count. As you can see, Lady Luck was smiling on both scenarios—both players were winners after five-hundred hands. Notice the larger number of deviations, or fluctuations, in the top line (bets with counting) versus the bottom line (bets without counting). Point "A" indicates the end of a four-hand winning streak when the unit bet was tripled or quadrupled. Point "B" highlights the end of a six-hand losing streak when the true count was high. The total difference between counting and not counting after five-hundred hands is annotated at point "C." In this case, the card-counter would have won $170 more than the normal player. If this were an actual scenario, and the card-counter quit sometime shortly after the winning streak at point "A," the difference between counting and not counting would have been as much as $500.

After finishing my simulation, and charting the results with pretty blue and red ink and perfectly centered and sized labels, I was anxious to share the results.

"Cadet Williams, I need to see you after class." Predictably, the other students "ooohed" and "aaahed" after I made this statement. They thought Williams was in trouble.

"Look at this," I bragged, after relating the story of how I had dealt five-hundred hands to myself.

"That's great, sir. Uh, but you know, I did that same sort of model on the computer with one million hands when I was in high school."

Awed again by Cadet Williams' brilliance, but not shaken by his actions, I retorted, "Yeah, but did you have a graph with pretty blue and red ink and perfectly centered and sized labels?"

"No, sir. Mine was black and white with no labels." He gave me a look that said, "You're cool, I'm not." That had been precisely what I wanted out of the conversation, since I was obviously not smarter than my own pupil when it came to blackjack.

Besides dictating the proper amount to bet, the true count can also signify when to play the cards differently. For instance, Basic Strategy dictates a player hit a thirteen when the dealer is showing a two. However, when the true count is +1 or more, the player should not hit. The probability of busting increases—for you and the dealer. A high true count can also justify buying insurance against a dealer's ace. Normally, buying insurance against an ace is a terrible move. You should refer to wizardofodds.com or a more advanced card-counting book like the type Cadet Williams owned to determine when to deviate from Basic Strategy with "index plays" during a high true count. It all depends on the counting strategy, rules of the table and/ or number of decks in play.

Before ending this chapter, I feel it is important to point out a common misconception regarding card-counting. Don't think for a minute that you'll win every hand when the unit bet is doubled, tripled or more. The odds of winning increase only a fractional amount (1-2%) by counting. Your goal should be to win the majority of hands when the true count is high. Winning two of three or three of five with a high count is well worth the effort. Sometimes, simply getting a blackjack or a winning double-down hand with a tripled unit bet can erase a whole hour of losses when the count had been relatively non-existent. In my opinion, the hardest part of counting is being patient while waiting for the card-counting "edge" to surface.

THE SHACK

January 28, 2001 was my first day living in "The Shack." It was also the day that my blackjack card-counting adventure officially began. I had played blackjack with family and friends since elementary school, and visited Las Vegas, Atlantic City and a few other casinos in the United States several times as an adult, but those visits were sometimes years apart, and for limited durations. When I counted cards at the Sandia Casino in Albuquerque, New Mexico, on the night of January 28, 2001, little did I know that it would be visit #1 out of 864 total visits in a seven-and-a-half year span.

Six months prior, my family and I lived in Colorado Springs, Colorado. I had been in the city five-and-a-half years on two successive Air Force duty assignments. When an Air Force officer stays in one place for that long, it is considered "homesteading" by military officials. Homesteading is supposed to have a negative impact on the career of a junior officer. Therefore, senior leaders and assignment personnel in the Air Force do their damndest to make sure officers get their ass moving to another duty location before the stigma of homesteading settles in the officer's permanent record. For me, the next logical assignment in my career progression as a Scientific Analyst was at the Headquarters Air Staff at the Pentagon. I didn't want to go there. Lori and the kids were happy in Colorado. All of my wife's family lived there. I liked the state as well, except for the ridiculous five-month golf season each year cut short due to inches or feet of some cold, white powdery substance.

My daughter, Sarah, expressed the most displeasure about moving from Colorado in the middle of her senior year of high school.

"I won't go, Dad!" she insisted, "All my friends are here. If I have to, I'll live with grandma and grandpa before I go to college."

I expected the reaction. No problem. In just a second, my gorgeous wife and best friend for life will say something like, "No, Sarah, we must support Dad and go where he goes."

Lori made her point clear without any hesitation, "I can't let my baby live in Colorado without me. I'm staying too!"

Just then, I looked at my son, Mitchell. My boy. My shadow. The fifth-grader who had made me so proud recently while playing second base because he stayed down on a difficult one-hopper that hit him under the chin, popping his head up for an instant, then bounced off his chest a yard in front of him. Mitchell grabbed the ball and threw the batter out at first base with a split second to spare. After the play, he had quickly spotted me in the stands and gave an exaggerated thumbs up all the while fighting tears that were leaking from his eyes just above his throbbing chin and red cheeks. My son, my ten-year-old genius. The kid who learned any and all sense of logic from me, not his mom or sister. I could depend on Mitchell—he certainly would be on my side of the dilemma.

"Have fun in Washington state, Dad." Some prodigy. Not only did he quickly join forces with the women, but he also had me moving to the wrong side of the country.

At least I could take Barkley, my trusty black lab. He would be my only friend in Washington D.C.

"Don't even think about taking Barkley either!" Lori and the kids chimed in unison.

I spent a few weeks wheeling and dealing on the telephone with the Air Force assignment teams in San Antonio, Texas. There were no options for me to remain in Colorado. I had to move. Fortunately, not far. After all was said and done, and a bird colonel at my current duty assignment cashed in a favor, I received orders to the Air Force Operational Test and Evaluation Center at Kirtland Air Force Base in Albuquerque. My report-no-later-than date was the end of January 2001. After serious discussion with Lori and the kids, we all agreed that it would be ridiculous to move Sarah during the last semester of her senior year. Plus, we had needed time to sell the house in Colorado Springs. It was jointly decided that I would live in an apartment by myself for five months. After Sarah had graduated, the whole family would join me, regretfully, but rightfully, in Albuquerque. I had never lived away from the wife and kids for more than a couple weeks.

What could I possibly do with all my time until June? Yet-to-be-known-answer: visits #1 through #118 to the casino.

I departed snowy Colorado the day after Sarah's eighteenth birthday. The present that I gave her, letting her finish high school in Colorado, was not material.

"Thank you for doing this, Daddy," Sarah said while hugging me. "I love you bigger than the sky."

After a teary goodbye to everyone, and a five hour drive south from Colorado Springs, I reported into my new unit. I had signed paperwork for fifteen minutes and was given the rest of the day and the next day off to get settled in town. I had used an apartment locator to find me the Shack earlier in the week before my arrival. The "Shack" got its name because the room was four-hundred-eighty square feet of nothing. The apartment was the size of a shack used to store garden equipment at a normal-sized home. The bed in the Shack folded into the wall. There were two wooden folding chairs, a kitchen table the size of a newspaper, and a lounge chair just slightly larger than a coach airplane seat. There was also a small sofa, but I had to move it each time the bed was pulled down from the wall. The kitchen was the size of a normal bathroom. The bathroom was the size of a normal closet. The closet was the size of a junior high school locker. The crappy heating and air conditioning unit kept the room bitterly cold in the winter and uncomfortably warm in the summer. Before I had purchased industrial strength room deodorizer, the Shack smelled like a mixture of bacon, cabbage and ass. There were a couple of roaches in the Shack, but even they disliked the small confines of the room.

The Shack was *awesome.*

Well, the Shack wasn't awesome, but the casino located less than five miles from the Shack certainly was. I knew the casino was there even before I had spotted it on the side of I-25 driving into town. I had been practicing card-counting hardcore ever since I learned of the pending assignment to New Mexico. Since my sister-in-law had previously lived in the state, I knew gambling was nearby on two or three Indian reservations just outside of city limits.

Sandia Casino is now a huge, luxurious resort with a championship golf course. Back then, the original facility was relatively small, dark, beat-up and unfamiliar. There were only four or six table games enclosed in a building roughly the size of a high school gymnasium. The first night that I visited the casino, there were only 20-30 people in the entire facility. I didn't mind. I would have visited Sandia even if it was in a cave or a prison and I was the only patron.

I considered myself a seasoned gambler at the time. However, before card-counting on visit #1 with a $5 unit bet, I was nervous with butterflies in my stomach. I had a limited budget for blackjack. Since Lori and I were a few thousand dollars in credit card debt, and since we now had to budget for both a house and an apartment, I could not afford to lose. Besides being low on card-counting capital, I was also extremely paranoid. *I wonder how long I can count cards before they kick me out?* I paced around the blackjack tables until I found a dealer who was beginning a new six-deck shoe. The first hand she dealt to me was a pair of aces. Destiny. No hesitation at all—always split aces. I split the pair, receiving a jack on one hand and a king on the other. I was beaming after I won $10 on the first hand. I was so giddy, I had forgotten to count the cards. *Holy shit. That's why I'm here.* I got up from the table and walked away.

When I resumed playing at a different table, I was much calmer. What the hell was I thinking a few minutes ago, acting like a 1960's schoolgirl who saw the Beatles for the first time? I studied the cards like a hawk. From all my math modeling and card-counting practice, I knew to be patient waiting for a high card-count. The first shoe hovered near a zero running count the whole time. When the dealer had shuffled, I was down $5. The second shoe was way in the negatives. I quit playing when the true count had reached –2. I went to another table, down $15 at the time. Midway through the third shoe, the running count hit +6. My first card-count betting increase decision. My virginity was broken on an easy one. Six half-decks remaining with a +6 running count, thus, a +1 true count. I had doubled my $5 bet, but it seemed like I was betting the pink slip for my car. The butterflies returned with nervous energy. I had fully expected to be dealt a pair of face cards. Instead, I had gotten some crappy hand that required four hits before I busted. The first card-counted extra bet was gone. It felt like I had *lost* the pink slip for my car.

I stayed cool. After the hand, the running count was +9. I could have justified tripling the bet, but I stayed on the safe side of the bet increase. With another $10 wager, I had received a blackjack, but so did the dealer, with a face card on top so there was no have a chance to buy insurance, or take even money. The next hand I lost, but the running count went higher. The true count had been +2, so I tripled the bet. And won. I played a few more hands at double or triple the unit bet until the penetration card surfaced, signaling a shuffle. I was up $20. I think I had won four of six hands with the true count being positive.

An hour later, I won four hands in a row with a positive true count. On the fourth and last hand, I had needed a win to break $100 in winnings. I won in dramatic fashion, hitting a sixteen against the dealer's ten. The count had been positive, so I just knew that I'd get a face card. It was a five. The dealer's twenty pissed the other players off, but not me. I cashed in on a high note. The butterflies returned for one last time that night as I had approached the cashier cage. *This must be where the armed guards jump out of the back room and grab me for card-counting.* Nobody jumped out of anywhere and grabbed me for anything.

On the drive back to the Shack, I stopped at a Domino's Pizza carryout restaurant. I had only wanted a few slices, but ordered an extra large. I lived by myself now, and could eat cold pizza for breakfast the next day. I also ordered cinnamon sticks and grabbed a couple refrigerator magnets annotated with Domino's phone number. I returned to the Shack that first night having doubled my money. I learned two valuable lessons on visit #1. First, it is good to end the night on a high note after a winning streak with a positive true count, and second, take a *right* on Academy Blvd. when returning to the Shack from the casino, otherwise you'll drive around lost in that stupid sub-division with all the speed bumps until you eventually find your way home to eat cold pizza and cinnamon sticks because the microwave sucks in the Shack.

The next morning, I ran a few errands around town and visited the commissary and base exchange at Kirtland. After purchasing groceries and other knick-knacks, I still had $50 more in my wallet than when I arrived into town the previous afternoon. *Sweet.* I was back at Sandia Casino for visit #2 by noon. As I entered the dark building, the butterflies in my stomach returned, along with the accompanying hope-I-don't-get-busted-for-card-counting paranoia. I played and counted, and counted and played blackjack all day long. A few times, I was painfully close to losing my entire $150 bankroll. But I was patient. When the count was good, I upped the bets. When the count was lousy, I quit the table. I remember quitting a shoe midway, but continued to watch as the true count went to –2, then –3, then –5. Near the end of the shoe, all the other players, including the dealer, received nothing but low cards. The players always stayed, and the dealer always made a pat hand. I had been overjoyed knowing that I quit before the deluge.

Around seven o'clock in the evening, I departed the casino another $100 winner. Doubling my money seemed like a realistic goal during those early visits. After shelling out $15 for an encore Domino's pizza and cinnamon sticks dinner, I returned to the Shack. During my phone call to Lori and the kids, they all asked me, in different ways, if I was "bored yet?" *Hardly.*

The next day, I had to go the work. What a nuisance. I also had to go to the gym because the effects of an all-Domino's-pizza-and-cinnamon-stick diet were starting to show on my body. The new job was interesting and challenging, and I naturally stayed later than necessary since it was a new assignment with greater career responsibilities. I exercised after work, then ate soup, sandwich, and a salad for dinner. I returned to the Shack at 9:00 p.m., and didn't even think about going to the casino. That's a lie. I *had* thought about it, but I didn't go. Until the next night.

I don't have details for every time I had gone to the casino during the Shack era, but there were several memorable visits and milestones:

Visit #4. After posting wins on visits #1 through 3, I lost for the first time. While there were many good true counts, I seemed to lose the big bet hands more often than not. However, keeping with my strategy, I quit after a relatively good streak on a high true count. I was down $40, and could not justify another fast food victory dinner. I ate a TV dinner back in the Shack.

Visit #6. Until this point, I did not have a player's card at Sandia.

I had always thought that giving my name and address would make it easier to track me as a card-counter. I changed my mind about the player's club card, however, when I heard two women discuss how they were able to get comped a buffet meal after playing $5 a hand for just a few hours. My initial comp was a $10 Sandia Casino buffet meal that I earned later that night. I had won again, for the fifth time out of six visits, and celebrated with a dinner that cost me zilch.

Visit #9. This visit wasn't memorable for the result—I lost $100 relatively quickly with crappy cards and no significant positive counts whatsoever. Instead, visit #9 became part of Shack history because I had created an Excel spreadsheet at the end of the night in the confines of the dreary apartment to track wins and losses on each of my previous casino visits. Before that night, I kept track of all the data by hand on a small loose-leaf binder emblazoned with the Sandia Casino logo that was given to me as a free gift for joining the player's club earlier in the week. The binder was no match for technology. In addition to tabulating the wins and losses on Excel, I was able to chart the results and use linear regression to forecast future winnings. As I watched the predictive line climb steadily on my computer monitor, I decided that an increase in my unit bet was warranted. I had known card-counting worked from when I modeled the strategy back in Colorado. I also had $560 in winnings after visit #9; I could easily afford a $10 unit bet.

Around the same time, I had also learned about the 6:00 a.m. pick-up basketball game played each Monday, Wednesday, and Friday at the base fitness center. Perfect. If I exercised or ran a few ball games in the morning before work, my evenings would be free. What could I possibly do with all my free time each night?

Visit #24. On the last day of February, after winning $225 at Sandia, I made a new entry on the spreadsheet to track win percentage and earnings by month. I finished the month of February with twenty-one visits, of which, fifteen had resulted in wins and six ended in losses. My winnings for the month totaled $1555. I didn't play blackjack for the next four days; I was back in Colorado celebrating Lori's birthday with the family.

Visits #25 through #51. The month of March 2001 was productive. On my first visit to the casino after returning from Colorado, I upped my unit bet to $15 a hand. Three days later, I upped it to $25. Playing for $25 a hand brought back the butterflies and paranoia. The fluctuation in daily wins and losses was far more dramatic. On three occasions, I won more than $1000 on a visit. On a few other visits, I lost my entire $500 bankroll for the day. Each time I had won big, I thought I would be kicked out for card-counting.

One scary day in March, the pit boss asked me, "What's the count?"

Since I had previously researched card-counting strategy and tips to avoid being banned, I was ready for the answer. I even practiced my response a few times in the Shack, "Oh, I'm up about $350." I made a comment about my chip count, not the card-count. My goal was to convince the pit boss that I didn't know what he was talking about. The pit boss simply nodded and smiled. After seeing his reaction, I think that he thought, that I thought, that I was tricking him, when in fact, he probably thought, that I thought, that he thought, my answer was phony, so actually, I wasn't fooling anyone. Whatever the case, I continued counting and he continued watching. Consciously, however, the paranoia increased big time. *Today I will definitely get banned.* It didn't happen.

Just to be safe, I started playing blackjack at some of the other casinos in the Albuquerque area. Casino Hollywood was approximately twenty-five miles north of town off I-25. The casino and a truck stop were the only facilities on the highway exit. Casino Hollywood offered single-deck blackjack, but the rules were screwy—the player could only double-down on ten or eleven, not on soft hands. I never really got into that particular game or the casino in general. I played at the Santa Ana Star Casino on the northwest side of the city and the Isleta Casino twenty miles south of Albuquerque. It was a pain in the butt driving back and forth to Santa Ana and Isleta, but I quickly learned that both resorts comped rounds of golf on their courses. I added them as regular stops on my card-counting circuit.

With good fortune throughout the month of March came great rewards. I had won enough to pay the monthly rent on the Shack plus all utilities with cash or locally purchased money orders. Lori thought something was wrong with our checkbook balance, because it never went down due to actions on my end. I was also making deposits into the bank a couple times a week. I opened a Bank of America account strictly for blackjack transactions. The conditions of the BOA ATM card were perfect. The maximum I could withdrawal per day was $500, the same amount as my daily bankroll. That way, I didn't have to carry large wads of cash to the casino. Carrying large amounts of cash *from* the casino was never a logistical problem for me to sweat.

I reaped other rewards. I continued my tradition of stopping at Domino's Pizza on the way home to the Shack on nights when I had won big. For variety, I alternated between Domino's and Pizza Hut. I never bought any big ticket items for myself, but I began the tradition of buying several new music CDs on the weekends. I remember the era of the Shack distinctly each time I listen to *Everyday* by The Dave Matthews Band, *All That You Can't Leave Behind* by U2, or the grossly under-rated album, *Pay Attention* by The Mighty, Mighty Bosstones. I also upped my collection of George Carlin comedy CD's to well over twenty with casino winnings from the timeframe.

March ended with impressive statistical results. My monthly winning percentage decreased from February, but the total winnings were almost $3000.

Visits #52 through #83. April 2001 was an absolute rush. It will always be remembered as the greatest single month of my blackjack card-counting adventure. At the beginning of April, I was playing with a $25 unit bet. At the end of the month, I was playing $100 a hand. With the exception of a three-day visit to Colorado Springs for my birthday weekend, I played every day in April. Even on the night of my birthday, as I had returned to Albuquerque late in the evening because I couldn't miss work the next day, I stopped at Sandia. I had been tired from driving, and didn't really want to stop. However, the Sandia Player's Club had sent me a promotional coupon earlier in the month for extra bonus points if I gambled on my birthday. I played five hands, winning four of them without counting. I was in and out of the facility in less than five minutes. My quick birthday visit paid for all the gas and munchies on both road trips to and from home.

Visit #68 was a watershed day. Before telling you about that visit, I must define a new blackjack gambling phrase:

magic shoe = a rare, multiple-deck blackjack phenomenon

in which the shoe unexpectedly offers cards that defy normal probabilities and winning expectations.

I entered Santa Ana Casino around ten o'clock on a Saturday morning. I was betting $50 per hand with a $750 bankroll. There was one other player at the table with me. On the third or fourth shoe of the day, all the stars and planets in the blackjack universe aligned to give me an unbelievable run of cards. Early in the shoe, the dealer gave me numerous double-downs and split hands. I won all of them. Later in the shoe, I had a run of five wins in a row, then one loss, then seven more wins in a row. Meanwhile, by mid-shoe, the true count was already +2. Toward the end of the shoe, I had a run of three or four blackjacks in a span of five minutes. Twice when the dealer had an ace on top, I insured my bet due to the count. The dealer had blackjack both times. Almost every time I had a twelve, thirteen, fourteen, fifteen, or sixteen throughout the shoe, I hit, and made a pat hand. Almost every time the dealer had showed a bust card, he busted. The shoe ended in dramatic fashion. The true count was a hair more than +3. On a $300 bet, I received a pair of eights against the dealer's face card. Always split eights. I hated my chances against a face card with a $300 bet, but I had to do it—splitting eights was a no-brainer. I had silently begged for threes, but I received a queen of clubs on both of the eights. Two eighteens.

As the dealer looked at his hole card, he smiled wildly, "This has been a pretty good shoe." A seven, for a total of seventeen. After coloring up, and tipping the dealer generously, I won $2800 on the magic shoe. *Holy jumpin' fuckin' catfish.*

The magic shoe had lasted only fifteen minutes, but the adrenaline lasted for hours. I was out of the Santa Ana Casino and on the Santa Ana Golf Course by noon. My golf swing was not hampered one bit by the thick wad of cash in my front pocket. I bought beer all round for the threesome of New Yorkers who had let me join their group. That evening, I purchased ten music CDs and a Mesa Airline plane ticket from Albuquerque to Colorado Springs for the following weekend. The days of my ten-hour, roundtrip automobile road trips were over.

April 2001 was also the month that my mother and father had

visited Albuquerque and stayed three days and two nights in the Shack. Despite repeated urgings to my own version of Mr. and Mrs. Seinfeld, Mom and Dad would not let me put them in a hotel. They shared the bed that folded out from the wall. I slept on the floor near the kitchen, because I could not fit on the couch. With the mountains and all the culture that Albuquerque had to offer visitors, there was no doubt where we'd spend most of the time during my parent's visit—Sandia Casino. Mom played bingo and the slot machines, Dad played slots and table games. When my father and I sat at the blackjack table for the first time, he started to purchase $100 worth of chips.

"Put your money away. I have some chips for you." I gave my dad a $500 stack of greens. He thought it was strange that the $5 chips at the casino were green. "They're $25 chips, Dad, not $5."

"Ohhh, get the hell outta here. I'm not taking this!" Dad said.

"Yes, you are. It's an extremely small down-payment for everything you gave me in life."

I'll never forget that moment. My father gave me a wonderful, grateful look that only a father and son could understand. The bond between he and I was stronger than ever—until he took a hit on a thirteen against the dealer's five.

"Dad, let's go golfing instead."

Visit #83. I lost $700 on the last day of April. Who cares? Because on the day before...

Visit #82. Remember the magic shoe from earlier in the month? Another one, albeit not as dramatic as the first magic shoe, happened on April 29, 2001. Another $2000+ day in less than a few hours. For the month of April, I won twenty-two of twenty-nine visits. My cumulative winnings for the month totaled $5235.

In addition to the cash, of which most went into Bank of America certificates of deposit, I also earned $900 in merchandise comps. From the Sandia Casino Player's club, I received two 27-inch Sony televisions and two DVD players. From Santa Ana and Isleta, I earned several free golf rounds. All these comps had been provided to promote my continued visits to the casino. No problem there—it was icing on the cake.

Visits #84 through #97. The month of May started in the toilet.

I lost my $1000 daily bankroll three times during the first five visits of the month. I don't think I had been doing anything differently strategy-wise. I can't explain why the run of relatively bad luck had occurred. I remember being angry and frustrated after the second big loss. Maybe it affected my tracking of the cards and betting amounts. I definitely hadn't been paranoid about being kicked out of the casino. What house would kick out a big loser? I took six whole days off from the casino to simmer down a bit. I played a lot of golf and surfed the Internet for hours since I had a high-speed connection for the first time.

When I returned from Colorado mid-month, I decided to lower the unit bet to $50 until a string of good cards returned. With only a few gambling days left in the month before I had taken a long vacation to attend Sarah's high school graduation, followed by my annual trip to Fort Walton Beach, Florida, with friends, I went into the positive winnings for the month. I ended May with total earnings of only $450.

Visits #98 through #118. I knew the days of living in the Shack were about to end. Lori sold the house in Colorado Springs at a tidy profit on the first day it was posted on the market. *Those were the days.* The plan was for her and the kids to move to Albuquerque in late June or early July depending on the success of our home search in New Mexico.

Unlike May, I came out of the chute in the month of June with strong wins at the casino. I flirted with $100 unit bets a few times during the month, but I mainly played a $50 or $75 unit. I was up a couple thousand by mid-month. Plus, I had earned three more comped DVD players and another 27-inch television.

During a week-long house-hunting trip, Lori and Mitchell joined me in the one-room Shack. Mitchell thought the Shack was the greatest place in the world. He liked it, not for the allure of the casino like his old man, but for the swimming pool in the apartment complex and the high-speed Internet hook-up on my new computer. Lori didn't like the Shack, but she had tolerated it. The search for a new house could not begin fast enough. There were plenty of homes for sale in northeast Albuquerque. Lori and I had two great homes in mind when her sister, Tanya, arrived for the weekend with our two nieces, Taylor and Haley. Lori wanted her sister's advice on the top house prospects. Keep in mind, the Shack slept one person uncomfortably. For two nights in June 2001, the Shack slept three adults and three children miserably, plus my seventy pound black lab, Barkley, who, by the way, violated numerous apartment covenants involving pet litter, drooling on furniture, and other prohibitions involving black hairs clogging the drain in the swimming pool.

When I awoke from a crappy sleep before sunrise on Saturday morning because my nieces played the movie, *Mermaids*, three straight times on the VCR from 7:00 p.m. until 1:00 a.m., and I tossed and turned after that, I decided to play early-morning blackjack at Sandia. Sitting on a blackjack bar-stool during visit #107 was more comfortable than sleeping with one of Mitchell's feet in my ear and Mitchell's other foot in my other ear. Sleep-deprived or not, I won $900 by 8:00 a.m. When I returned to the Shack, everyone was still groggy from their uncomfortable evening. There were blankets and sleeping bags everywhere covered with Barkley hair. The place smelled rank. I didn't mind. I planned to cheer up the temporary Shack residents.

I threw the door open allowing the morning sunbeams to shine directly into the room. I then entered the Shack shouting, "I have an important announcement to make!" Lori and her sister knew where I had been, but they had no idea what I was about to say. "There will be toy buying today!"

Mitchell and the girls screamed in unison, scaring the hell out of Barkley and the next door neighbors. After breakfast at Weck's Restaurant, there was plenty of toy buying that day, plus we found a gorgeous home a 7-iron away from the fifth green of the Tanoan Golf and Country Club. The $10,000 Bank of America CD that I had invested from casino winnings went toward the down-payment.

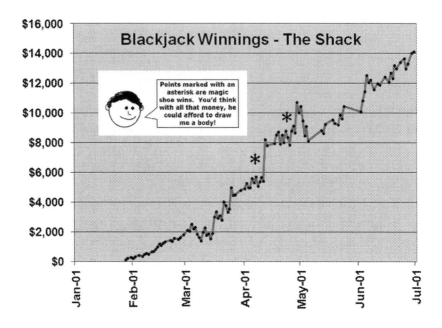

I ended June 2001, and my stay in the Shack, with thirteen wins out of twenty-one total visits. I won $3670 for the month. My cumulative winning percentage for the 118 visits between January 28th and June 30th was 68.3 percent. Cumulative earnings = $14,145. The estimated value of all comps earned during the period = $1400. The total number of times that I was banned for card-counting = 0. The number of music or comedy CDs purchased = 42. I think the count was forty-two—sometimes Sarah would liberate some of my music when I returned to Colorado for visits. The total number of Pizza Hut or Dominos carry-out orders placed = 40. The total number of bottles of Febreze that I had purchased to spray smoky-smelling clothes after returning from 118 casino visits = 7. The amount of sheer exhilaration that I had experienced in demonstrating that card-counting was fruitful over a long period of time = could-not-be-measured-on-any-Excel-spreadsheet. The Shack ruled.

THE GREED

I wish all my blackjack adventures had lucrative endings like the Shack winning streak. That was a fun story to tell. I don't like relating what happened post-Shack.

After the wife, kids and dog joined me in Albuquerque, it was obvious that my visits to the casino would be now limited. After all, I had been going almost every day during the five-month heyday of the Shack. Plus, I had never been limited on time while playing at the blackjack tables. Sometimes I went for twenty minutes, sometimes the visit extended eight hours or more. Patience was a much appreciated virtue as I waited for a good card-count or winning streak. With all of us back under the same roof in the same city, many things changed. First of all, I no longer had a huge gambling budget. All my winnings from the Shack went toward the down payment on our new home in New Mexico. Lori and I still had some credit card debt and Sarah was starting college that fall. I could no longer afford or justify playing $100, $75, or even $50 unit bets. I didn't have the cash. When I returned to playing $10 a hand, the mystique was no longer there. I imagine it was like a Major League Baseball player who had suited up with the Boston Red Sox—then all of sudden, he was sent down to playing Double-A ball for the Portland Sea Dogs. Blackjack buddies of mine at the Sandia Casino $25 table gave me strange looks because I was now frequenting the crowded $5 tables.

I also had difficulty adjusting to the sharp decrease in the number of visits to the casino. Long gone were the days when I came home from work, changed clothes, grabbed a piece of fruit, and played blackjack thirty minutes later. Family time was my new priority at six o'clock each evening. I loved playing with the kids, sharing details of our day with Lori, and throwing a tennis ball two-hundred times to Barkley in the park; but, for awhile, I felt something had been missing in my life. I know it was selfish.

I decided to frequent the casino only twice a week, early on Saturday and Sunday mornings. I would leave and return before anyone woke in our household. The routine was fine for a few weeks, but Lori sensed my anxiousness to visit the casino in the middle of the week. She knew me better than I knew myself. She was also quick to pick up on the subtle clues that I had given her.

"I want to go to the casino!" I said rather loudly one Wednesday night after a stressful day at work.

"So go," Lori replied, "but only after you walk Barkley and help Mitchell with his homework."

"Thanks, honey," I said as I kissed her cheek.

I jogged Barkley around the block for twenty minutes instead of giving him the normal one-hour leisurely stroll along the perimeter of the fifth through eighth holes of the Tanoan golf course. Instead of instilling basic math concepts to Mitchell for an hour, I simply provided answers to most of his homework problems. He finished the assignment in record time.

As I proceeded out the door for an unexpected weeknight casino adventure, Lori instructed, "Two hours should be plenty of time."

"Okay, bye, I love you." I was rather giddy as I headed to the car. However, I returned to the house and stuck my head into the door for clarification of an issue, "The two hours start when I get there, not two hours from now." I quickly slammed the door and ran to the car just in case my last declaration was met with a non-negotiable counteroffer. The drive to the casino was eight minutes. Exactly two hours and sixteen minutes later, I returned.

Lori greeted me in the kitchen, "Did you win or lose?"

I had not been accustomed to this type of inquiry when I returned to the Shack. "I lost."

"Too bad. You should have stayed home, like you said you would do on the weekdays. Now go see if your dog is alive. He's been passed out on the patio rug every since his walk. Then you need to take a shower. You smell like smoke."

Oh, yeah. Big adjustments would be needed.

Most Air Force personnel stationed at Kirtland Air Force Base had been given the day off on the Friday before Labor Day weekend. I was especially happy that day because the house was empty. Lori was visiting her sister, Brenda, in Scottsdale, Arizona. Sarah was at Colorado State University. Mitchell was my responsibility for the long weekend, but he was on the yellow bus headed toward school. Barkley and I played fetch for awhile, until he kindly licked my face and gave me a look that said, "Go, go. You know you want to go to the casino." I did.

I had a $1000 bankroll, and at least seven hours before Mitchell's school bus would be returning to our cul de sac. As I drove to Sandia Casino, I knew that patience was the order of the day. I did not have to rush to meet anyone's timeline. I had no monetary goal in mind for winnings, but I wanted to win at least enough to get a Domino's pizza and some music CDs, like the glory days of yesteryear. When I started with a $25 unit bet, I had butterflies in my stomach. *Awesome*. That was the sign of unbridled enthusiasm. Around midday, I had been dealt a partially magic shoe. More nostalgia. I won more than $1000 in just a couple hours. I took a break. I was hungry as hell, but didn't want a take-out pizza and cinnamon sticks. Instead, I used Player's Club points to get a voucher for buffet lunch at the casino restaurant. While eating, I pondered whether I should quit or not. On the plus side, the big win would provide a much-needed buffer in my tiny gambling budget. And, the positive effect the win would have on the Excel spreadsheet trend line would be impressive. On the minus side, I still had a few hours to kill for the day. And, with Young American Football League games beginning the next weekend for Mitchell, I would not have Saturday mornings free to visit the casino until late November. I decided to stay.

After lunch, I played a $75 unit bet. As I had fully remembered, the high and low fluctuations were plenty at those stakes. My stacks of green and black chips had gone up and down, then back up after a seven-in-a-row winning streak. During the next shuffle, I was up $1900 for the day. I set the alarm function on my cell phone to ring at 3:00 p.m. That would give me plenty of time to depart the casino and greet Mitchell's bus at 3:45.

For one last ride down memory lane, I upped the unit bet to $100 a hand. The cards on the next shoe provided the most phenomenal count fluctuation that I had ever seen at a blackjack table. Early on, the dealer handed out nothing but small cards. After three or four hands, the running count was already +15. I doubled my bet. After losing one hand and winning the next, the running count was +22. The shoe was not halfway complete. I had to pause a few moments to make sure I calculated the true count correctly. I bet a $500 purple chip, something I had done only once previously throughout the entire Shack era. I had a blackjack, but so did the dealer with a face card on top.

The running count had gone down a hair, but I left my purple chip bet on the table. The next hand would be a nightmare, but I didn't know it yet. I was dealt a pair of nines against the dealer's five. I split the nines according to Basic Strategy without any hesitation. On the first nine, I had received a three. Stay. On the second hand, I had received a six. Stay. I was extremely nervous, but I continued to tally the other player's cards at the table. I couldn't believe my eyes. The running count was +26. No face cards were in play. The dealer had another five underneath. *The next card had to be a face card.* It was.

I didn't panic. I'd been playing smart all day, and would not deviate from the game plan now after losing a grand on one hand. The running count was still +26 with five half-decks remaining. True count, +5. I had to think. Is that nine times the unit bet? It was. I bet $900 on the next hand. I had a twenty. So did the dealer. Remarkably, however, there were enough small cards in the other player's hands to keep the running count the same. I had never seen it this high toward the end of a shoe. I left my $900 bet on the table. *Please, just one blackjack or a double-down.* Didn't happen. Instead, the dealer gave me a 10-9 but dealt himself a K-J. *This isn't happening.*

The running count went down to +20, but there were only four half-decks remaining. A true count of +5 still. *Mercy.* I had never seen anything like this. This had to be the last hand. I bet everything in front of me, a conglomeration of black, green, red, pink, and white chips. Excluding the $5 incentive toke that I had placed in front of the betting circle, the wager was $1115, the largest in my blackjack career. If I won, I would end the day more than a thousand dollar winner. If I lost, it would be the end of one of the most bizarre shoes that I had ever experienced at the casino. The dealer commenced with the dealing. As expected, the yellow penetration card was the third one out of the shoe—last hand. My first card was an ace. I actually stood up from my stool and grabbed underneath the table with both hands as I waited for the next card. *It had to be a face, it had to be a face.* It was not. It was another ace. The dealer had an eight.

I had to split the aces, but I didn't have the money "I have to split 'em!" I panicked aloud. "But I don't have the money."

The dealer responded sympathetically, "If the other players don't mind, I can wait while you go to the ATM or write a check at the cashier's cage."

I didn't have a credit card or check. I never took them to the casino. "I don't have a credit card or check. I never take 'em to the casino," I pleaded aloud. I called the pit boss over to the table. "Do I have any options for getting credit? You know me. I've been coming here for months."

"Of course I know you, but we don't extend credit. Sorry."

"You know I can't hit these aces, especially with..." I stopped before I said, "You know I can't hit these aces, especially with all the face cards left."

Like the dealer, the pit boss was sympathetic to my situation and offered a suggestion, "Can you borrow the money from someone here?"

I hadn't thought of that. "Give me just a second." I had an idea. As I departed the table, I addressed the other players, "I'm sorry about all this. If I win the hand I'll make it up to everyone." At the time, I had no idea what that comment meant, or how I would keep the promise. I was too busy looking for someone I had seen earlier. There was another guy at the casino that day who was an Air Force officer at Kirtland Air Force Base. I'd seen him around the casino in the months prior, and I also saw him at the base in uniform periodically. He was a major, the same military rank as I was. I spotted the other major at the roulette table.

"Hi, we've never met. My name is Glen. Can you help me with a big problem?"

"I'm Edward. You're at Kirtland, right?"

"Yes, usually, but now I'm at Sandia in a bit of a bind." I fully explained the situation to Edward, hoping, (1) he had the money to lend me, and (2) he would lend me the money he had.

Edward was the third sympathetic man in this peculiar situation, "Sure, I can do that. But I need to stop at the ATM."

"Okay. I'm at that table over there." I pointed to the table where all the chaos was taking place. "It is the table where everyone is looking at me right now like I'm a zoo animal."

I returned to the table, winded, nervous, and apologetic. "I'm sorry again, everyone, but you gotta understand—I have to split this hand."

The wait for Edward was painstaking. *Where is he?* The player waiting at first base said he had to go to the bathroom. He asked the dealer to watch his bet. The lady to my right tried making small talk with me, but I couldn't concentrate on what she was saying. I was busy looking in the direction from which Edward should have been approaching. The pit boss used the extra time to hit me where it hurt.

"What if you get another ace?"

Holy Hell! I hadn't thought of that. At Sandia, you could split aces three times, for a total of four hands. On any other day, at any other blackjack table, I would absolutely *love* another ace or two on a pair of split aces. Today, I would simply be happy with two face cards. I silently prayed not to get another ace.

Edward approached with cash in hand, "Sorry, I have $1000 exactly. That's not enough for you to split."

Before I could ponder the dilemma, the lady to my right, the one who had been trying to chat with me earlier said, "I'll cover the rest." As she slid the required number of chips along the table in my direction, she continued, "But it isn't a loan. I'm investing in your hand. I get to keep the winnings."

"Thanks."

After what seemed like an eternity, the moment of truth came. Edward, the pit boss, the dealer, the lady to my right, the man to her right, the other man at first base who had returned from taking a pee, plus a new dealer who had been waiting to take over the table from the current dealer a few minutes earlier, all watched. I asked for the cards to be dealt face-down, so I didn't have to look right away.

"We can't. You might get another ace." The pit boss laughed. Another cheap shot. Actually, it had been the same cheap shot, just repeated.

"I know, I know. I forgot." The suspense was killing me, but simultaneously excited me like no other previous experience at the casino. I resumed grabbing underneath the table with both hands. On the first ace, I received a three. *Okay, I can still get one twenty-one.* On the next ace, I received a six. With a shitload of face cards remaining, the shoe with the highest running count that I had ever experienced went even higher because I had gotten a three and a six. *Astonishing.*

Naturally, the dealer had a face card underneath his eight. I had two high-priced, losing hands. I angrily and forcibly tried lifting up the table with both hands. It was bolted to the floor, but I still budged it a half-inch or so, enough to shake everybody's chips.

The pit boss, who had been smiling and joking moments earlier became stern, "You need to calm down, sir!"

"I know. I'm sorry. It will never happen again." Until that point, I had never been ashamed of my actions in a casino.

Edward had been right there by my side when it was over. For a split-second, I forgot why he was still hanging around the table. *Oh yeah, I remember.* I told him that I could go home and bring back a check. Actually, it would be a credit card check. I didn't have enough cash in my blackjack stash or the checkbook to cover the loan.

Edward was pretty cool about everything, "That's not necessary. You can pay me at work after the long weekend."

What a looooooooong weekend it was. I scrutinized all my actions from the Friday casino visit. I had counted the cards flawlessly. I had never deviated from basic blackjack strategy. I had bet correctly according to the true count. What happened? Was it poor money management? Was it simply the result of a stinky boot?

stinky boot = my new term for the opposite of a "magic shoe."

Was there a simpler answer? Yes. Greed. I could have quit several times during the day, even toward the end when the count was unbelievably high. There is no rule, written or unwritten, that says you must continue to play when the count is high. Greed got the best of me. Regrettably, it wouldn't be the last time.

Things were not the same at the casino after that Friday before Labor Day visit. I had limited time to play blackjack and a limited budget when I did play. Instead of enjoying myself in the lush surroundings of plentiful cards, friendly dealers, and colorful stacks of chips at the casino, I was constantly looking at the clock on my cell phone to see how much longer I had for the duration of a visit, or I was scrutinizing my short stack of red chips to see how long I could remain in the game without going broke. Lori and I mutually agreed that my visits shouldn't go for more than 2-3 hours at a time. I had a good reputation as a loving husband and father. I couldn't jeopardize that status by excessive gambling.

August 2001 was my first losing month since the beginning of the card-counting adventure. I had won a few dollars overall in the month of September, but it was modest. October was the second losing month. November and December were small winners. Analyzing my win/loss tally on the Excel spreadsheet at home was depressing in the post-Shack era of blackjack gambling. The trend line on the graph no longer had a nice, gradual increase. Instead, the line was relatively flat. In my first 118 visits to the casino, I won $14,145, with an average win of $125 per visit. For the thirty-eight visits in July through December 2001, I won a total of $350; an average of less than $10 a visit. During that stretch, there were many occasions when I lost my entire bankroll on a visit. That rarely happened during the Shack era. In the first half of 2001, I would regularly quit after a good winning streak with a positive card-count. In the second half of the year, I found myself quitting only when "time was up" or when I went broke. If I had won early in the visit to the casino, I stayed, sometimes giving my winnings back to the house. My whole routine was *fakakta*. Greed was the reason, plain and simple.

> Hey blackjack boy! Something's missing. Where is your fancy graph of winnings for this chapter? You know, like the graph at the end of the Shaq story? Where?

THE 1536 FREE WATERS

"No mor water for yoo, ever!"

With these words, Yong, a Korean immigrant waitress employed at the Pueblo of Sandia Casino in Albuquerque, New Mexico, had ended one of the most successful casino scams in the history of organized gambling. The perpetrators of this endeavor had not been a group of *Ocean Eleven* experts financed by a wealthy millionaire to exploit a casino owner or a team of MIT students dedicated to exposing face card-rich blackjack shoes for an overwhelming probabilistic advantage. No, a single military man staged this prolific campaign now known as the "1536 Free Water" scam. The motive: quenching his wife's thirst.

The adventure started in June 2001 when Lori uttered four little words, "This water tastes funny." She made this assertion on her first day in New Mexico. In the previous five and a half years, water quality was never an issue in our household. The public water system in Colorado offered some of the cleanest and best tasting water in the United States. Why else would Adolph Coors have started a brewery there in 1873? Adolph would not have unhitched his wagon in Albuquerque for two reasons: 1) The water quality can, at best, be described as "skunky," and 2) "Albuquerque" is too hard to spell. Can you imagine typing out "Albuquerque" on the wireless telegraph all day? Screw that. While New Mexico bordered Colorado, and both states featured snow-topped mountains providing watery goodness below, the contrast in water quality was obvious. I faced the ugly fact—for the next three years, I would be buying bottled water for my lovely wife.

I've always followed a fundamental strategy for casino gambling. Never drink alcoholic beverages while gaming. It is fun to receive a free beer, wine, or gin and tonic from your host, especially when you're out on the town with your date or friends. But, there is an obvious reason why alcoholic beverages flow so freely in the casino. An impaired player is bad player, a forgetful player, and more likely than not, a losing player. Think about the excessive drinkers that you've seen at the tables. In any other public place, drunks are shown the door. In a casino, they are given comps. Don't fall for it. Unless you are pretending to be drunk to throw off the scent to a pit boss suspecting you of card-counting, drinking and betting is a bad combination. The casino has enough advantages over the player already. When I'm playing blackjack, I drink water or soda. Occasionally, I'll celebrate a winning night by downing a beer, but only after cashing out and heading for the door.

Sandia, like many other casinos, followed the latest trend of providing cold bottled water to players on demand. Bartenders, waiters, and waitresses preferred bottled water over tap water served in plastic cups. Less mess. Some casinos, like Sandia, even went as far to bottle their own water, or contract from an existing bottled water distributor. They added their casino logo to every bottle label, subconsciously reminding the patron that water can give life to the gambler, but the casino can take it away.

During the previous four months, the timeframe of the $14,000 winning streak, the Sandia waitresses and I had a wonderful "player-to-server" relationship. I say "waitresses" because 98% of the servers were women; no offense intended toward the couple of men who worked there. The waitresses would bring me a cold bottled water or soft drink every fifteen minutes or so. I would tip them a white $1 chip or a red $5 chip if the cards were in my favor. I wasn't the biggest tipper, but I was a constant tipper. The servers appreciated me. Some players complained that they never saw the wait staff. These had been the same cheap bastards who were often rude to their servers or never tipped. Not me, I had always tipped, even when I was losing. How else could I guarantee free drinks throughout the visit? Like I said, my relationship with the waitresses had been great—until I became greedy.

After a few weeks of losing at the table more than winning, a funny thing happened to my tipping habits. Instead of tipping $1 or more per drink, I began tipping one or two dollars a visit. During a couple losing sessions, I didn't tip at all. Some of the waitresses asked me, "Are you okay?" I'm sure they wondered if I was the same person who had been tipping all those months. Yup, same person, but now the wads of green were getting smaller. Coincidentally, I noticed that it took me longer to get served. *Hmm, I wonder why?* Had I turned into one of those aforementioned cheap bastards? Instead of facing the puzzling looks and mild scowls of the tipless waitresses, I began leaving the blackjack table between shuffles in search of the self-serve concession stand. Many a cheap bastard practiced this tactic.

I remember Yong giving me my first truly "free" bottle of water. Being in her late fifties or early sixties, she didn't walk the floors like the traditional waitresses. Her duty was to hand out complimentary soft drinks, juice, coffee, and water, all without leaving the confines of her post. Although there was a tip cup next to her station, I didn't fill it on that first visit. I wasn't going to pay for a drink that I had journeyed to obtain. I made several trips to Yong that night. I ended up tipping her at least once before I departed the casino for the evening. No need to be a total prick. She smiled broadly and said, "Thank yoo" with a rich Korean accent.

Sometime during my next couple visits, I had the novel idea to get two bottled waters at a time from Yong, or one of the other waitresses that distributed drinks at the self-serve concession stand. That way, I didn't have to leave the blackjack table as often. One cool summer evening, I had a full bottle of water in hand when I returned home.

Lori, knowing that I didn't usually buy bottled water for myself, said, "Where'd you get that?"

"At the casino," I replied, as I offered the water for closer inspection. "See, they bottle their own."

Obviously she was uninterested in the fact there had been a picture of the Sandia Mountains and a Pueblo of Sandia logo on the label. Lori replied with a hint of attitude, "I'm glad *you* have water." She then opened the refrigerator door to show me an empty shelf next to the gallon of milk where her supply of bottled waters usually resided. It appeared I had been neglectful in obtaining the required weekly ration from the commissary at Kirtland Air Force Base. A few minutes later, as I was driving to Wal-Mart, the nearest inexpensive bottled water source, I had the greatest brainstorm of my gambling career. You know those light bulbs that appear above Wile E. Coyote's head when he has a brilliant idea? My idea lit up the interior of the car and blinded the driver next to me in the Wal-Mart parking lot. *Why not procure a few free bottles of the elixir of life from Sandia each time that I visited?*

Yong greeted me the next day with a smile. "How yoo today, Mister Glen?"

"Fine," I replied, as I lifted two of the Sandia bottles. Visibly putting a $5 bill into her cup, I asked, "Yong, how many waters am I allowed?"

Yong saw my uncharacteristically large tip, "Oh, yoo can take as many yoo want."

I grabbed four more bottles, putting a total of six into my T-shirt upturned from the waist, a makeshift cloth shopping bag. As I departed Yong's station, she said, "Ooh, yoo drink lotta water, Mister Glen."

I returned to the blackjack table and placed the six bottles at my feet. It had been a pain in the ass babysitting the water throughout the evening, transporting them from table to table when the negative card-count dictated a move. However, I successfully managed to leave with the bottles intact.

Lori was happy. Free, crystal clear, readily available water, just like in Colorado. Wile E. would have been proud. Since I had accounted for every bet and comp made while gambling, I decided to also account for the number of free waters that I accumulated. The easy rule that I established: if I drink it at the casino, it doesn't count. I only counted the bottles that came home with me. I had rationalized that the waters I brought home were "free" since I accounted for all tips, whether to the dealer, or to the water-providers in my win/loss tally for each visit.

I established a solid routine for procuring water over the next couple months. Lori drank approximately half a case of bottled water per week. I visited the casino roughly two times a week. Therefore, with each visit to Sandia, I would bring home six bottled waters, always storing them in my upturned T-shirt. In the course of time, I made several efficiency improvements in my water-gathering methods. I learned to wait until the end of the casino visit to retrieve the six bottles. *Duh.* I also began telling Yong, "Well, I lost tonight. At least the water was free." Simple psychology—If Yong was under the impression that I had lost, she would be more understanding when I didn't tip. A guy standing to my side, wearing sweatpants and a torn leather jacket, smirked when I had made the comment. Even among the cheap bastards, I was a cheap bastard.

After awhile, I started stuffing a small plastic shopping bag into my pocket before leaving the house. That way, I could carry the water easier. Plus, I didn't always look like a hunched-over moron with bottles bursting out of his shirt. It hadn't taken me long to realize that the average plastic shopping bag could hold roughly twelve waters. I decided to double productivity. I started taking six waters from the self-serve concession near the bingo room, before getting six more from Yong's station. Yong gave me suspicious looks every once in awhile, but she always provided the goods. I was now bringing home two cases a week. With this increase, I was considerably outpacing Lori's consumption. The refrigerator had remained full, so water bottles began piling up on the workbench in my garage. The statistical water count increased as well. I especially enjoyed the way the blue line on the graph constantly climbed. It was quite a contrast from the sporadic win/loss line chart.

Approximately six months after the water scam began, Yong gave me some bad news, "Yoo in trouble, Mister Glen. Yoo taking too many water home!" I tried flashing some green her way, a fiver, but it didn't work this time. She pointed to a new sign behind her workstation that read "CUSTOMERS ARE LIMITED TO TWO REFRESHMENTS."

Was the sign created because of my actions? Did house policy change for little ole me? The thought pleased me and disturbed me at the same time. I was flattered that a lowly blackjack player's actions could cause this giant establishment to dictate policy changes. I pictured a large group of Native-American tribal elders discussing the unexplained increase in their monthly bottled water requirements. I was disturbed, however, because there was now a huge obstacle hampering my future water gathering abilities. Lately, coming to the casino was more about the water than anything else. The water count seemed more important than my win/loss tally. I don't care if I won $500 for the evening? How many waters did I get? I was strung-out like a crack addict. *I gots to have my water fix.*

A change of strategy was in order. Wile E. Coyote never quit, so neither would I. With a simple ten-minute reconnaissance mission, I learned there were several water sources in the casino of which I had been previously unaware. For instance, they served bottled water in the poker room and at the deli counter near the ticket booth. There were also two more self-service concession stands buried deep in the slot machine and video poker areas. With six sources, I could get two waters from each and meet my daily quota. The scam continued. For the next few months, I mastered the routine of walking the shortest route encompassing the six water sources. I replaced the plastic shopping bag with a black, cloth recyclable bag, the type of bag those environmentally friendly people used as they were giving you dirty looks in the supermarket checkout lane. Who cared if I looked like a man with a purse? I was getting my water fix. To make the collection interesting, I started timing myself to see how fast the route could be accomplished. My best effort was three minutes, eight seconds. I tried beating the record once, but I almost floored an old lady in a walker rounding the corner near the nickel slots. Yeah, time to slow things down. I decided that a four-minute pace was adequate.

My efficiency was top notch. The water flowed and flowed. Meanwhile, the physical bottle count increased at the Wiggy household. At one time, I had 50-60 bottled waters in the back of my car. Another hundred or so bottles filled a corner in the garage. My daughter, Sarah, once experimented by using a couple bottles to wash her hair. Our dog, Barkley, enjoyed bottled water in his bowl. I suppose I should have interpreted these as warning signs of me getting greedy again. But I couldn't stop. Getting the water had been more addictive to me than the gambling. One Saturday morning, I drove to Sandia before realizing that I had left my wallet at home. No cash to play blackjack. However, I still made the rounds to get a dozen waters. When I returned with my wallet thirty minutes later, I made the bottled water rounds again.

One sweltering day in Spring 2002, Yong was the bearer of bad news again, "Because of yoo, there is new sign." Above her workstation, it read "CUSTOMERS ARE LIMITED TO TWO BOTTLED WATERS PER VISIT." *Oh crap.* They upped the ante this time. Wile E., what am I going to do now? After racking my brain for a few minutes, and finding no other acceptable alternative, I decided to run my usual twelve-bottle route. Why not? Maybe the policy changed for some other reason. Maybe "per visit" meant, "per visit to where each sign was posted."

Just two days later, I learned the truth. A casino floor manager personally visited me at a blackjack table to inform me that, yes, the policy was enacted because of me. And, yes, it meant two waters. Total. Per person. Per day. In fact, he advised me of another new policy that was crystal clear—something to the effect, "Glen Wiggy is prohibited from receiving any bottled water at all. He has the option of getting water served to him in a plastic cup." The floor manager also advised that I should not try to beat the system or I would be banned from the casino. *Wow, a banning.* And to think, I had always expected it would be because of card-counting. I won a couple hundred bucks that day, but I felt dejected as I drove home waterless for the first time in over a year.

I checked the statistics on the free water tally—1536 bottles. Not bad for ten months of effort. During the same period, my gambling winnings totaled only $1730. Not too impressive for a card-counter. My run-in with greed during the summer of 2001 reduced the profits. During the period of the great water scam, I nearly brought home more bottles than dollars.

The next week, Yong greeted me at the self-service concession stand with the unforgettable words, "No mor water for yoo, ever!"

Instead of resigning myself to drinking water from a plastic cup, I asked Yong for a Diet Coke. She handed a cup to me as I tipped her a $5 red chip. *It had been a long time since I've tipped that much.* As I sipped the Diet Coke, I asked Yong, "Do you have this in to-go bottles?" She laughed, but I was serious.

THE ONLY TIME THAT I CHEATED

Card-counting while playing blackjack is not cheating. That item is important enough to repeat. Card-counting in blackjack is not cheating. If it were, I would have gotten the hell beat out of me by disgruntled casino staff members long ago. Card-counting is strategy, just like memorizing the cards played in spades or pinochle, thinking ahead several moves in chess, buying every possible property in sight in the game of Monopoly, or giving your opponent a two-stroke penalty in golf because he incorrectly removed a pine cone from a green-side bunker before playing a shot. Cheating is when you mark the back of the cards in spades or pinochle, move a chess piece while your opponent is using the crapper, steal fake money from the absent-minded banker in Monopoly, or when you "foot-wedge" your golf ball a few feet to the left so you could take a full swing without hitting that big cottonwood tree trunk in your line during the ninth grade divisional golf tournament at Dornick Hills Golf and Country Club in Ardmore, Oklahoma, because there were only two holes left and you had to make up three shots on freakin' goodie-two-shoes Kevin Whipple who won every damn tournament anyway since he was six years old and deserved to lose once in his life, just once, but still won because while you birdied one of the last two holes and made par on the other, Whipple also played the final holes one-under par and won by three strokes anyway. None of those things happened to me, by the way—just some random examples of cheaters.

When I play blackjack in a casino, I am a card-counting strategist, not an immoral or illegal cheater. I am a craftsman and a statesman, representing all my fellow counters. I am predictable with the next move, yet puzzling with the next bet. I am cautious, yet bold. Saying all that high-and-mighty bullshit, I must admit that I did cheat once at the game. I cheated rotten. And, oh yes, it was quite illegal.

I cheated in front of five other players, the dealer, the pit boss, the eye-in-the-sky, and approximately eight spectators surrounding a packed casino blackjack table. Nobody caught me either. I wouldn't have cared if I was caught. I was livid. Before I tell you *how* I cheated, I must first tell you *why* I cheated.

In the summer of 1999, Lori, Sarah, Mitchell and I went on our first ocean cruise vacation. Because the story I'm about to tell involves illegal activity and some details that might be taken out of context, I cannot divulge the name of the commercial liner who hosted us for the cruise. I wouldn't want the bastards to try to sue me for libel or to pursue a criminal case for larceny. So, I won't tell you the name of the cruise company—let's just say the company promised us a "carnival-like" experience on our first "carnival-like" vacation, except, the "carnival-like" experience that the "carnival-like" marketers and "carnival-like" employees promised us was not "carnival-like" because most of the staff had lied out their "carnival-like" asses. The cruise sucked.

Let me set the stage before the trip. My lovely wife, Lori, hates natural bodies of water; more specifically, she hates anything that might be swimming or living in the water. She always has. Lori is a land lubber. However, she is perfectly comfortable on the beach because she looks good in a swimsuit and fancy new beach hat. She never goes into a pond, lake, or ocean. She will violently use her little fists to thrash anyone who tries to push her into the surf. When the subject of our next vacation was discussed a year earlier, Lori didn't want a cruise, but was outvoted three to one by Sarah, Mitchell and me. Since Lori was a team player, she decided that a cruise was okay as long as she did not have to look overboard. She'd be fine sunning on the deck or relaxing in the hot tub. She was also looking forward to the shops and sights on the ship and in the ports along the cruise route.

Sarah was sixteen years old during the summer of the cruise. Sarah does not dread the water like her frightened mother, so she expressed genuine excitement in going on the ship and visiting the ports, beaches and waters of Cozumel, Mexico, Ocho Rios, Jamaica, and Grand Cayman Island. She was athletic and conscious of her health at that age, so she greatly anticipated using the various exercise equipment and workout facilities advertised on the cruise brochure. All those great qualities notwithstanding, Sarah possessed a slight bit of teenage angst at sixteen. I was concerned that she might not like the confines of our small cruise ship cabin. No worry. There were supposed to be plenty of recreational areas and planned activities on board.

Mitchell was nine years old at the time, and really had no idea what to expect on the cruise except what I told him and showed him in the cruise brochures. He was excited about the many swimming pools and a giant water-slide perched on the top deck of the ship. Mitchell was mostly looking forward to the free video games in the ship's arcade. He was told that the games were free by me, because I had been told that fact by the customer service operator who helped us book the cruise. I specifically asked the "carnival-like" operator if the video games were free; she replied, "Oh yes, the arcade games are free to everyone." Good thing, because that boy could go through the quarters faster than an old lady stuffing a slot machine.

I was eager for the night life on the cruise. While my exhausted kids would be resting in the cabin, I planned to eat and drink everything in sight with Lori and then hit the casino. I knew Lori wouldn't want to stay long in the gambling parlor, so I planned to fill the void with blackjack after she had returned to the cabin. I wasn't a card-counter then, but blackjack had still been my game of preference.

We all had our sights set on a good time. As you can imagine, the anticipation factor for our first "carnival-like" cruise was high—right up to the point where we actually got on the big, fat, stupid boat. In reality, the "carnival-like" cruise sucked for the following reasons:

- When we dropped off luggage at the designated point early in the morning before entering the ship, we were promised that our luggage would be delivered at our cabin doorstep in less than a few hours. It took almost fourteen hours. It was after dinner before we received luggage. Meanwhile, since we were rookie cruisers, none of us stowed away bathing suits, workout clothes or needed toiletries in a carry-on bag when we had boarded in the morning.

- Maintenance personnel told us that the closed-circuit television with round-the-clock movies in our cabin was inoperative on our side of the ship. There were only two channels of television viewing; one was mainly sports, which was no fun for Lori, Sarah, or Mitchell, and the other channel was non-stop, repetitive, canned promotional advertisements sponsored by the "carnival-like" company in an attempt to get vacationers to spend all their money on the many pay-as-you-go items that accompanied the vacation cruise.

- The closed circuit radio promised in every room was not functioning either. However, we did have the pleasure of entertaining ourselves in the room with two plain, white bath towels artfully folded into the shape of swans. That entertainment lasted forty-six seconds until Mitchell started playing with the towels. Then the swans looked remarkably like plain, wrinkled, white bath towels.

- The workout room was great, just as the brochure had described. However, the minimum age for entry was eighteen years old unless accompanied by a parent or guardian. Sarah was livid. She couldn't go to the gym unless her mommy or daddy had been there to guarantee her safety on the *twedmill* in the *widdle* workout *woom*. She also couldn't attend any of the aerobics classes with adults. Her only option was to participate in the kids programs.

- The free arcade was not free. And, most of the machines cost fifty cents, even the old crappy throwback machines from the early eighties like Tron and Space Invaders. When I told a third-world national steward on board that the cruise planners had said the arcade was free, he responded in broken English, "Yes, yes, arcade free to use by everyone" meaning it was not restricted to just adults. Mitchell was livid.

- The first time Lori tried the hot tub or the swimming pools, she learned they were full of salt water. Lori hates salt water, because it reminds her of the things that swim or creep beneath the surface of the ocean. When we inquired about the salt water to the "carnival-like" employees, they said, "Sure, all cruise ships use salt water in their pools and tubs.

Everyone knows that." We didn't. None of the brochures had mentioned the fact. Lori was livid.

- Mitchell sure loved the giant water slide—loved *looking* at it. For five out of the six days on the cruise, the water slide was closed due to high winds. The winds topped out at barely 10 MPH, yet the requirements for safely operating the slide had called for lighter winds. On the one day that the slide had been operational, there were 2,371 kids waiting in line. It was like Disneyland, Coney Island, or Six Flags on a Fourth of July weekend.

- Lori and I played bingo one night in the main entertainment area. The cards were $20 apiece for one game. The prize was $1000. There were at least five-hundred people in the auditorium. Do the math—a nice profit for the greedy, "carnival-like" company.

- The special programs advertised for the kids Mitchell's age and the young adults Sarah's age were lame, lame, lame. All of them were nothing more than glorified attempts at babysitting while most of the parents got wasted on free alcohol and gorged on fourteen different meal opportunities throughout the day. Sarah and Mitchell pleaded for us not to send them to the special group activities. Lori and I listened, and kept the kids with us.

- Since the big-ticket venues failed to impress my family and me, we searched for fun in the form of shuffleboard, ping pong, hitting golf balls into a net, and getting our photos taken while dressed sharply for dinner. The shuffle-board sticks, or poles, or whatever the hell you call 'em, were all bent or broken, the ping-pong balls were crushed, the golf balls cost something like $50 for fifteen minutes, and the wonderful photos, of course, were free when taken, but came at a price if you wanted to actually take the photos home with you. The big, fat stupid boat was, in my opinion, a money-grubbing, floating accumulation of bilge water.

It has been several years since the vacation, so I might have gotten some of the details wrong in the preceding list of calamities that we had experienced on the cruise. Good thing I didn't mention the cruise ship company by name. However, the main point of my story should be crystal clear at this point—the "carnival-like" cruise was not even close to the fun or value that had been expected or advertised. The ports we visited were exciting, but returning to the ship was a drag. Sitting in the room with nothing to do was the worst. Lori and I are great at entertaining each other and the kids. We had plenty of fun jumping on the beds, telling stories, laughing at the each other's lame jokes, and having pillow fights. However, we could have generated all that entertainment at home instead of paying out the ass for a big, fat, stupid boat to drag us around the Caribbean. When I stepped into the casino to play blackjack on the last full day of the cruise, I didn't plan to cheat, but it felt really, really good when I did. Here is how it happened.

Each day of the cruise, the table games area in the casino advertised a blackjack tournament for a $25 entry fee with a chance at a thousand-dollar first prize or smaller awards for second, third, fourth, and fifth place. In almost every other casino where I witnessed or participated in a blackjack tournament, the contest format was basically the same. A large number of players systematically competed with each other until one player beat everyone else. For instance, the blackjack tournament started with 125 players at twenty-five different tables, with each of those table winners advancing to the next round, then the next, until only five players remained. The winner among the five players at the last blackjack table was crowned the champion, with payouts comparable to the total that had been generated in tournament entry fees.

The "carnival-like" casino staff did not run their blackjack tournament in this manner. Instead, the tournament advertised that the five players with the highest chip totals at the end of the day would earn a seat at the final table. Upon paying the $25 entry fee, each player would be given $200 worth of fake chips for which to bet ten hands of blackjack against the dealer. The minimum bet was $10 of the fake money; the maximum bet was $200. Players could bet as much as they wanted on each hand following standard blackjack rules on double-downs, splitting, etc. How players fared against one another at a table was not relative. You were competing against all players, all day. Only a high stack of chips at the end of ten hands mattered. A whiteboard posted behind the blackjack pit tallied the five highest totals as the day progressed. There was no limit to how many times you entered, as long as you paid another $25 for a fresh stack of chips, and started back at $200 in fake money. The format of the tournament was genius, for the house, since it could charge hundreds, maybe even a thousand players, $25 each, all day long, then pay out only a couple thousand in prizes at the end of the day. What a money-grubbing, big fat stupid boat.

I played in the daily blackjack tournament for the first time early on the third day at sea. Since it had been my first attempt, I didn't know what chip total would make the top five. I started with $200 in play money and finished with approximately $900 after a great run of cards. When I left the table at 9:00 a.m., my tally was the second highest. Not bad. The leader was at $1150.

Lori, the kids, and I spent a wonderful day in the Cayman Islands. The food and beach were both great, but Mitchell and I enjoyed swimming with sting rays the most. At the end of the day, all of us dreaded the return to the big, fat stupid boat except me. I was anxious to see if I had a shot at the final blackjack tournament table at the end of the evening. Not even close. The leader was at some ungodly total, like $2100. Fifth place, and a spot at the final table, was around $1700. I did the math in my head. These players would have almost had to wager the table max on every hand—and win. It didn't make sense.

"It doesn't make sense," I told the pit boss. "Did some players win every hand?"

He responded, "Not exactly, but most players who make the final table split tens and double-down on weird two-card totals. Also, some of the guys on the list try a dozen times or more before making the final five."

I couldn't afford that crap. My budget allowed me to play once, maybe twice a day. The pit boss, one of the nicer employees that I had met on the entire ship, told me that the cut-off point for making the final table each night was usually $1700 or so.

I didn't play in the blackjack tournament during the next two days. We were too busy in port. Plus, each time I checked the high scores on the whiteboard toward the end of the evening, I saw that the cut-off for fifth place was unbeatable, in my mind. It must not have been my destiny.

On the last full day of the cruise, I made my own destiny. It was noonish when I had watched a few other players try their luck in the tournament. A disgruntled guy from somewhere below the Mason-Dixon Line had roughly $300 in fake chips and change going into the last of the ten hands. Instead of making a final bet, he simply said, "Ah, screw it. I ain't winnin' nothing" and pushed all his chips into the middle of the blackjack table. As he angrily shoved the pile, one of the fake, black $100 chips fell to the floor behind his seat. I nonchalantly picked up the chip and palmed it into my pocket. Nobody noticed. Then, I got a wonderfully wicked idea, just like the Grinch Who Stole Christmas when he got his wonderfully wicked idea. I might have even smiled like the green Grinch when I got the wonderfully wicked idea. I bought into the next tournament game for $25 in real currency. During the first few hands, I did not stack the chips neatly on the table in front of me, like most blackjack players did. Instead, I kept some of the chips in my hand, and splashed the others in a mostly unrecognizable stack. I won six hands out of the ten. Not coincidentally, however, there was only $80 in fake red and green chips on the table in front of me when I left the table. Hmm, I wonder where the other chips went?

I hung around the blackjack pit area for awhile, feigning interest in other players' attempts at the tourney. I then nervously left the casino on the big, fat stupid boat, and ducked into the first men's restroom that I could find. Safely in the confines of a stall, I pulled out the chips that were in the oversized pocket of my baggy shorts. I had the original black, fake, $100 chip from the Southerner, plus $550 worth of other fake chips from my game, mostly green $25 tokens.

I then sat atop the stool and pondered how to get these chips into the next game without anyone noticing. I figured that I would have to do a lot of crazy splitting and doubling down, while keeping the chips splashed in front of me. I also figured that I should wait until a dealer and pit boss change, so the new shift wouldn't suspect anything. I spent a few hours with Lori and the kids. They were all tired that day, as the miserable trip was coming to an end. I, on the other hand, was getting a second wind.

At approximately 4:00 p.m., I paid $25 and received a fresh stake of fake chips and real cards from a new dealer named Elsa. A new pit boss stood directly behind her. I nervously waited for the opportunity to bet crazy and fluctuate my chip count to accommodate "supplemental chip intrusion" as I had coined it. I never got the chance. I kept getting hard eighteens and nineteens, or low two-card totals like 4-3 or 5-2. Nothing I could split or double-down. After ten hands, I actually had only $300 in fake money. I slid $200 of it back to Elsa, secretly keeping another fake black $100 in my hand.

Dammit. I'd have to buy in for another $25. Since the end of the trip was near, my wallet was pretty light. I barely had enough cash to buy another stack of chips. As luck would have it, the next ten hands were highly eventful. The first hand, I bet $50 and received a pair of threes against the dealer's five. I split the threes and got a seven on the first. Double-down. Face card for a twenty. On the other split three, Elsa dealt me an ace. Double-down. Another face card, for a crappy fourteen, but the dealer busted. *Bingo.* There was a lot of chips on the table after just one hand. I swept them all into a big lump of green and red plastic. The next hand, I bet $200 in green chips. Blackjack. Most excellent. I asked Elsa to pay out in black chips. I splashed the dark chips with the rest. My unkept pile looked like a pepperoni pizza with green peppers and black olives. I lost the next hand, but won $400 on the following hand after a double-down on a hard seven. Note: Never, *ever*, double-down on a hard seven in a regular blackjack game. The odds are horribly against you. Such a goofy play is only permissible in a blackjack tourney. The crazy play worked for me only because the dealer busted. I then won a few more hands, each highlighted with strange betting and chip color combinations to add to the pizza toppings.

By the ninth hand, I had been able to execute full supplemental chip intrusion. My pockets and palms were empty. Nobody questioned my collection of chips, because it still looked like a Ken's pizza. On the tenth and final hand, I bet $100 and lost on a hard nineteen against the dealer's twenty. No worries. My total had to be over $1500. Since none of the other players had chips worth tallying, the plan worked great. Nobody was suspicious. I was feeling good. I hadn't been the least bit worried about cheating until I saw the pit boss leaning over Elsa's shoulder while she colored up the chips. Oh, no, what is he doing? As Elsa counted the stack and reported, "1815," the pit boss stared straight into my eyes momentarily. *Yikes.* For the briefest moment, I recalled how I felt when I was ten years old and the manager of the 7-11 in our neighborhood caught me shoplifting 9-volt batteries for my handheld Mattel football game. I think I might have soiled my pants just a bit—not when I was ten years old in front of old-man elephant-face at 7-11, I'm talking about soiling my baggy vacation shorts right there in the big, fat, stupid boat casino in the year 1999.

"Good job" the pit-boss commended, as he cracked a slight smile for the first time. "What is your name?"

I think I said, "Glen," but it might have come out "Gleempth." I was still nervous, but felt much better when my name bumped "Carl" from second place on the whiteboard. The pit boss said I should probably make the final table with that tally. Yeah, or I'll be arrested and forced to walk the plank.

When I returned to the cabin, Lori and the kids were getting ready for dinner, albeit at a slow pace. All of them were drowsy from a long nap, but I breathed some excitement into the room when I explained my pending entry into the final round of the blackjack tournament at the end of the night. I promised Sarah and Mitchell cuts from the winnings, while Lori reminded me not to count my chickens before they are hatched. Of course, I didn't tell my lovely family that I cheated. I wouldn't want them to be accomplices after the fact.

I made the final table in the tournament. My final chip count of $1815 was third best for the day. I wish I could conclude the story with a dramatic tale how I had won first prize and $1000. Nope. The final table was actually rather boring and uneventful because the dealer won seven of the ten hands. Two of the players went broke quickly, and I was never able to catch the other two guys who bet conservatively early in the game. I finished third, and won $200 in real money. For the trip, I bought into the game four times, so my profit was a mere $100. Of the profit, I think Mitchell got a $10 cut,

Sarah got $25 and Lori ended up with the rest. I consider the $100 a small, but well-earned, compensation for all the failed promises and inconveniences that we had experienced on board the big, fat, stupid boat. Actually, the last morning of the cruise vacation seemed "carnival-like" because we were finally going home.

A few years ago, a "carnival-like" cruise ship embarked on a trip where almost everyone onboard got food poisoning and explosive diarrhea. Is it wrong that I enjoyed hearing that news?

THE LIES

During the first fifteen years of marriage, I can honestly say that I lied to my wife only twice. Two lies, that's it.

On the first occasion, I was playing softball with a bunch of degenerates from work. It wasn't the standard game of softball. "Beerball" rules were in effect. For every run scored by a player on the opposing team, my teammates and I had to chug a cup of cold beer tapped from a keg strategically located behind home plate. Imagine the carnage stemming from a game in which the final score was 14-12. Our team scored the least number of runs, but both sides won in the display of drunken athleticism. When the designated driver pulled into my driveway in Bossier City, Louisiana, from what I'm told, I had to be dragged from the back of the Chevy Caravan all the way to the front porch. I was also informed that my cadaver-like sleep was deep enough for me to spend a couple hours sprawled out on the warm concrete.

My buzz had worn off, because I distinctly remember Lori slapping me in the face with a wet washcloth screaming, "Wake up, you fool! Wake up!"

I awoke, stumbling immediately toward the bathroom. Regrettably, two bodily functions were ready to involuntarily erupt from both ends of my inebriated torso. I'll spare the nasty details. Let's just say I had to go number one and number puke. When I finished, an incensed woman waited for me outside the doorway.

"Are you drunk?" Lori demanded to know.

"No," I mumbled, "Just a couple beers." [DING, let's ring the bell for each lie.]

The second lie that I told Lori occurred a few years later while we were stationed at Ramstein Air Base, Germany. After only a few weeks in the foreign country, Lori became extremely homesick. She missed her American mother, her American sisters, her American house, American food, American shops, American TV and America. In an effort to take her mind off the recent domestic tragedy of uprooting to the middle of the Rhineland, Lori decided to pursue serious baking as a hobby. The kids and I thought it was a great idea. Cakes, cookies, muffins, pies—bring it on. Lori's first effort at a made-from-scratch chocolate cake, however, was hideous. God bless her for trying, but the cake looked, smelled, and tasted like dirt. Evidently, Lori used an excessive amount of the prescribed baker's chocolate.

"I thought I bought the wrong ingredient," she would later plea with tears in her eyes. "It didn't taste sweet."

After taking my first bite of cake, Lori asked me with the sweetest and dearest expression, "How does it taste?"

"Good," I managed to mumble without choking in the difficult situation. DING, lie number two.

Two lies in fifteen years, that's it. I defy you to find a better husband. Ward Cleaver, Cliff Huxtable, even Ned Flanders, I had them all beat. I proudly maintained an incredibly staunch record of nuptial honesty and integrity. Until I started playing blackjack. Since then, I've lied to Lori 647 times—DING, DING, DING, DING, DING...

I don't know why. The casino is fun and exciting, but it tends to make liars out of some decent folks. Maybe the smoke affects the portion of the brain that controls honesty. Whatever the reason, shortly after moving out of the Shack, I found myself lying to Lori about wins and losses. It all started innocently when I realized Lori wasn't tolerant of the normal win/loss fluctuations experienced by me or any other frequent gambler. I'm not exaggerating the following conversation that once occurred in our household:

[Sunday, as I returned home from the casino]
LORI: How'd you do?
GLEN: I won $125.
LORI: Good.
[Tuesday, as I returned home from the casino]
LORI: How'd you do?

GLEN: I won $175.

LORI: Good.

[Friday, as I returned home from the casino]

LORI: How'd you do?

GLEN: I won $140.

LORI: Good.

[Saturday, as I returned home from the casino]

LORI: How'd you do?

GLEN: I lost $100.

LORI: You lost a hundred bucks?! How could you lose that much? We need that money! Do you know how many groceries that would buy? What a waste. I could have bought three pairs of shoes.

GLEN: But I'm still up $340 for the week.

LORI: It doesn't matter. You lost $100. I'm calling my mother!

It was painfully obvious to me that "frequenting the casino" and "telling the truth" would not mesh well in our household, especially as I tried to repeat the magic of my winning streak during the five months that I had lived alone. My wins had been more dramatic, but so were some of my losses. As a safeguard to maintaining marital bliss, I began under-reporting wins and losses to Lori. If I had won $600, I would say that I won $300. DING. If I had lost $500, I would say that I lost $100. DING. Since I demanded mathematical accuracy in recording all data on wins, losses, streaks, and comps, I simply maintained two Microsoft Excel spreadsheets, the real one, and the one that I showed Lori from time to time. DING. Despite the alternate data tabulation, I never lied about the monthly or overall win/loss tally. I simply lied about the fluctuations. DING. For more than three years, the system worked fine. I had been a closet liar, but I likened the situation to lying about the taste of a putrid chocolate cake. I was tactfully diffusing the truth to make things easier on both my wonderful wife and me. I wasn't in the Husband Hall of Fame anymore, but I was still an okay guy. DING.

The lies increased. DING, DING, DING. Maybe it was because I started to get bored with the casino—card-counting was no longer a mystery to me. Or maybe, just maybe, I was frustrated because I couldn't replicate the great winning streak of the Shack era. Whatever the reason, I found myself telling more and more lies from late 2001 all the way through the summer of 2004, not only to Lori, but also to other family members, friends, and co-workers. Strangely, all the falsehoods stemmed from my actions in, around, or near the casino. Here is a sampling of the lies that emitted from my bell-ringing mouth:

To my military supervisor, who asked why I had been sleepy at work lately: "We just got a new puppy. Damn thing keeps me up at night." DING. The truth: a dealer named Lewis, who was notorious for offering extremely deep penetration on a double-deck shoe, started working the graveyard shift at the casino.

To my son Mitchell, who asked why I was thirty minutes late in picking him up from baseball practice: "I was stuck at a car dealership looking at a new Mazda Miata for your mother." DING. "Don't tell her I was late. If I get the car, I want it to be a surprise." DING. The truth: I waited at the casino an extra thirty minutes to see if I won the "Beat the Summer Heat, Win a Mazda Miata" promotional give-away. If I won the car, that baby would have been mine.

To my golf buddies, who asked me why I had no-showed for our weekly Saturday morning tee-time at Tijeras Arroyo Golf Course: "Lori wasn't feeling well, so I stayed home with her." DING. The truth: Early morning heads-up blackjack action. The casino was practically empty at eight in the morning on a Saturday. By the way, Lori thought I was golfing with the guys. DING.

To my dog, Barkley, who gave me a look of death when I was four hours late in giving him his daily walk: "Sorry, buddy, I had to work late." DING. The truth: After-work casino shenanigans. I don't speak dog, but I believe Barkley replied something to the effect, "Bullshitruff!"

And to lovely Lori, I spun more and more lies: "Crap, I forgot my cell phone at the casino." DING. The truth: I came home to get more money from my stash because I lost the first bankroll. I will now return to the casino for more glamorous blackjack action. "I didn't have enough comp points to get your sister that DVD player for her birthday." DING. The truth: I didn't have enough comp points because I used a one-time promotional offer to convert player's club comp points for cash. "I didn't take money out of our checking account." DING. The truth: I *had* taken money out of the checking account, but I'll be damn quick in putting it back there from some other source before you find out about it.

Yeah, I had turned into a lying sack o' shit, but I rationalized that the little white lies had all been for the sake of keeping the peace among those persons closest to me. DING. Like an alcoholic, crack head, chain-smoker, or Civil War re-enactment enthusiast, I had a severe problem and needed a sharp jolt of reality to bring me to my senses. Citibank provided the jolt.

From the beginning of my gambling venture, I made a strict, internal pact not to take credit cards or ATM cards to the casino. I didn't need the added temptation. I prided myself in maintaining the utmost discipline by leaving the plastic at home. That was not the case a few months after the Air Force relocated us to Nebraska. I returned home from a week-long military TDY (temporary duty) with credit cards in my wallet. I caught an earlier return flight, so I had a couple hours before Lori and the kids expected me home. Since I hadn't satisfied my weekly dose of blackjack fever, I popped into the Harrah's Council Bluffs, Iowa, riverboat, conveniently located across the river from Eppley Airfield in Omaha. *Just a few shoes.* DING.

I withdrew $1000 from my Citibank credit card, with every intention of depositing it back, plus cash advance fees, the next day. To my delight, I won $500 in just a few minutes at the Harrah's $100 table. If I had left at that time, I could have surprised Lori by arriving earlier *and* richer than expected. Nope. Something unexplained happened to me. DING. All right, all right. There's an easy explanation. I got greedy again. Fifteen minutes later, I lost the winnings and the initial $1000. Back to the ATM, courtesy of Citibank. I withdrew another $1000, but I made the bank wad last awhile. DING. Okay, I lost it fairly quickly. On the next visit, the ATM only let me have $500, which I lost in three straight hands. I must have reached my daily cash advance limit. I left Harrah's in an adrenalin-induced rage. During the twenty-minute drive home, I knew my screw-up was a biggie. How big, however, wasn't apparent until Lori greeted me at home.

"You smell smoky," she exclaimed with a straight face. "Were you at the casino?"

I was so frazzled from my horrific loss and the question posed before me, I didn't even realize that Lori failed to greet me with a kiss or hug. "Yeah," I replied, "just for a minute." DING.

She snapped back with a noticeable increase in the tone of her voice, "Let me get this straight. You were TDY for a week, then you flew back, but you stopped at the casino before coming home to your wife and kids. You're so inconsiderate!"

"Yes, I did stop," I said. I had the nerve to get slightly offensive, "But only because I had a $20 cash-back coupon that expired today." DING. "I didn't want it to go to waste." DING. "I'm still here at the time you expected me." True, strangely—no ding.

Lori's tone of voice increased again as she stepped toward me, "Did you play blackjack? Did you lose?"

My retort, "I played a few hands." DING. "I lost, but not much." DING. "I didn't even have that much cash left from the TDY." Again, technically true, at one time, but not really. DING.

My beautiful wife's face wasn't beautiful anymore. Her neck, cheeks, forehead, and eyes turned Satan-red. Her tiny, normally fragile hands were clenched in powerful fists. Her breathing reminded me of how she had looked in the last phases of childbirth. She took a final step closer, just inches from my face, repeatedly pointed a finger in my chest, and let it all out with an unmistakable crescendo, "*Oh Yeah?! Citibank called. It appears that someone withdrew $2500 at Harrah's. Either your card and PIN have been stolen, or you are a big, fat, inconsiderate, idiot, golfing, gambling, liar!*"

It was the latter, although I hadn't understood how the "golfing" insult fit into Lori's tirade. Boy, she would have looked silly if my credit card and PIN had been stolen. But, alas, she was right on all accounts. I was busted, and in a big way. Looking back, I suppose I could have lamely responded, "But I'm still winning for the year!" Luckily I didn't. Instead, I solemnly lowered my head in shame and despair. For days and weeks, I apologized profusely. Needless to say, there were a few trust issues in our marriage after that. Eventually, Lori forgave me for my transgression, but she will never forget. Neither will I. I don't deserve her.

After a couple months of mending the relationship, Lori allowed me to return to the casino. However mad she had been because of the great "Citibank Lie of 2004," she realized that my card-counting was a profitable venture—when I was disciplined. Either that or she simply wanted me out of the house so she could quietly re-evaluate her options to leave me. I couldn't complain. I had to take what I could get. So, as I said, I was allowed to go back to the blackjack table. However, I wasn't allowed to go back to my lying ways. From that point, there has been only one spreadsheet. And the truth is always told about wins and losses, no matter how severe. And when Lori makes a hideous dessert, I'm allowed to truly say, "Honey, these Christmas cookies taste like sewage." I may get a dirty look, but I won't hear any bells ring.

THE $1500 BOWEL MOVEMENT

Try not to be repulsed by the title of this chapter. I don't want you thinking, "How the hell will this guy interweave a story plot about blackjack gambling and the high-dollar, bodily act described in the title? I know he's twisted, but he doesn't seem *that* twisted." We'll see. Actually, I could have entitled the story, *The $1500 Tinkle*, but you probably wouldn't have wondered about the plot as much. I could have also entitled the story, *The Time When I Returned to the Casino When I Shouldn't Have Instead of Quitting When I Was Ahead and Leaving the Casino When I Should Have.* But in that case, the title, albeit quite lengthy, would not have been specific enough to describe one of several occasions in which I didn't leave the casino when I should have instead of returning to the casino when I shouldn't have. Got it? No? Okay, let's start over.

You are free to be repulsed by the title of this chapter. However, don't worry—I promise not to use explicit graphics to describe the aforementioned high-dollar act as it relates to gambling. I simply wanted to relate one of the times in which I lost a large sum of money playing blackjack. I am definitely not a hypocrite. I've bragged many times in this book when I won money. It is only fair to share tales of significant losses as well. Even the most experienced and disciplined gamblers get carried away once in a while. Big losses occupy a place in your long-term memory as vividly as big wins. The biggest wins often accumulate gradually. The biggest losses usually happen in seconds.

I have experienced four significant losses at the blackjack tables— not bad, for twenty plus years of playing legally. There have been numerous winning days interspersed between the big losses, but the defeats are always more memorable than the victories. I already told you about the great Citibank Lie of 2004. I also told you about the day when card-counting angst first humbled me in *The Greed*. Those two losses were biggies, both financially and emotionally. I have one other tale of a relatively large blackjack loss which wreaked havoc with my finances and my psyche.

In the fall of 1991, well before I knew anything about counting cards, I gambled at Atlantic City for the first time. I was a typical twenty-something college graduate. I thought that I knew everything. I grew up in the Wiggy household, where my father constantly reminded me, "Gambling money has no home." Through betting at golf, football, poker, craps, cribbage, gin, and every other possible way to win a buck, my father instilled the concept in me, "Never wager more than you can afford to lose." I knew perfectly well what that meant. As I approached the hotel and casino skyline of Atlantic City with only $100 in cash, no checks, and no credit cards in my pocket, I was absolutely positive the day could not end a big loser. If I lost everything, I would only be down $100. No pressure. I went there to have fun.

I stepped foot on the boardwalk at 10:00 a.m. I had been to Las Vegas once as a legal adult, and lost money, so I wasn't too eager to visit the second largest collection of casinos in the United States just yet. I wanted the day to last. Before doing anything, I ate a slice of New York style pizza and drank a beer while staring across the ocean. I then visited several of the boardwalk shops, but failed to make any purchases lest my gambling bankroll would decrease. My only other purchase for the day involved forty-five fun-filled minutes playing the video game, Galaga, on a single quarter at the covered arcade on the pier. High score, just like ten years ago. *You still got it, Wig.* Hopefully, I would have the same luck with the gambling games.

Around noon, I stepped into the oceanside entrance of the Caesar's Palace Casino in the middle of the boardwalk. After lunch, I had $94 total bank. I played the nickel slot-machines for a few minutes, winning a couple bucks and simultaneously noticing out of the corner of my eye that the waitresses at Caesar's wore sexy toga outfits. One of the Roman goddesses smiled at me while taking a drink order. She walked away. Wow, if I weren't happily married, I would still have absolutely no chance with that girl. I cracked myself up. After a 200-credit jackpot on the nickel machines, I won back my pizza and beer expenses and bravely tempted the quarter slots. Soon after,

I re-lost my pizza and beer money, plus $5 more, and wallowed back to the nickel slots. When the waitress returned with my drink, she didn't know that I had left the low-stakes machine momentarily.

My total bank was $90 when I approached the craps table. I made a single $5 bet behind the pass line, and played that way for awhile, going up and down, up and down, but never below $75 and $125 total bank. *Make the day last. Make the day last.* I left the craps pit with exactly $100 before walking inside the adjoining Bally's casino. I played three-card poker, but quickly realized that I wasn't good at the game. I would stay with a ten or jack high and get beat by the dealer every time. I lost $25 in five hands. *Shit.*

I needed a break. I found a pay phone to call Lori and the kids on the same pier where I had played Galaga earlier. Seeing the arcade again, I realized I could always play video games for hours if I lost much more cash at the casinos.

"Hi honey. Guess where I am?"

"Fort Dix, New Jersey," Lori said, "training with the Army, where you are supposed to be." I could hear my two-year-old boy, Mitchell, making some sort of fuss in the background. Lori was irritable.

"Nah, remember when I said we had a day off coming? It's today. I drove to Atlantic City."

"Great. I'm happy for you. When's my day off?"

At this point in the phone call, I had two options. I could respond: (1) "You don't work—every day is your day off," or (2) Anything better than stupid option number one.

"I'm sorry, sweetie. I'll be home in just a couple weeks. You'll get plenty of days off then. I miss you!"

Lori returned with a more pleasant tone, "I'm sorry too, honey. I didn't mean to sound grumpy. Mitchell had a rough night, and your dog has poopy-drawers. I really wish you were here."

During the rest of the call, I learned that Mitchell had a bad cough. My daughter, Sarah, was spending the night at Grandma's so she wouldn't get sick the day before Halloween and miss out on being the prettiest princess in her sparkly costume. My dog at the time, Lucky, was sick from eating a whole mini-bag of chocolate donuts that were left unattended on the family room coffee table. I also learned that Lori's brother, David, was ejected from a Denver

Bronco football game for throwing a draft beer on the head of a visiting Seattle Seahawk as the player walked to the locker room. Finally, I learned that Lori missed me terribly and was anxiously looking forward to my return. I missed her too. She was, and still is, my best friend. I think about her constantly. After the phone call, I couldn't help but wonder how Lori would respond if I brought home a Caesar's Palace sexy toga outfit for her to wear.

I felt extremely homesick when I ventured into the Merv Griffin Resorts Casino. My self-inflicted misery lasted a whole thirty seconds, until I saw a casino sign with a large red arrow pointing to BLACKJACK. *Hey, lookee there.* Don't judge me—I couldn't do much to help Mitchell's cough from New Jersey.

Blackjack was my game, even way back then. Craps and slots had been fun, but blackjack was serious fun. I remember the first time I saw the unique chips at the Resorts Casino. They were ceramic on the outer edge, like every other casino chip at the time, but the center was metallic. *Neato.* I bought in for $50 and played the minimum $5 a hand. I started nervously because I was not accustomed to the fast pace of play. The dealer was snapping cards out of the shoe faster than I could think. I racked my brain early with decisions. Do I split sevens against the dealer's three? Do I hit on a soft eighteen against the dealer's nine? Do I stay on twelve against a two? I hadn't heard of Basic Strategy back then, but I knew most of the fundamentals from watching my father and others play the game. I think I made the correct move most of the time, although I doubt I ever doubled-down with a hard nine back in those days. In fact, I know I hadn't—I previously only doubled-down on ten or eleven or soft totals.

Whatever the case, I was doing pretty well. After an hour at the table, I doubled my money. I distinctly remember the milestone hand that put me over $200 total bank. Split aces against a ten. I hit twenty-ones on both. I left the table and colored up with two handsome black chips and a paltry red one. I tipped the dealer the red. Until that point in my gambling life, I don't think I had ever touched a black chip or tipped a dealer. Two professional firsts. I stared at the black chips for awhile, and continued to check my pockets every few minutes to insure the pair of chips was still there as I walked along the beach for some fresh air. I pondered my next move.

It was around two o'clock in the afternoon when I grew tired of ducking the seagulls that flew dangerously close to me everywhere I went outside. I decided to rejoin the gambling action inside. I planned to cash in my original $100 and play exclusively with the other $100 in profits. I had wanted to see a different casino, so I cashed in at Merv Griffin's place and walked toward the relatively new Trump Taj Mahal. Back in 1991, The Donald was married to Ivana, and only said "You're fired!" to employees in private. His casino was new and glamorous. *Then.* Have you seen it lately?

I went straight to the blackjack tables and muttered some curse words under my breath while passing the three-card poker table. Unlike earlier, I sat down without the slightest bit of nervousness. I doubled my money once, I could do it again. I even foreshadowed greatness by buying in for $50 in red chips and $50 in green. I wanted to vary the color of my bets. The next few hours were highly enjoyable. I hit three black jacks in a row at one point, and watched the dealer bust four hands after that. I had never experienced such a streak. At 5:00 p.m., during my first bathroom break, I had $450 total bank. *Awesome.* I tipped another $5. In my mind, I was becoming a big shot.

The good fortune increased exponentially. At 8:00 p.m., I had $1100. *Holy bat, holy cat and holy rat shit!* I called Lori again.

"Hi honey. Guess where I am?"

"Back at Fort Dix, New Jersey," Lori said, "where you are supposed to be, getting ready for tomorrow's training."

"Nope. I'm still in Atlantic City. I'm on a *huge* blackjack winning streak. I've won a thousand dollars!"

"Really!" Lori was getting into the spirit of things now, "Wow, you're my hero. I'm so proud of you. You're leaving now, right?"

There was a long pause. I didn't want to quit.

"How's Mitchell's cough?"

"Fine." Lori continued with a slight sense of urgency, "You're leaving now, *right?*"

"Pretty soon. I'm gonna eat first, and then play just a few more hands."

"Okay, but leave soon." Total trust, then. "We could pay off our Discover card. Or take a trip."

Lori was right. A trip would be fun. We hadn't been on a vacation since Mitchell was born. On the other hand, I was still enjoying a mini one-day vacation that I didn't want to end. I pondered my next step again as I ate a spicy gyro and drank another beer on the boardwalk. Note: It hadn't dawned on me back then to get a comped meal. It would have been a cinch. All I had to do was ask the pit boss for a meal after playing awhile. The seagulls were bothering me again, so I went back to the casino after tossing the birds a few scraps of pita bread.

Next stop, the Showboat Casino north of the Trump Taj Mahal. Before sitting down at the table, I folded $700 in Ben Franklins and tucked them away into my velcro wallet. No matter what would happen at the Showboat, I was assured to end the day up $600. That was the new master plan. I bought in at my fourth different blackjack table of the day. This time, all green, $25 chips. I was downright cocky at this point in the adventure. Early on at the table, I remember scolding the old man next to me because he hadn't split eights.

I'll never forget his response for the rest of my life. With a puzzled face, the old man said, "What have you been eating? Your breath smells like shit!"

Three hands later, I was the one to get a pair of eights. I split them, placing another $50 on the table to cover my original bet. I covered my mouth while looking at the old geezer and muffled, "See—always split eights."

I received a ten on the first split hand. Stand. I then got another eight. Split again. Next, I received a two and doubled-down against the dealer's nine. I got a nine of my own for a total of nineteen. On the third hand, I got another eight.

The old fart looked at me and said, "You're in trouble now, sonny."

I wasn't worried in the least. Another two green chips on the felt betting circle. The dealer gave me an ace first, for another nineteen, and a three on the second hand, for another double-down. Still, I was totally confident in the strength of my hands, although I was unconfident about the strength of my breath. I doubled-down again, and received a seven. I surveyed the table. I had $300 in total bets with hands of eighteen, nineteen, nineteen, and eighteen. The normally fast pace of the table seemed unbearable slow as the dealer finished dispensing cards to the other players. Finally, the moment of truth. *Don't be a face card.* I was hoping he had an eight or a nine underneath to match his other nine. Before turning over the hole card, the dealer glanced at it, and then stared directly at me.

"Sorry, guy," he claimed as he showed the entire table an ace. Twenty. My twelve green chips were whisked away in a flash.

I was stunned. The whole hand took forever to pan out, but seemed like a quick blur once it was over.

The old guy sitting next to me didn't say a word. He'd probably been in that position himself at one time. He had a lot of class in holding his tongue. I would learn how to act that way at the blackjack table, but not until years later.

I had $100 in green chips remaining. Oh well. Let's go out in a blaze of glory. I bet the entire stack on the next hand. I had never bet $100 on a single hand in my life. Another first. When I was dealt a pair of queens, I actually smiled. Nice comeback. Maybe I'll ask for a black chip on the payout. The dealer had a queen as well. *With an ace under that crown-wearing bitch.* Blackjack for the dealer.

Stunned again, I walked away from the table hot. I lost four-hundred bucks in two minutes. Another first.

As I stepped outside on the Boardwalk, I was not impressed by the sound of the ocean, the cool breeze, or the bright lights on all the storefronts and amusement areas. I wanted to vent my frustration by kicking a seagull. I also wasn't feeling well in the stomach. I decided to call it a night. Unfortunately, I had to walk about a mile or so to where my car had been parked. I thought about using one of those guys who drove the bicycle carts with passengers up and down the boardwalk, but I didn't have any bills except hundreds.

As I strolled, I realized that I was still a big winner for the day. Lori might be upset that I had lost $400, but she would realize that a $600 gain was still impressive. Plus, any anger she had toward me would pass in the two weeks before I returned home from training. Things would be fine. I walked past the Taj Mahal where I had a nice, steady financial gain, past Merv Griffin's Resorts where I had quick fortune on a miraculous streak, and finally to Caesar's Palace where the whole thing had started at the nickel slots. I saw the toga-wearing waitresses one more time as I looked for the route to the parking garage.

Then it happened. To be honest, I can't really describe what "it" was, but the urge to play blackjack again was overwhelming. All the rational thoughts that I just had while walking on the boardwalk disappeared when I set foot in the casino again. I had to play. I didn't want to leave on a bad note. I sat down at the blackjack table intent on playing just a few hands. I removed two of the $100 bills from the folded seclusion of my wallet. I started with a $25 win. However, I lost four in a row after that, one of which was a double-down. Crap, another $100 loss in minutes. I bet the remaining four green chips and lost. Without thinking twice, I reached for the remaining folded bills in my wallet. I bet $200, all in cash, no chips.

The female dealer announced, "Two-hundred, money plays."

The pit boss echoed her, "Two-hundred, money plays."

I had a sixteen, and stayed against the dealer's four. She had an ace in the hole. *What is it with all these sunuvabitchin' aces underneath?* Things looked decent when she hit a face card for fifteen. But then drew a two. Her seventeen was weak, but it beat the hell out of my sixteen.

I reached for the folded bills again—all of them.
The dealer yelled, "Three-hundred, money plays." From way over yonder I heard the pit boss echo, "Three-hundred."

I had a hard five. I hit and hit and hit again, and still only had sixteen against a face card. I knew it was over. I hit for the last time, and busted with a looooovely total of twenty-six. The next few seconds began one of the longest days, weeks and months of my life. It started with me throwing up in the parking garage trashcan. The gyro and beer didn't agree with me or my loss of composure.

The car ride from Atlantic City back to Fort Dix was absolutely miserable. The two-mile run at training the next day seemed like a marathon. Plus, all of my Air Force and Army classmates constantly asked how I did in Atlantic City. I muttered, "I lost a hundred," but I lost a whole lot more. I lost willpower, pride, attitude, and confidence, not to mention hero status from Lori. To this day, she brings up the incident anytime *The Apprentice* is on TV or there is a reference to Merv Griffin or there is a scene in a movie filmed on location at the Atlantic City boardwalk. We can't watch *Beaches* together. Maybe that isn't a negative. Also, I can't look at anyone wearing a toga without a gut-wrenching gyro taste coming back to my mouth.

So, that explains everything you need to know about the $1500 bowel movement. There was nothing disgusting or graphic in the... Wait a minute. That wasn't it. This was *The $1100 Gyro and Beer Throw-Up* story. I guess I'll have to tell *The $1500 Bowel Movement* story another time. Sorry.

TAKING ADVANTAGE OF
THE GRAY AREAS

As I discussed earlier, card-counting is not cheating. If it were, I would have been thrown in jail or had my thumbs broken years ago. Card-counting is a mathematical art form practiced by the proudest, most sophisticated, and most attentive gamblers—*hey, what's that on the ground? A red $5 chip.* Instantly, dignity, style, and grace go out the window as I slide one of my size eleven Reeboks over the chip. Never looking down, I am perfectly still for a minimum of thirty seconds. I casually search in all directions for the unwilling owner of the lost gaming token. The coast appears clear. In a careful, but deliberate manner, I bend one knee to the ground as I untie, and re-tie, my left sneaker. I gingerly palm the chip in my right hand as I raise upright. I draw my hand toward my denim pocket as I deposit the chip into the confines of my faded Levis. Just for show, I take out my car keys and twirl them once. Mission accomplished. At this point, I legally declare the formally lost chip as property of the Glen Wiggy Estate. I begin to walk away, but I quickly remember the golden rule: Anytime you find money on the ground, check to see if there is more. I taught this valuable lesson to my children soon after they learned to walk. I turn around and scour the floor again with my eyes, just to be sure.

Am I a petty thief for taking someone's dropped chip? What would you have done—turned the $5 into the casino lost and found? The way I see it, a gambler should take advantage of any and all opportunities to make a quick buck within the confines of the casino. I'm not talking about stealing a handful of quarters from an eighty-six-year-old lady's slot machine cup when she isn't looking. I'm referring to certain situations that fall in the gray area between right and wrong, ethical and unethical. Think about how you'd react to the following situations that happened to me:

Situation #1: In Council Bluffs, Iowa, I noticed a blackjack dealer periodically flashing a card. The dealer's nametag read "Samuel," but he went by "Sam." Sam would occasionally show the corner of the next card as he prepared to pull it from the shoe for the next hitting player. I quickly deduced that Sam wasn't doing it intentionally. I think arthritis had been taking its toll on his hands. Sam was old enough to have dealt cards to Abraham Lincoln. I followed Sam from table to table throughout the evening. I witnessed him flash a card four more times in a one-hour period, but I was never seated in the right position to take advantage of the flub.

I learned that Sam routinely worked the 6:00 p.m. to 2:00 a.m. shift. I arrived at the casino promptly at six o'clock the next evening. I scrunched down in my chair and patiently waited until I saw him flash my next card. It was a queen. I had a hard thirteen against the dealer's nine. I obviously wasn't taking a hit. Sam's hand was not pat. He drew the face card and busted. I won $50 that I shouldn't have. For the next few weeks, I tried my best to be seated at third base on Sam's table. I was able to take advantage of the "pre-cognitive" next card several more times. Although, there were a couple times when I couldn't openly take advantage, like when I had a hard nineteen and the next card was an ace. If I'd taken a hit, the gig would have been blown. Sam quit dealing shortly thereafter, or maybe he was fired. The fun was over. Interestingly, there was another player who knew of Sam's flashing flaw. I remember the guy well because he was the spittin' image of the late Jerry Garcia, leader of the band, The Grateful Dead. For roughly a week, Jerry Garcia and I always seemed to end up at Sam's table at the same time. We'd share a glance and a smile each time Sam flashed a card.

Situation #2: I bought in at a table for $480, all in twenty-dollar bills. The dealer lined up my cash into five columns of $100 each, but one row was clearly $20 short of the others. After stacking sixteen green $25 chips and twenty red $5 chips, the dealer yelled to the pit boss, "Changing five-hundred." *If the pit boss doesn't catch the boo-boo, I'm staying quiet.* The pit boss appeared to observe the transaction, but echoed back, "Five-hundred." *Sweeeeet!* As I started to drag the chips to my position, the lady seated to my right looked at the dealer and said, "You gave him too much." The dealer quickly fixed the error. I wanted to lash obscenities at the damn do-gooder lady, but I would have looked like a jerk. Instead, I faked a surprised expression and said, "Oh, did you give me too much?"

Situation #3: A young female dealer accidentally turned over her first *and* second cards. She quickly flipped one back over, but I saw that it was a five of hearts. Her up card was a ten. There was only one other player at the table, a NASCAR fan wearing an extremely loud orange, red, and black leather coat, adorned with racing endorsement patches. NASCAR guy didn't see the dealer's five because his head was momentarily turned. He was about to hit to a thirteen when I had mentioned that I knew the dealer's other card. I could have kept my mouth shut, but I felt a moral obligation to expose the obvious glitch to my brother-in-arms. Just to let you know, I considered writing "...brother-in-hands" in that last sentence, but it would have been the stupidest pun in the book. NASCAR guy trusted me and stayed put. For the only time in my life, I split tens. I received a nineteen on one hand, and a seventeen on the other. Neither hand was as good as my original twenty, but the dealer ended up busting as I had predicted. NASCAR guy and I shared a high-five.

Situation #4: Okay, this one was really dishonest, but I was hungry. A floor manager at a riverboat casino in Tunica, Mississippi, approached me less than fifteen seconds after I had entered the building. He said, "There you are, Mr. Lewis. Here are your comps." He handed me two vouchers worth $25 each at the casino's upscale restaurant. At first, I thought it was a promotional stunt, but it was merely a case of mistaken identity. A few minutes later, I was ordering a sixteen-ounce ribeye, medium well, baked potato, loaded, and a side salad with ranch dressing. Even after padding the bill with an unnecessary dessert, two drinks, and a nice tip, there was $15 credit remaining on the voucher. I used the balance to buy fifteen packs of chewing gum near the register. I pocketed a couple packs, but distributed the rest to three rows of video poker players and one casino custodian. The people were appreciative. They thought Mr. Lewis was a pretty neat guy.

Situation #5: I finished a marathon session of blackjack that ended at 4:30 a.m. Regrettably, it was one of those nights where I should have quit hours earlier. I was flat broke, losing $400. *Pitiful.* I deprived myself of sleep at a cost of roughly $50 an hour. I made one last visit to the men's room. I splashed water on my face as I prepared for the sleepy drive home. As I passed a row of slot machines near the escalator to the parking garage, I noticed an unattended machine with 120 credits. I shook my head violently and made that horse-blubbering sound with my lips—you know, the sound actors make in some comedy movie scenes. I took a closer look. Yup, 120 credits. The story gets better. It was a dollar machine. I glanced around the area. There wasn't a player within 50 feet. I waited a couple minutes to see if anyone came running out from the bathroom in desperation. I wouldn't want to defraud an old lady who had an unexpected accident. Nobody came running. As final confirmation of my good luck, I hit the COLLECT button and listened to tons of metal $1 tokens clanking in the tray. As I scooped my newfound fortune into a nearby plastic cup, I was now wide-awake. I decided to check the status of other machines in the deserted area. Maybe other sleepy gamblers had similar lapses of inattentiveness. Bingo. I discovered two other machines with unattended credits, one with six quarters, and another with three nickels. I couldn't care less about the $1.65 fiduciary gain, but I was pleased to see that my sleepy-gambler hypothesis was supported. Ever since that night, any time I'm in a casino after two or three o'clock in the morning, I do a quick walk-around the electronic machines to see if credits remain. I've hit paydirt several times. I once discussed the situation with a security guard. He frequently saw unattended credits on machines late at night.

Situation #6: No doubt about it—this one was downright theft. I was playing at a blackjack table that was part of a pit containing eight tables arranged in an elliptical manner. On the opposite side of the pit, I noticed a dealer drop a green, $25 chip. The chip, approximately twenty feet away inside a roped area, remained on the carpet for a couple minutes without anyone noticing. I sat next to a regular blackjack player who I had shared many a table with over the years. I whispered to him confidently and pointed, "I bet I can get that chip."

He looked to where the green chipped rested on the carpet. "No way!" he exclaimed, "You can't get anywhere near that chip without someone noticing." I grabbed three green chips from my current stack and began walking around the pit to the opposite side. As I approached the table with the green chip beyond it, I intentionally bumped into the barstool at first base and fell to the side of the table, dropping my three green chips in an exaggerated manner. The dealer called, "Chips down." This action immediately got the attention of the pit-boss, who came to my aid. "Crap," I muttered, "I dropped my chips." The pit-boss scoured the floor near me and the back of the table, producing four green chips. "How many did you lose, four?" she asked, handing me the chips. "Yeah, thanks." As I walked back to the original table, my cohort shook his head in disbelief saying, "Un-fuckin'-believable!"

Situations in general: Every once in awhile, I'll get paid too much on a winning bet, or get paid after I pushed with the dealer. Once, I even got paid on a twenty-two, when the dealer thought I had twenty-one. *It's not my responsibility to total the cards in a hand.* These types of situations happen to everyone eventually. You should watch the dealer carefully, in case there is a mistake that costs you. When a flub results in my favor, I always take the extra loot without giving it a second thought. I consider it part of the game. When I make a mistake, like not quitting when ahead, the casino takes my money. Why shouldn't I capitalize on their mistakes? Karma is a concept that doesn't belong in a gambling establishment.

> Why don't you tell them how Situation #5 ended? He lost the $120 back in an attempt to regain his previous $400 loss at the blackjack table. He also lost an another hour of sleep. Maybe he should rethink that karma comment.

> By the way, that horse-blubbering sound effect mentioned in the story is spelled, "blurabulbrabulblurabulbrabulblurabul."

THE HAND

"Pay attention to your own hand."

This was one of the lessons that my father taught me nearly twenty years ago, but I remember the advice as if it was given yesterday. He didn't want me to be distracted by the hands of fellow blackjack players at the table. Dad would say, "Don't worry about some guy who can't decide whether to split those eights or not. Focus on what you got." Good advice for the beginner. Eliminate all distractions. However, my old man knew nothing about card-counting. I obviously had to scrutinize all the hands around me, at all times, to tabulate the correct running card-count. Otherwise, my money at the blackjack table would decay at a chaotic rate of 1-2% a hand.

The Ameristar Casino riverboat was grounded in Council Bluffs, Iowa, but technically, it floated on the Missouri River between that city and Omaha, Nebraska. Legally, the river could be exploited to bring gambling pleasure to numerous Middle Americans longing for the corruption of the East Coast or Las Vegas. I was playing an uneventful shoe at the Ameristar for nearly an hour one bustling Friday night. My current bankroll matched my original $300 buy-in almost to the chip. Although the casino was jam-packed, the action at the table was extremely boring as hand after hand passed without a significant fluctuation in the count. Things changed with the addition of a distracting new player to the table. I should have taken my dad's advice when the new guy entered the game.

A grizzled old man climbed onto the seat at first base. I'd seen tens of thousands of hands in my lifetime, but never one like this. The man, who later introduced himself to the dealer as Jake, was missing the three middle-most fingers on his left hand. *Holy crap! What happened to this guy?* Was it a birth defect? Couldn't be. His mangled limb contained geometrically perfect scars where sutures once were.

Jake was obviously the victim of some sort of accident or operation. Was he in a war? He was too young for World War II, but too old for Vietnam. Korea, maybe? I pictured Hawkeye or Trapper operating on him, but not Winchester or Honeycutt. I prefer the earlier seasons of M*A*S*H. Was Jake involved in a nasty farming accident? Could be. The casino was smack dab in the middle of corn country. I pictured three detached fingers lying in the cornfield directly behind my house. Then, I pictured something worse—three mangled fingers floating in my daughter's cornflakes.

I jumped a little when Jake said "Hi" to everyone at the table. He bought in for $50 in red chips. Play began, with Jake betting the $5 table minimum. My $15 unit bet from the previous hand remained. The true card-count was neutral. As the dealer distributed a pair of cards to each player, I tried to regain my focus. No luck. My eyes were glued on Jake's hand. Not the fourteen, a nine plus five that was face-up on the felt in front of his betting circle. I'm talking about the "five minus three" hand sitting atop his left wrist.

The outrageous thoughts continued. Did Jake qualify for a handicap sticker on his car? I doubt that his driving ability was impaired, although his ability to flip-off other drivers in a fit of road rage certainly was. Could Jake throw a baseball? Maybe, if it were a split-fingered fastball. Was he married? No ring was showing. *Stop it.* You're supposed to be an adult. Instead, I was acting like a fifth grader who teased and bullied the first girl in class who grew boobs. I quickly shook my head, focusing my eyes toward the ceiling. While looking up, I thanked God for blessing me, and every other person I had seen or known for my thirty-seven years, with two full-functioning hands. Back to the cards.

The dealer was showing a ten of spades. My hard eighteen wasn't impressive, but it was pat. Jake disobeyed Basic Strategy by standing on his hard fourteen. He waived his good right hand over his fairly lousy hand of cards. All other players were pat. The dealer uncovered a hard fourteen also, and drew a six for twenty. Jake, that was your card. I lost. No biggie. The running count turned positive, but still not high enough for me to change my bet.

Jake's next hand was similar to his first. Another hard fourteen, but it was an eight and a six this time. I had a total of ten and felt that wonderful tingle in my gut when the dealer showed a five. Perfect double-down time. Jake, in his elderly, twisted wisdom, decided it was now time to take a hit. It had been painfully obvious to me, and the other players at the table, that Jake was blackjackally challenged. He possessed not only a physical handicap, but also a gambling handicap. Jake busted when he drew a king. Poor guy. Life just isn't fair for some folks. After the dealer passed a few more cards to the players in between Jake and me, it was my turn. Three of hearts. *Great.* I doubled-down to get a lucky thirteen. The dealer drew a three as well, adding to his now upturned fifteen for a total of eighteen. A couple of players won at the table, but not the player who had mattered most, me. On quick inspection, it appeared that Jake's second snafu against Basic Strategy was to blame. I lost because of his play again.

All three players in between Jake and me departed the table at that point. The Taiwanese husband and wife made a few remarks in their native language while gathering their chips. The man in the business suit hadn't spoken, but made some sort of grimacing gesture to the dealer as he colored-up. I wasn't leaving. Statistically, players making bad decisions will help your hand as much as they hurt it. You just don't remember the good occurrences like the bad. Besides, the running count had made a hefty jump with all the small cards that surfaced on the last hand.

Although the casino was packed tighter than a can of sardines, only Jake and I remained at the six-person table. I tripled my bet in response to the +2 true count. Jake was dealt a pair of aces against the dealer's seven. Surely, Jake would know to split aces. You always split aces. Everyone knows that. Not Jake.

Despite the dealer explaining the split option, and then recommending it, Jake waived him off saying, "Nah. I don't wanna double my bet. Just hit me."

Jake received a Queen. He was about to motion for another hit, but instead stayed with an ugly twelve. I hit on a fourteen. Ten, I busted. The dealer uncovered a five, then drew another seven to make nineteen. If Jake had split his aces, the last seven would've been mine for a perfect twenty-one. I lost three hands in a row lost because Jake didn't know his ass from a hole in the ground.

Patience. The true count was still high. I calmed down as much as possible, trying not to be distracted by Jake's play. Maybe I should purposely distract myself to keep from losing my cool. As I doubled the unit bet, my thoughts turned back to Jake's two-fingered hand. This time, however, I found myself being vengeful in wondering how Jake's accident had occurred. Maybe he had been caught cheating at poker and lost his fingers to a knife-yielding member of the Yakuza mafia. Maybe he wrecked a motorcycle on a dangerous curve after cutting off a school bus full of children returning from a tour of the pottery factory. Maybe he was high on LSD and decided to carve himself just for kicks.

Next hand. Jake drew a blackjack, and I drew a soft twenty against the dealer's face card. No way Jake could mess up this hand. He collected his $7.50 with a huge smile. I pushed when the dealer uncovered his twenty. At least I didn't lose.

Jake chuckled, "Boy, I needed all of that one, heh, heh." He really was a nice fellow. Maybe I had been too hard on him. After all, losing a few bucks didn't compare to losing a few digits. Maybe Jake lost fingers trying to save that baby Jessica who fell into a well a long time ago. What a decent man.

Although the true count decreased by one, I left my bet from the previous wager. The shoe was nearly ready for a shuffle. I added a two-dollar incentive toke for the dealer. Jake was dealt an eight and a three. Me too. The dealer showed an eight. It was a good double-down situation for both of us, but Jake might not have known it. In the friendliest tone that I could muster, I said, "Jake, if you didn't know, this is a good double-down hand."

He replied, "Nope. I don't wanna double my bet."

"You know, you are going against Basic Strategy."

Jake was incorrigible. "You play the way you want. I just wanna hit."

After motioning to the dealer for another card, Jake received a two. He then hit again and busted with a face card. *My* face card. I received a four, for a total of fifteen. The dealer upturned a jack, for an advertised eighteen. Loser for me, again.

Jake turned to me and said, "See, I would have lost either way." I wanted to scream it aloud, but I kept the thought in my head. *But I wouldn't have lost, stubby! Why don't you go flash the "hang loose" gesture to someone!*

I knew probability theory. I knew myth from reality. I knew that the actions of other players don't affect my cards in the long run. But Jake's blackjackally challenged actions were unprecedented in my mind. Four bad plays in a span of two minutes. I wasn't the only sore loser. The dealer, who lost a double toke, gave me an I-understand-what-you-are-going-through look. The shoe was over, and so was my tolerance for further torture. I needed a walk on the riverboat deck to cool down and prepare for a financial comeback. Before I could leave, however, I had to know why Jake was disfigured. It must be a result of his stupidity.

As I pushed my chair into the table to depart, I pointed to Jake's nub and asked, "I was just wondering. Were you in some sort of accident?"

Jake replied, "Yup, had my hand in the garbage disposal clearing it out. I hit the run switch instead of the light switch."

"Tough luck," I said.

THE LA COCINA INCIDENT

With Jake, I kept angry thoughts in my head. I couldn't stay quiet regarding another gentleman.

A neighbor of mine in Albuquerque named Gene was the poster child for white, Catholic, rustic America. Everything that Gene said and did revolved around the church and its traditional influence on the surrounding population. On the outside, Gene appeared to do everything perfectly with the best intentions. Besides working for Saint Joseph of the Sacred Heart church, he also volunteered at Habitat for Humanity and coached Little League baseball. Gene diligently maintained the greenest yard in the neighborhood, easily carried a two-handicap in golf, and somehow kept his car spotless every day of the week. He was friendly, well-dressed, polite, and handsome. Gene never cursed unless the Texas Longhorns lost a close football game. "Those darn refs had it in for us!" he would claim, while making a half-hearted pounding fist gesture. Even at times like this, however, his mock anger never lasted long. "Oh well, I guess God wanted the other team to win on this day."

I hated Gene. The real Gene was extremely boring, overly opinionated, and a closet racist.

Gene's wife, Linda, became good friends with my beautiful wife, Lori, shortly after we had moved into the Tanoan community. Their relationship started innocently enough as just a Lori-and-Linda thing. They went shopping together each weekend and chatted over coffee or by phone almost every day. Lori and Linda car-pooled the boys once school started. Naturally, the wives added their spouses to complete the neighborly group dynamic.

I discovered that Gene was a real horse's ass the first time we met. My son, Mitchell, attended a birthday party for Gene and Linda's twin boys, Jacob and Matthew. While the kids were playing kickball in the park, two black kids wanted to join the game. Gene told them "No" saying something like, "the game was just for the birthday party kids." I overlooked the remark at the time, thinking that maybe Gene had a bad run-in with those two particular boys on a different occasion. However, from that point forward, I always looked at Gene suspiciously, similar to the way Larry David looks at everyone on the HBO show, *Curb Your Enthusiasm*.

It also didn't take me long to realize that Gene was the most boring person in the world. At the same birthday party, he cornered me near the soft drinks table and explained in great detail how and why ice cools drinks in bottles quicker than aluminum cans. Size, shape, texture, quantity, clearness of the ice, source of the water, relative humidity, the amount of sunlight shining on the ice in the cooler, and day of the week, apparently, were key factors in the cooling process. Before I had a chance to pull away from that one-sided conversation, Gene transitioned into a ten-minute soliloquy about weather patterns, likening the story to why Greenland and Iceland were named the way they are. Thankfully, one of his sons, I don't know which the hell one of them it was, fell off a trampoline and scraped his elbow. Gene rushed away to help, granting me parole from his gripping personality. When I later spotted the kid holding a homemade ice bag on his scratch, I couldn't help but think that the soft drinks would be less cold now since some of the ice was used for non-soft-drink-cooling purposes.

"Don't plan anything for Saturday night," Lori told me while we were dressing for work one morning, "We're going to La Cocina with Linda and Gene." Obviously in a good mood, she gave me a sharp pat on the butt as she announced the dinner date.

Crap. Linda was fine, but I dreaded dinner with Gene. Ever since the birthday party months earlier, I went to great lengths to minimize my time in the presence of boring Dudley Do-Right. At parties or gatherings with the kids, I either stayed close to Lori or Mitchell, or occupied myself with something else. At dinners, however, with just the four of us in the small confines of a restaurant table, it was all-Gene-radio, all the time. One evening at the Olive Garden, I almost fell asleep as Gene explained how the situation between Israel and Palestine affected his ability to purchase a good car stereo.

Don't ask me how he argued the connection between the two issues. His arguments never made sense. Besides, I had been barely holding onto consciousness as it was. The only thing that had kept me awake was listening to the restaurant staff loudly singing some Italian-style birthday song to a guy in the corner booth with reddish-orange hair who resembled Conan O'Brien.

"Why are we having dinner with them again?" I asked Lori. "Didn't we go out with them last week?"

"That was almost a month ago, and you've been complaining about it ever since. If I hear that Conan the Barbarian story one more time, I'm gonna throw up."

"It was Conan *O'Brien*," I retorted, as I imagined Conan the Barbarian with the other Conan's freakishly reddish-orange hair and head.

When Saturday came, I prepared myself for the pre-dinner date ritual that Lori always made me endure.

It started with a bang when she said in one breath, "Wear your long-sleeve brown shirt and the new green tie, fix your hair in the back, and make sure you sweep the leaves off the front porch before Linda and Gene pull up into the driveway." After dispensing my chores, Lori also made it a point to remind me of all the things I should and shouldn't say throughout the course of the evening. "Don't tell them that we went drinking with my sister; Gene and Linda don't drink, so neither should we. Be sure to mention that Sarah made the honor roll. Linda doesn't know that I started working again, so don't tell her yet; I'll tell her when I'm ready."

When Lori paused a moment to retrieve a dropped earring, I thought the litany of rules was finished. Nope. She continued while simultaneously threading the earring in place, "No arguing, no cussing, no discussing religion, no slouching at the table, no eating food that falls on the floor. And for God's sake..." her voice became noticeably louder, "...don't tell Gene that you go to the casino!"

That last instruction bothered me. I took great pride in my phenomenal blackjack card-counting abilities. But Lori never wanted me to talk about gambling, even with friends who were morally less conservative than Gene and Linda.

"Why can't I talk about something I like?" I asked in response.

"It's better than listening to Gene talk about how driving five miles less than the speed limit on the interstate increases gas mileage."

"Be nice, he's not that bad," she said, bringing her vocal delivery down several notches. I was briefly distracted as I noticed the finished product of Lori's evening preparation. She looked stunning in a little red dress that had teeny-tiny straps supporting the whole thing.

Sexy wife notwithstanding, I quickly responded, "Wanna bet? I had her attention as we walked downstairs. "I'll bet you anything that Gene will make some stupid, inane comment less than thirty seconds after we get into their car."

"Okay, I'll bet," Lori replied confidently. "If he does say something silly in the car, I'll let you have *dessert* after the date."

By the way she batted her eyes while saying "dessert," I knew she meant something that was *not* on the menu at La Cocina. Maybe this night wouldn't be so dreadful after all.

"However," she emphasized cruelly, "if he fails to say something goofy, you aren't getting any for a month!"

A month? That was a bold raise in the stakes. The thought of Lori being a sexual camel for a month worried me, but I remained confident in the wager. Although I couldn't mention it in mixed company, I *was* a gambler.

"Agreed," I replied, "but dessert better be really good."

As Gene's spotless 2005 Lexus pulled into our driveway, I felt that Lady Luck was with me. Why? Because while Lori was approaching the car with me hand-in-hand, she had failed to notice that the porch was still leafy. *Hee-hee.* Sometimes I neglected my chores on purpose—and got away with it. Even with good luck apparently in hand, I made a final subliminal gesture as we walked closer. *Gene, Gene, you predictable shit, if you can read my mind, make sure you say something ridiculous.*

"Hey you guys," Linda greeted, as she lowered her window.
"Hi Linda, hi Gene," Lori followed, "Are you hungry? I'm starving."

As the girls finished their greeting on the starboard side of the car, I approached the port side, gave Gene an obligatory male half head-nod, and then mumbled, "Hey."

Gene slowly placed the car in reverse, fumbled with the knobs while muting the stereo, draped his right arm behind Linda's headrest, deliberately turned his head, looked at Lori and me with a huge smile, and proclaimed, "We were just discussing how Texas Longhorn fans are the best fans in the whole wide world."

Booyah! What a lame comment.

I looked at Lori and smiled even larger than Gene. The next few hours might be filled with boring conversation, but things would liven up when I returned home. Lori's eyes widened for a moment, apparently shocked that I won the bet so fast. Or maybe, she was thinking about later too. She gave me a subtle wink.

As the car quickly pulled away, and as overjoyed as I was, I still remembered that it was my solemn duty as the only not-boring guy in the car to say something witty in response.

"You know, Gene, every team thinks they have the best fans. Just because some sports announcer made that comment twenty years ago doesn't make it scripture."

Lori squeezed my hand sharply, indicating that I said something that I shouldn't have. This was another social ritual of my wife's. Anytime I had said something she didn't like, I would get a reminder-squeeze on the arm. If we were sitting side-by-side at a table, I might get a reminder-squeeze of the thigh. If I really went overboard, I might get a quick kick in the shin. That shit doesn't just happen on TV sitcoms, you know.

On quick introspection, I realized this squeeze of the hand was for my saying the word "scripture," a potential springboard to a religious discussion. Fortunately, Gene didn't steer the conversation down that avenue. Instead, he spouted out another ridiculous comment that made his first one seem tame.

"I guess the best fans are the ones who support the team from the heart."

Are you shittin' me? I gotta get out of this car.

Lori smiled straight ahead, but squeezed my thigh, way harder than she squeezed my hand a moment earlier. I interpreted this as a logical sign to let Gene have the last word. Linda then made a comment about Lori's scarf. Luckily, the girls consumed the next several minutes of conversation by discussing fashion and holiday decorations.

At the La Cocina restaurant, the hostess attempted to seat the four of us in the corner booth adjacent to a large row of decorative windows. I happened to notice an African-American family of five seated in the booth next to it. Gene asked the hostess if she had another table.

"I don't want to be near the window with the sun setting," he justified.

Suspiciously, the sun was shining at such an angle that it wouldn't have been a nuisance to any of us. By the way Gene had abruptly turned his back to the black family of five as we moved to another table, I sensed a serious racial overtone on his behalf. It had been extremely subtle, but it was there. *What a jerk.*

As we took our seats at the new table, Gene stated, "They make the best enchiladas here. I think the chef is an illegal alien." Before he finished the sentence, Lori was squeezing my thigh hard. How can she do that with such little hands? *It feels like a bear is tearing into my flesh.* This was going to be brutal. At this rate, I would need a thigh-transplant by the end of the night.

The next two hours went by at a snail's pace. I felt like I was back in college. I pretended to be interested in everything, when I was interested in nothing. Anytime Linda, Lori, or I initiated some great conversational tidbit, Gene would soil it with his meaningless insight. He never ran out of words. He went on and on and on. To keep from nodding off, I distracted myself by observing peculiar sights and sounds in the restaurant.

I couldn't tell you all the details of Gene's boringness, but the lowlights included:

- How there were too many unhealthy breakfast cereals marketed solely for kids. His two boys were forbidden from eating them. During Gene's tirade about Lucky Charms and Cap'n Crunch, I noticed a tortilla chip on the floor that was shaped exactly like the state of Florida.
- How there were "bad, really bad places" on the Internet. During this rant, I stared at the clock on the La Cocina wall, next to the chili pepper painting. It was missing the one in

front of the zero where the ten digit should have been on the clock face.

- How the Catholic priests and cardinals were getting unfairly scrutinized in the wake of the recent molestation and sexual misconduct allegations. Here, I noticed that everyone in the restaurant was beginning to make faces at Gene while he rambled incessantly. It was fun to count how many heads I could see shaking in disbelief at the same time. The record was four.

- How the residents of Mississippi and Louisiana devastated by Hurricane Katrina were "asking for trouble" by living near the coast. In the middle of this one-sided conversation, Lori gave me a sharp kick to the shin because I instinctively said "Yes" when the waiter asked if we wanted margaritas. As I winced in extreme pain, Lori quickly corrected me to the waiter.

- How supermarket lines with one feeder queue were more efficient than separate lines for each individual cashier. I became sad during this story, because a busboy stepped on the Florida tortilla chip, smashing it to bits. I planned to pick it up and eat it later.

- How he and Linda quit going to the movies because the prices were so high and there was nothing but sex on the screen. My thoughts were X-rated during this rant. I can't divulge them here.

After dinner, well over an *hour* after dinner, Gene excused himself to go to the restroom. Seconds later, Linda had received a cell phone call, and also excused herself from the table. For the first time of the night, Lori and I were alone.

"Do you believe this bullshit?" I angrily asked Lori. "He's killing me tonight."

"I know, I know," she agreed, "but you're being really good." She stroked my face with the back of her palm and continued, "I love you for not arguing or making smart-ass comments. Thank you."

Lori always had a knack for saying the right thing to calm my nerves. Without her, I would have no acceptable social skills.

"I love you too," I relented, kissing her hand.

As I turned my body to make a sophomoric attempt at kissing her fully on the lips, she straightened up and whispered, "Cut it out. There's Gene!"

"Wow, those hot-air blowing machines make a lot of noise," he beamed.

"Yeah," I said with mock excitement, "Noisy."

Linda also returned to the table, looking distraught. She mentioned something to Gene about somebody "having trouble with the petition."

Lori asked, "Is everything okay?"

Gene responded with attitude, "It makes us so mad that they're trying to build casinos outside of the Indian reservations. Linda and I are leading initiatives to keep the riff-raff from coming into the city."

For the first time that evening, Gene said something that piqued my interest. "What riff-raff?" I responded. At the same time, I defended several violent kicks coming at me from under the right side of the table.

"The casinos and the stupid people who go there," Gene said. He continued, and so did Lori's attempted kicks, "Gambling is for idiots just wanting to lose their money. Then comes the gangs and drugs and violence. Just look at the reservations. They are fraught with ugliness and people emancipated from their money. I hate the fact that..."

I loudly interrupted, "Fraught? Emancipated? Those are powerful words from someone who has his head up his ass!" By this time, Lori had stopped kicking me because she knew the launch sequence was already in motion. Getting even louder, I continued. "I gamble, Gene. Are you calling me an idiot? Do you think I want to lose my money?"

"No, err, I um..." was all he could muster in a much timid tone.

"Have you even been to one of the casinos?" I asked Gene. I noticed that I was drawing attention, so I lowered my voice. "You know, for someone who is so prim and proper and godly, you really should know both sides of an argument before you start blabbering like a fool!"

Lori and Linda were shocked. Lori was shocked because I was letting Gene have it in the middle of the crowded La Cocina restaurant. Linda was shocked because Lori was married to a gambler.

I continued with Gene, "The casinos on the Pueblos employ hundreds of employees and bring in millions of dollars in tax revenue to the rest of the state. They also provide a great form of entertainment."

Gene countered, "But gambling is addictive. If you eliminate the problem, you can eliminate the addiction."

"Alcohol and cigarettes are addictive too," I replied, all the while setting him up to say something silly to the effect, "Those are wrong too. They *should* be eliminated."

"Those are wrong too," he whined, as if a trained seal, "they *should* be eliminated."

I quickly countered again, "Caffeine is addictive, so is food. Are you saying that all people subject to some type of addiction should be prohibited from legally indulging in it? Are you petitioning Starbucks? Are you trying to eliminate all the supermarkets so the fat-assed members of your congregation can overcome their addictions? I agree that gambling addicts need help, but you are talking about a small portion of the gambling population."

Gene remained wide-eyed with his jaw slightly hanging open. He didn't attempt to answer any of my questions. Just then, the waiter approached.

"Two margaritas for me and my wife, please. No salt on mine." I was on a roll. "Plus, bring me one of those big-ass Budweiser drafts in the special La Cocina orange sombrero mug." Turning to Linda, I asked, "Do you want anything?"

She shook her head, quickly and repeatedly.

"Since you are remaining silent, Gene, I'll continue. Let's talk about the *emancipated* part of casino gambling that you mentioned." While I utterly hated the nerdy gesture of making quote marks in the air with your fingers, I made the gesture three inches from his face while saying "emancipated" for Gene's benefit. "I know a lot of people who lose money at the casino, but they see it as a form of entertainment. Suppose an elderly couple pays $100 for two seats to see the Longhorns pad their record by beating some Division

II-A opponent for three hours. Now suppose there is another elderly couple who spends $100 playing slot machines for three hours at Sandia. What's the difference?"

Gene finally had the courage to respond, "But football is a *morally acceptable* form of entertainment." He smiled and looked at the girls, like he had made some fascinating and overwhelming argument.

"Who says? I like football as much as anyone else, but how can you say that a bunch of guys knocking the hell out of each other is morally acceptable? Plus, football is dangerous. I've never seen anyone taken away from the casino on a golf cart because their vertebrae were snapped." Truth be told, I *had* seen numerous patrons taken from the casino on a stretcher, but it was usually due to injuries involving old age.

That last argument hadn't been my best, but I still had plenty of momentum. I rewarded myself by immediately chugging half of the Budweiser in the special La Cocina orange sombrero mug.

While I was drinking, Linda chimed into the argument, "Society, voters. We're the ones who decide what is acceptable. There is nothing wrong with petitioning others who share our point of view."

"I agree, Linda." I smiled at her, clearly conveying that she was not the overly boring and overly opinionated member of her household who was pissing me off. I pointed at her and playfully said, "You make good arguments. I like you. You good." She smiled back at me, and blushed slightly. I suspect she was unfamiliar with the concept of a man exhibiting charm.

Turning my pointed finger toward Gene, I scowled and claimed, "I no like you. Your arguments suck shit!"

Hearing my choice of words, Lori gulped her entire margarita and then started on mine. I noticed a small crowd of La Cocina employees and a few customers turning their attention toward our table. Gene was visibly shaken by my last comment. I guarantee that nobody ever told him, "suck shit" in one of his previous conversations. He'd probably have to go to confession for just hearing such a phrase.

Like an out-dueled prizefighter ten years past his prime, Gene weakly stood up and came back at me with a flurry of verbal punches that he thought would be effective. "No matter what you say, gambling is an immoral activity that cheats old people out of their retirement money, robs welfare recipients of their benefits, and leads minorities to gang violence and drug dealing. Everyone knows the casino has the advantage. I can't believe someone with your education would gamble. You *must* be dumb." He looked at Lori and finished, "You must be dumb, too, for letting him gamble."

Lori's expression indicated that she was about to erupt like a volcano. She is the best at standing up for me or the kids anytime that some prick says something negative about us. This time, I was the one to squeeze her thigh.

I immediately turned to Lori and whispered, "Don't worry, honey. I got it."

I stood up from the table, finished my Budweiser in the special La Cocina orange sombrero mug, wiped my mouth with a linen napkin, proceeded two inches from Gene's panting, scared face, and angrily replied, "Sit down!" He sat down. "You don't deserve a response, Gene, but I'll answer your points with numerous counterpoints. I recommend that you don't interrupt me."

I straightened my long sleeve shirt and loosened the new green tie. I sauntered a few feet back toward my side of the table while I prepared a one-sided conversation of my own. I tried to take a sip of my margarita, but Lori must have finished it while I was in shit head's face. Instead, I looked a bit silly trying to drink from an empty glass. I glanced at Lori. She was wiping her mouth.

"Number one," I directed toward Gene, "If there are any old people being cheated out of money in this area, there's a good chance most of them have been playing bingo at your church, Saint Joseph-what's-his-face. The last time I took my mother there, bingo games were twenty dollars. Simple math shows that two-hundred old ladies, times twenty dollars each, minus a thousand dollars in prizes, equals a 75% advantage for the Catholic house. That's not gambling. That's organized crime."

Our waiter stopped in his tracks after hearing that argument. He and two of the busboys inched closer to our table in an attempt to hear the rest of my lecture.

"Number two. If welfare recipients rush to the casinos after getting their monthly checks, it is probably because the support they get from conservatives in this area is paltry. It may not be right that they try to double or triple their money by playing slots, but I can understand why they do it."

A young mother of four kids, approximately aged four, three, two, and one, was sitting a couple of tables away from us. After this argument she yelled, "Right!" Meanwhile, our waiter was quickly trying to interpret my English to Spanish for one of the busboys. More of the La Cocina crowd converged toward our table.

"Number three. Gang members and drug dealers don't hang out at the casino. They're not morons—armed security guards and cameras are everywhere. And if one or two of them do show up to play games of chance, good, at least they're not on the streets causing trouble."

Gene looked like a deer in headlights.

"Number four. FYI—this was another nerdy term that I never used. Gene used it incessantly—the casino doesn't have the advantage over me. I count cards in blackjack. I have an edge over the house whenever I play. Besides being entertaining, going to the casino is a lucrative venture on my part."

Linda appreciated the power of the buck. Her eyes perked up when I made that last comment. She looked at Lori for confirmation.

"It's true," Lori exclaimed. "He kicks ass."

Gene sunk in his chair. His six-foot-one frame appeared to measure three-foot-one. He was obviously destroyed by my arguments. Nobody had ever called bullshit on him in such a passionate way. I sensed that mercy was now required on my part. There was no need to go further. *Oh hell, who am I trying to fool?*

"Numbers five through ten," I went further. Gene's eyes widened, then closed, as he realized I was only halfway done. "Just because you don't like Fruit Loops, don't ruin the fun for your two boys, Rod and Todd Flanders. It's called 'porn' Gene, and yes, the Internet is full of it. Deal with it like a man. There's probably as much sex between priests and altar boys as there is on the movie screens. Deal with that too. Were you actually talking about supermarket lines two hours ago, or was I dreaming that, because you put me to sleep talking about supermarket lines? Didn't your dad lose the roof off his house in a tornado twenty years ago? I suppose he was *looking for trouble*—I made the air quotes in his face again—by living in Tornado Alley.

And finally, Gene, nobody ends an argument by saying, 'You must be dumb.' If you run out of things to say in an argument, and you still want to save face, at least you could have the balls to shout, 'Fuck you!' like a man."

The crowd that accumulated on every side of our table applauded. The women with the four kids tried to cover their eight little ears, but she realized the task was impossible. Instead, she clapped, too. Lori also applauded. Then she barked a "Woof, woof" while circling her little fist in the air. The whole scene was glorious. I felt the same way that I did after being dealt from a magic shoe.

Gene rightfully buried his head in shame. Linda subconsciously, but noticeably, scooted a few inches away from him. Unfortunately, she would have to stay by his side during future lame arguments. Maybe there wouldn't be as many of them now.

I extended my hand toward Lori. She was beaming at me as I helped her up from the chair. She was satisfied by the way that I had defended her honor and mine. Once Lori had gotten on her feet, I gave her a big hug.

We started to walk away, but I returned to the table to make one more remark to Gene. While sliding a piece of paper under the arms supporting his lowered head, I said, "Number eleven. You're paying the bill, you racist son-of-a-bitch!"

Lori and I proceeded down a row of four tables filled with La Cocina customers offering high and low fives. These were the same people who were shaking their heads during Gene's ramblings throughout the night. The show was over, and the public got its money's worth.

Near the door, we could hear Gene weakly yell, "Oh yeah?! You're not getting a ride home!" *Good one, Gene.* We didn't even acknowledge him by turning around.

Lori and I exited the restaurant to discover a wonderful night sky: full moon, cool air, beautiful stars. We both agreed the conditions were perfect to take a stroll home. The walk would also be a perfect way to build an appetite for dessert. Of course, I would have to sweep the porch first.

THE SMOKE

When I was in eighth grade at Monroney Junior High in Midwest City, Oklahoma, I had the biggest crush on a girl named Tiffany Herbert. It was lunchtime on the first day of school when I met her. Tiffany was a seventh grader. Half the eighth graders had lunch scheduled with the freshman, while the other half of us had lunch with the younger class. When I first saw Tiffany, my stomach felt queasy. Lunchtime would now be a dilemma for me. I couldn't eat. She was the prettiest thing I had ever seen in my life. She had that effect on me for weeks, so I continued to sneak around the parking lot at lunchtime just to get close enough to see her without being caught staring like the little perv that I was.

Naturally, Tiffany had the attention of all the boys, including many of the fellas in our junior high who were obviously now "men" judging by their introductory facial hair and increased body mass which tragically dwarfed my 90-pound frame. I knew that if I ever had a chance to get close to Tiffany, and eventually make her my girlfriend, as I imagined destiny intended, I would have to compete with many from the masculine masses. Luckily, I had a secret weapon—I was a goofball who brimmed with an unusual amount of confidence. If I was rejected by the opposite sex for any reason at a party, dance, after-football pizza dinner, or anywhere else, I quickly thought of something funny to say or do to play off the situation without embarrassment. For as long as I could remember, I never had problems trying to start a conversation with a girl in hopes of sparking up a childhood romance. If I struck out, it was no big deal. I'd crack a joke and move on to the next female challenge.

Tiffany made me change strategy. She was special. If I just blurted out that I was hopelessly in love with her, it might have come across as weird. I had to think of a different approach. In time, I became a

144

friend by association with Tiffany because her circle of friends and my circle of friends overlapped. During lunch or after school events, I was afforded many opportunities to chat with Tiffany or make her laugh. Her flawless smile always made my heart beat quicker. I watched dozens of guys try to win her affection, and learned something from each schmuck who was unsuccessful. In late January, when I was positive that Tiffany didn't have a boyfriend, I finally got the nerve to ask her to a school Valentine's Day dance.

"Sorry, Glen," Tiffany explained with the utmost amount of seventh grade style and grace, "I'm already going with so and so. Besides, I only like you, you know, as a friend."

Ouch. I can't recall being able to say something funny to ease the pain. Tiffany rejected me as nicely as possible, but I was truly heartbroken for the first time in my life. I thought I did everything correctly. So much for destiny.

Eventually I got over Tiffany, but not before getting the same type of rejection from a handful of other girls in junior high and the first year of high school. Sometimes I got rejected rather rudely. I know I had been a smartass at times, but was I that undesirable? Someone once asked me if I was ever going to have a serious girlfriend. Believe me, I tried. In fact, I had tried so hard, unsuccessfully, that I began to lose confidence. Finally, in the spring of tenth grade, when I was hanging out in the parking lot at Ken's Pizza before my part-time shift in the restaurant, I learned something about myself from a girl named Lisa.

Lisa had a gorgeous face, topped with a skunky blond streak of dyed hair that ran down the middle of her otherwise brunette head. She was fun and attentive; we talked for quite awhile. Just as I was preparing to ask her on a date, however, Lisa told me rather bluntly, "You know, you shouldn't smoke."

"I don't smoke."

"Oh, you smell like you do." She then buried her nose into my shirt just to the right of my Ken's Pizza nametag and asked, "Do your parents smoke? You reek!"

My parents did smoke. I hadn't really thought about how much until Lisa and I delved into the issue. My mom smoked about two packs of Raleigh Filters a day; my dad always had a short, fat cigar, either lit or unlit, sticking out of the corner of his mouth. When I was young, I remember my parents driving with a carload of us kids in a station wagon to Pennsylvania with the air conditioner blaring and the windows rolled up while they smoked. Mom sent me across the street to 7-11 to buy cigarettes when I was about ten years old. Nobody checked ID in those days. I didn't *have* ID at that age. I recall my dad frequently stepping on his cigar with golf spikes after he threw the stogie on the ground prior to making a golf swing. Funny. I remember both of my parents smoking in the Ridgecrest Elementary School gymnasium when I had participated in a sixth grade Christmas program. Not so funny.

When I told Lisa all of this, she replied, "Wow, that is bad! Sorry you have to live that way. I can't stand the smell." She then walked away, but turned one last time to add with a smile, "Too bad, Smoky the Bear, you're cute." With that, Lisa left.

I lost track of my thoughts after that quasi-rejection, and eventually had to hurry inside for work. While I spent the next several hours making pizzas, preparing salad bar toppings and washing dishes and pans, I constantly put my nose to my own shirt taking a whiff of the smoky smell. *I did reek—and this shirt was just cleaned yesterday.* Could it have gotten that smoky just by hanging overnight in our laundry room? As I became attuned to the distinctness of the cigarette and cigar odor on my body, I noticed it was stronger than all the various pizza smells in the restaurant kitchen.

When my mother picked me up from work in her 1978 royal blue Monte Carlo, I noticed a cigarette in her mouth. I absolutely love my mom more than anything, but I grimaced when I saw the thick smoke hovering in the front seat since the windows had been closed because of the cooler-than-normal spring air. I got in the car and immediately thought I would suffocate in the gray cloud. Was that smoke always there? I coughed and coughed. Mom thought I was sick.

Upon arriving home, I changed clothes and took a shower. For some reason, I was appalled by the stench that was on my shirt where Lisa's nose had been. After my thirty-minute marathon shower session, spent washing, rinsing and repeating several times, I noticed that the clean bath towels still smelled smoky. Then, I went into my bedroom; it smelled smoky. I bent over to smell the bed. Linen—smoky. Pillow—Raleigh Filters. I went to my closet. Golf shirts—cigars. Ken's Pizza shirts—ashtray.

Where in the hell had this odor been the last sixteen years of my life? Surely it hadn't been surrounding my very being since I was born. As I lay in bed that night, nauseous, I thought about how smoke and its stench might have adversely affected the last few years of my life. The next day, I called my friend, Bruce LaBrie, to get his opinion of my odor.

"Oh yeah, you stink, Wig," Bruce explained matter-of-factly.

"For how long?!" I asked in a panic.

"I dunno. Forever," Bruce reckoned. He then gave me a ration of shit only a friend like Bruce could have given, "In fact, I can smell it through the phone line."

I then called Elizabeth Knight, a girl that I had always wanted to be more than friends with since fifth grade, but we never, ever, became more than just friends, despite my repeated asking, because she always told me that we were good friends, but we could never be more than just friends.

"Hi, Liz. This is Glen. Can you be honest with me? Do I smell like anything?"

"Smoke!" she said rather loudly and quickly, catching me off guard. "You always smell like smoke."

"Oh my god! Why didn't you ever tell me?"

Liz said, "I don't know. I thought you knew it."

The call ended with me feeling worse than I had the previous night. I was a smoky-smelling fucker and, apparently, had been that way throughout my adolescent life. *Had this been the only reason that Tiffany Herbert didn't become my valentine?* To this day, I don't know.

It is amazing how all these thoughts come back to you while waiting for a six-deck shoe to be shuffled in a smoky casino with a burly 280-pound man standing next to you crumpling a Marlboro soft pack and tossing it to the floor next to his recent flicker of cigarette ashes. Other thoughts come to me as well. I wonder if tonight is the night this fat bastard rightfully dies of a stroke or a coronary embolism. I usually keep thoughts like that to myself. *Usually.*

For the record, I don't mind smokers as a group. I love the fact that smokers, along with people who have tattoos, people who pierce their bodies—not with normal earrings, but with hoops, ball bearings, spark plugs or small woodland animal bones—and people who wear tailor-made suits and clap like idiots at the opening bell of the stock market, do all these ridiculous things on their own free will. I love that these groups justify the existence of their odd habits with passion and, almost always, illogical thinking. I respect the rights of these folks, as a group, to do all these silly things, and don't really care when and where they do these silly things. I just have a problem when these people are near me or my family. Why do they do that? Why, for instance, had the Marlboro Man chosen to sit next to me at the blackjack table this very moment? I was just minding my own business at third base, trying to double my stacks of red and green chips. I had just won four out of five hands with a high true count to end the shoe, so in general, I was in good spirits. Why then, did this sonuvabitch take a seat next to me with a cigarette in one hand, and another cigarette in the other hand just in case the first one happened to go out without warning? Why, I ask you, why?

Don't answer. I already know the reason. Everyone knows the reason. That is why I hadn't asked him the same question directly. Instead, I did my usual routine and simply moved to the other side of the blackjack table or to a different table. However, after I did so on this occasion, Marlboro Man immediately went on the defensive.

"Do you have something against smokers?" he asked.

"No. I have something against weak people."

"Are you calling me weak?" the chubby smoker answered back with a slightly louder tone.

I countered, without raising the tone of my voice one bit, "No, I didn't call you weak. I just said that I had something against weak people."

"I know what you meant, asshole! Just because I smoke doesn't make you a better person than me."

"I disagree. Since I don't smoke, I have a healthier heart, healthier lungs, and a healthier brain. I also don't stink. I think that is the very definition of a *better* person."

"Well, if you don't like it, you can just move."

"I did that a minute ago, professor," I retorted. "In fact, I moved without saying a word or making an ugly face at you, yet you still had reason to question my intentions."

"Okay funny guy, if you still don't like it, maybe we should go outside."

"Nope. That won't help," I quickly shot back, since I was in the safe confirms of a heavily alarmed and guarded facility. "I won't like you any better out there."

"You're an asshole!" he said, as he gathered smokes and chips and went to another table.

Success. He moved. But later, I would have to be extra careful while walking to the parking lot.

To reiterate, I have nothing against smokers at the casino per se, but I feel that many of them don't like me for some reason. Sometimes I draw their ire simply by waving a hand to fan the smoke away from my face. Why would that action cause a smoker to go on the defensive? It's not like I'm blowing the smoke back at them, which I had also done on occasion—bad example. For the most part, I keep to myself any time a smoker sits next to me at the blackjack table. I never cast the first stone or say something overtly inappropriate. Quite often, I don't give smokers a second thought because the shoe is running a positive count, or there are no other seats at an otherwise crowded, smoky table games area. I deal with the situation just like the casino staff. I could leave if I wanted, but I choose to be there next to Mr. and Mrs. Smoky Smokerson. You will have to make that tough decision also, if you want to count cards. You may be fortunate to live near a non-smoking casino, but the chances are slim. The reason casinos don't ban smoking is because the mindset of addictive smokers makes them perfect customers to participate in an addictive activity like gambling. If casinos banned smokers, they'd be banning a good chunk of their loyal clientele. Casinos and smoke go hand in hand. Accept that fact, as I did long ago, and enjoy three more blackjack and smoker stories.

The Horseshoe Casino, Bossier City, Louisiana, May 2003: After participating in a two-day conference with other Scientific Analysts at Barksdale Air Force Base, I took a day of leave, military speak for "vacation day," and hit the casinos on both sides of the Red River in Shreveport and Bossier City. If you ever strolled through the main casino entrance at the Horseshoe in Bossier, you know about the 10,000 hundred-dollar bills displayed under glass on the wall, showing every customer what a million dollars looks like. For the record, I once saw a million-dollar bill adorned with Bill Clinton's portrait behind the counter at a Gas-n-Go, but I suspect it was not real currency. The Million-Dollar Wall at the Horseshoe was more impressive. Upon entering the blackjack table area, I was greeted with another equally impressive spectacle, a single-deck blackjack game. When I started my card-counting adventure more than two years prior, I had researched single-deck blackjack, and created a few math models on the game, but I never had the opportunity to play single-deck for real.

The table games area had approximately eight blackjack tables, but there was only one single-deck game. It was 11:00 p.m. The table was packed with five players, all smokers. Two men and one woman waited to play. I didn't mind the smoke, or the queue; I was filled with adrenaline. The wait also gave me time to observe the other players and try to remember how to play single-deck correctly. Luckily, after a few moments, I remembered the small, laminated card in my wallet that showed Basic Strategy for one deck action. As I alternated between studying the card and watching the game, I learned the rules for the table. The cards were dealt face-down so the players could touch them. This is called a "pitch game" of blackjack as opposed to a "shoe game"; a shoe game is where the players are forbidden from touching the cards dealt face-up. Blackjack at the single-deck game paid three to two, players could double-down on any two cards, and the dealer stayed on soft seventeen. All good. However, aces could not be split more than once, and the player could not double-down after splitting. Not as good. I also noticed that the dealer dealt two hands before reshuffling. That meant I only had one hand for which to alter the unit bet on a positive count. The most startling aspect of the single-deck game concerned the table minimum, $50. Yikes. That was a little rich for my blood given that I only had $400 in cash. If I started on a small losing streak, it wouldn't take long before I did a premature exit down the corridor containing the Million-Dollar Wall.

Midnight. I still waited, but a husband and wife had just left the table together leaving me next in line. At 12:30 a.m., I finally got my chance to play. The table was occupied by all smokers, except me. On the first hand, I bet the table minimum of $50, doubled-down with eleven against a seven, drew an eight for a decent nineteen, rooted for the dealer to have a face card down, gasped when he had a four for an eleven, and muttered, "Shit" when he drew a king for twenty-one. In less than a minute, I was down $100. Worse, the true count was +4, so I was supposed to bet $350 on the next hand. I couldn't do it. I didn't have enough green chips. Instead, I bet the minimum again. And won. If I had adjusted the bet correctly, I would be up $250 instead of down $50.

As I nervously waited for the next hand, I looked around the room for the waitress. My mouth was dry and my lips were getting chapped. I must have been distracted, because the other players were yelling at me to place my bet; it takes less than a minute to re-shuffle a single deck. Play resumed. Coincidentally, I had another double-down hand, and lost, again. *Crap!* The true count was +2, but I still bet the minimum $50. Won. *Double-crap!* "Why am I afraid to bet correctly accordingly to the count?" I said to myself. "Because you don't have the bankroll to be playing a $50 game, shit head," I rudely answered to myself.

After only two more hands, in which I pushed once and lost $50 on the other, the pit boss notified us that they were switching cards; it would be a few minutes. He recommended that we all take a bathroom break or get a drink. I had other intentions. I ran out to my rental car to retrieve a small jar of Carmex for my chapped lips. I also stopped at the ATM machine to withdraw $2000. I had only one night with high-dollar, single-deck blackjack action; I needed to be properly armed for battle.

I was the last player at the table to return, but my seat in the middle of two chain-smokers had been reserved. I waved the smoke away as I sat, which obviously offended the smokers because the one on my right told the one on my left something like, "He can't hang with us." I ignored the comment. I had other things on my mind. I bought ten, black $100 chips and two purple $500 chips, then began betting $100 a hand. This time, I could afford to play correctly. The next couple hours flew by with incredible fluctuations in wins and losses. Single-deck does that. I was up $900, down $500, up $700, down $800, and up again over a thousand dollars after a ten-minute run of good cards, including at least three or four blackjacks. I never experienced such a fast pace of gambling emotions while my purple and black chips went up and down like a lie-detector test administered to a steroids-era Major League baseball player.

The heavy smoker to my right, however, was experiencing more of a straight-line fluctuation, pointing downwards. He lost a bunch. He hadn't used Basic Strategy and tended to chase losses with larger bets. In the span of an hour, he had gone into his pockets a half-dozen times, pulling out wads of hundreds and throwing them down angrily each time with his right hand while relentlessly smoking cigarettes with the left hand. He bitched and complained about everything while he huffed and puffed on his cigarettes. He even verbally abused the dealer, a tiny woman named Cici.

"I can't believe this!" he shouted at poor Cici, "I was winning when Joel was dealing. What's the matter with you?"

At this point, the pit boss came over, "Calm down, sir."

"I'm sorry, I'm sorry. I won't do it again."

Fifteen minutes later, after another reach into his pockets for cash, the guy yelled at Cici again while she started a new shuffle. This time, however, the pit boss was 30-40 feet away; he began walking toward the table when he heard the ruckus. At the same time, I reached into my pocket for another dose of Carmex. When the pit boss returned, I had my eyes down as I applied a nice, new shiny coat of lip protectant on my masculine, but kissably soft lips.

"Sir, sir!" the pit boss said loudly as he approached. *Boy you're gonna get it now, you smoky, blackjackally challenged loser.*

"Sir, you can't use that here." The pit boss tapped me on the shoulder. "You must walk out of the casino to use that product."

He was referring to me and my masculine, but kissably soft lips, and the jar of Carmex. I never heard of such a rule.

"What are you talking about? My lips are chapped."

The pit boss continued, "You can't touch anything that can be used to mark the cards."

As he explained the odd rule to me, I noticed that the smoky loser guy was grinning at me because I got yelled out by the pit boss and he didn't.

"Are you kiddin' me?" I pointed to the right as I spoke, "This disgusting prick can smoke all night, touch the cards with his filthy hands, burn tiny holes in the fabric table top, then yell at Cici, but I can't put Carmex on my lips once an hour?"

"That's right," he replied.

The pit boss then told me to calm down and repeated the rationale behind the prohibition of using any kind of product or displaying a device that could be used to mark the cards in a pitch game. Meanwhile, the other players, all smokers, reveled in the unexpected twist of fate which saw me as the bad guy, not them. That was a good stopping point for me. I tipped Cici $10 and left. Oddly, I was perturbed as I walked past the Million-Dollar Wall at 3:30 a.m. a big winner. I got over it.

In case you are wondering, not all of my smoking and blackjack stories involve yelling and ugliness. Here is a friendlier tale.

Pueblo of Isleta Casino, Albuquerque, New Mexico, August 2007: My son and I just finished playing a round of golf at the Isleta Golf Course. The links at Isleta featured twenty-seven holes of golfing pleasure made even better by the fact that I had been comped two rounds as a frequent casino player's card member. After playing eighteen holes, Mitchell wanted to play the third nine holes. I was exhausted and sun-burnt after playing the first five hours, so I let him play the third nine by himself.

"I think I can find something to do for two hours," I told Nacho. "Nacho" was Mitchell's nickname, given to him at age six by his Mexican grandma. At the time, all the other grandkids were learning how English names were translated into Spanish.

"John would be Juan," Grandma Gloria said, "Michael would be Miguel."

"What would my name be, grandma?" Mitchell asked.

Grandma Gloria, known for her quick-thinking and nonsensical wit, said, "Hmm, I think it would be Nacho."

Everyone laughed and laughed. Eleven years later, Mitchell was known to most family, friends, classmates, sports team members, co-workers and several members of the general public as "Nacho." In fact, a ninth-grade teacher once told Lori and me at a parent-teacher conference, "Nacho is such a joy in class."

Back to the Isleta Golf Course.

"I think I can find something to do for two hours," I told Nacho.

"Gee, Dad, where would you go?" Mitchell responded sarcastically as he looked 200 yards past my shoulder at the Isleta Casino across the street from the golf course. I agreed to meet him back in the parking lot in two hours.

At the incredibly comfortable casino, which was air-conditioned at approximately sixty-five degrees, I sat at a six-deck blackjack table that was occupied by only one other player, a friendly looking woman of 80+ years old who resembled Estelle Getty's character from *The Golden Girls*.

When I sat down at the table, the lady said, "Thank goodness, now someone can help me." Her name was Lee. She was visiting family in town, and was apparently left at the blackjack table by them in favor of eating at the casino restaurant. "I'm not hungry," Lee spoke and smiled while touching my arm just above the wrist, "so they left me here to lose money."

I was in an especially good mood since I had just spent a great day golfing with Nacho. We both played like dog shit, but we found something to laugh about on almost every hole. Since I was feeling good, I told Lee, "Well, we're not gonna lose money now that I'm here."

Lee chuckled, "Do you know how to play?"

"Sure. In fact, I keep really good track of the cards, so if I bet more, you bet more. If I bet less, you bet less." Lee was giddy.

The dealer, Luis, was from Las Vegas. He knew that I counted cards, and I knew that he knew that I counted cards. Therefore, I didn't mind telling Lee my trick. Besides, I wouldn't get thrown out for card-counting playing $10 a hand.

When play began, Lee asked me whether she should hit or stay almost every hand. On the good plays, she got genuinely excited and grabbed me playfully on the arm. After awhile, I was starting to get a rash over the sunburn from golf. When the dealer unexpectedly won, Lee moaned and produced enough drama that you'd think her cat had just died. Win or lose, every hand was an adventure.

After twenty minutes of action on the blackjack table, and a lot of fun chit-chat about family and home states, Lee and I were both about even. "Wow," she exclaimed, "I played a long time and my chips are still here! That's something new for me."

Lee took a pack of cigarettes and a lighter out of her purse. I was slightly surprised because smokers her age usually aren't walking the earth, at least without an oxygen canister.

"Uh, oh, Lee," I said in a sad, slow voice, "I don't know if I'll be able to help you anymore if you smoke."

"Okay," she replied, and put the cigarettes and lighter back in the purse, "I should quit anyway." Success, and I didn't have to be a jerk.

As luck would have it, Lee caught a good winning streak soon after with a relatively high card-count. Lee won five hands in a row betting $20 instead of her usual $5. She had a blast. I was up a few bucks myself. I swear, at one point, Lee actually placed both of her hands on my chest and rubbed a couple circles on my golf shirt. I think her last name could have been "Robinson," because Mrs. Robinson, or more like Great-grandmother Robinson, might have been trying to seduce me. Luckily, before Lee had a chance to disrobe me, her family returned from the restaurant. She held two big stacks of chips in front of the three younger family member's eyes and announced, "You got full bellies. I got a full wallet because of my new friend, Glen." It was a pleasant, feel-good experience.

In the car later, Nacho asked why I smelled like old lady.

The final smoky tale is utterly disgusting. Harrah's Casino, Council Bluffs, Iowa, January 2005: If I graded Harrah's riverboat casino on a scale of one to ten, with ten being the best, the establishment got a perfect ten for comps awarded to players. As a Harrah's Reward member, I quickly moved from basic Gold Status to a full-fledged

Diamond Member in less than a year. The casino Marketing Department sent me weekly cash comps ranging anywhere from $10 to $50 depending on my play from the previous month. They also had special drawings or promotions almost every day of the week. During my assignment at U.S. Strategic Command, Offutt Air Force Base, from June 2003 until May 2006, I earned more than $3000 in cash comps from Harrah's or their neighboring property in Council Bluffs, the Horseshoe Casino. I also earned another few thousand dollars worth of golf course, hotel or merchandise comps from the Harrah's Rewards Club catalogue. Our kitchen today has a stainless steel Cuisinart toaster and blender that were awarded to me as incentive to play blackjack at the casino where I already enjoyed an edge over the house. I also own a Sony digital video recorder and a Sony digital camera that were lovely parting gifts from Harrah's, just so I could be persuaded to return to the gaming establishment more often. I didn't need the added incentive.

On the other hand, if I had to rank Harrah's Council Bluffs on air quality inside the casino, they would score a not-so-perfect zero. As of my last visit, the riverboat that houses all the table games and slots had a horrible venting system relative to every other casino I had visited. Several dealers and waitresses openly complained about the working conditions. The air flow was poor, so the smoke hung in the air like fog. Anytime I played blackjack there, Lori would make me take off all of my smoky clothes in the garage and head straight to the showers. I used an entire bottle of Febreze every few weeks to spray the car, garage and anything else that came in contact with my smoke-riddled body. Our new Lhasa Apso puppy, Newman, wouldn't come near me when I returned from the casino because I reeked so much. I truly pitied the employees who worked there every day. On a few occasions, I went into Harrah's for two or three minutes just to redeem a cash voucher that would expire that day. I didn't play blackjack on those days, but still smelled bad enough to warrant a naked walk from the garage up the stairs and into the shower stall, followed by a Febreze mission back to the garage and car interior. It was a disgusting and tedious process, but the comps were well worth the trips to the smoky riverboat.

After a few weeks playing at Harrah's, I purposely altered the times when I frequented the casino. I learned to visit first thing in the morning, between six and eight in the morning when the boat had fewer customers, thus fewer smokers, and, hopefully, less smoky, foggy mist in my face and lungs. On one Saturday morning, I was playing at a table on the far end of the first floor of the riverboat. In between hands and shuffles, I watched two maintenance men at the other end of the first floor table gaming area climb a long, twenty-foot ladder and perform some sort of work on the ceiling. At first, I couldn't see what they were doing, but it was obvious to see, and hear, that the two men moved the large ladder a few feet at a time to systematically service every square foot of the ceiling.

Every once in a while, I would curiously glance at the men to determine exactly what they were doing. After about an hour, the men had worked a third of the way toward the end of the first floor where I was sitting. At this point, it looked as though they were painting the ceiling. One man held what appeared to be a flat paint applicator on the end of a six-foot pole. He worked back and forth across the ceiling in a systematic manner, while the other worker held a large bucket on the ladder shelf a few feet below the first worker who was standing four or five rungs from the top of the ladder. Both men wore white coveralls, and I could faintly see the change in color on the ceiling where they had been.

More time passed. Now the two men were half way done with the ceiling. They must be efficient painters to cover so much ground, I mean *ceiling*, you know what I mean. Now, I could clearly see that the men were painting the ugly gray ceiling some shade of blue. I love blue, don't you? I still couldn't see the exact color, but the sharp contrast of the ceiling between the blue where they had been compared to the gray where they hadn't been was obvious. I looked at the ceiling directly above me. Gray. I'm not the type of person who can look at a color and spout off the Sherman-Williams type name for it, like "Burnt Umber" or "White Eggshell." Instead, I always used a sports uniform reference. Let's see, the current color looked like a cross between Oakland Raider silver and Pittsburgh Steeler Black. If I had been at home with Lori, I would use a different frame of reference. I might have said, "Honey, the ceiling at Harrah's was definitely a Newman Gray." Remember the dog that I mention three paragraphs ago? He's gray—and cute.

Even more time passed. The maintenance men got closer to my table. They were about two-thirds finished with the length of the room. *North Carolina Tarheel Blue.* The new paint color was definitely North Carolina Blue. It was a dramatic improvement to the old color. I approved. Maybe a new coat of paint would also make this place smell better.

The men methodically moved closer. The pit boss told the players at our table that we'd have to move to another blackjack pit when the workers were close. He estimated that we had another 10-15 minutes.

During the next shuffle of the six-deck shoe, I checked progress once again. The workers were only 40-50 feet away. Here comes the disgusting part of the story. Can you guess what I discovered? The men hadn't *painted* the ceiling—they *cleaned* it. I couldn't believe my eyes. I wanted to vomit. The ceiling had not turned from Newman Gray to Tarheel Blue because of paint. It changed colors because of soap and water. That explained the speed at which the two men did the entire room.

I swore then and there that I would start going to another casino. However, I had a $25 cash back coupon that was good for the next day only. I had to come back. I had to return the next week as well. And the week after that. And the week after that. And the next month. Stupid high-dollar incentive comps.

That story reminds me of a joke that I heard back in the Great Depression: What is gray and smells like blue paint?

Gray paint.

THE PUPPIES

A blackjack player, or any other type of gambler, experiences a wide range of feelings and emotions after repeated wagering. Sometimes the feeling is sheer exhilaration, other times it is a disappointment beyond belief. One of the absolute worst feelings occurs when you quickly lose your entire bankroll after having been up hundreds or thousands of dollars just minutes previously. If you gamble long enough, it happens. When it happens to me while playing blackjack, blaring and irritating thoughts immediately fill my head. Why didn't I quit ten minutes ago? Why was I so greedy? I can't believe I lost it all.

I had this ill feeling crop up on me unexpectedly while playing at the MGM Grand casino in Las Vegas. I was up $900 and lost eight of nine hands while the true count was high. In the course of a few minutes, I lost all the winnings and my entire $400 bankroll, a $1300 swing. I was hot. Everything I saw after that pissed me off: the ninety-four-year-old lady jumping up and down because she just won $50 on the slot machine nearest to the table games, the security guard near the men's room telling me to "Have a nice day," the ten-second wait for the elevator to arrive from the second floor, and the fifty-something immigrant custodian cleaning the ashtray canister. I just lost enough to pay your salary for a month. The everything-was-pissing-me-off theme continued. The sign inside the elevator advertising the all-you-can-eat seafood buffet, and the mini-billboard in the parking garage promoting the Englebert Humperdink shows on August 28th and 29th. *Screw Englebert, and screw Mr. and Mrs. Humperdink for naming him that. While I'm thinking about it, screw the month of August, you hot bastard with no holiday!* I was hot, and getting hotter. The loss of thirteen black chips, coupled with the 110-degree heat, combined to create a satanic-like sweat that emitted from every pore of my body. I couldn't imagine feeling worse, until I saw the puppies in the covered parking garage.

Five puppies were crammed inside a kennel cage barely big enough to hold one of them. Some grade-A, uncaring, moron left five infant animals caged in the back seat of a thirty-year-old, piece of crap Impala. Left them with no food or water. I was fuming. The car was shaded, and the window was cracked a few inches, but the interior temperature must have been near 125 degrees. The puppies were lifeless. I had to quickly get these puppies some water and food, and then find the idiot responsible for their predicament. I ran back into the MGM Grand. Luckily, I had been away from the confines of my home-court gaming establishment, the Sandia Casino in Albuquerque, otherwise Yong and the rest of the water police would have given me grief. I snagged six bottles of water from the self-help concession stand, holding them in the upturned bottom of my linen shirt. I also grabbed the Styrofoam bowl used to hold an ample supply of Sweet-and-Low packages. *Damn coffee drinkers. Because of you and your need for artificial sweetener, laboratory rats had to die.* Everything was pissing me off. Finally, I grabbed a plate of half-eaten french fries from the dozen or so small tables just outside the main gaming area.

As I ran back to the piece of crap Impala, I hoped that the shit head who abandoned the puppies hadn't yet departed. Nope, the car was still there. I yelled proudly, "Don't worry, babies, Bobby Boucher is here with some fine quality H_2O." If you weren't aware, that was a reference to Adam Sander's movie, *The Waterboy*. Why don't you watch a movie with your kids once in awhile instead of gambling? *Geez, everything is pissing me off!* As I yelled, a couple of the puppies sprang to life. Although the Impala doors were locked, it only took a few pounds of force to push down the partially opened window. Was I breaking and entering? I doubt it. Any police officer or judge would sympathize to what I was doing. I poured a bottle and a half of the water into the Styrofoam Sweet-and-Low bowl. The dogs knew what was coming. I opened the cage door. It was like someone turned on a happy meter inside the car.

I placed the bowl of water on the backseat and watched the fireworks. The puppies immediately quenched their thirsts. One of them, whom I had named "Michael Phelps," actually got all four legs into the Styrofoam Sweet-and-Low bowl and did half a lap before getting head-butted out of the way by another puppy. I called that one, "Bull." Each time I refilled the bowl, the puppies playfully competed to get a drink. Rightfully so, they went nuts with delight. At this point, I figured it was safe to add french fries to the menu. "Michael Phelps, no swimming for twenty minutes after eating." Dinner concluded with the puppies licking my face through the partially opened window in appreciation. I was happy. They were happy. It was a wonderful after-school-special moment.

I basked in the glory of my friendly deed. What now? Maybe these little guys didn't deserve their current situation. Maybe these puppies were destined to leave the prestigious MGM Grand parking garage with me. I quickly dismissed that scenario. As much as I would have liked the immediate adoption, our family was about to go through another one of those wonderful moves that the Air Force believed in putting us through every two to three years. Plus, we already had a large Black Labrador at the time, Barkley. He wouldn't want to be a momma. He liked the current one-dog-to-four-person ratio in the Wiggy household. Finally, I thought about the security cameras in the parking garage providing damning evidence in the dognapping case that could be filed against me. Nah, these dogs would have to stay with their current owner, as sad as that person might have been.

My second idea was better. I once heard that puppies had to "go" only ten minutes after eating and drinking. What better place to go than the floorboards and seats of a powder blue, rust-accented, piece-of-crap Impala. I waited and watched. No kidding, as soon as I thought of the impending pee sessions, one of the puppies immediately started leaking on the back seat. I named that one "Squatter." The rest of the puppies bolted in every direction and found a spot of their own to urinate or defecate. The largest one jumped through the open window into my arms. I named him "Jumper." I gave Jumper one last kiss before returning him to the Impala romper room. I then raised the window almost back to its original state, but gave the puppies a few more inches of breathing room than they had previously.

My plan worked like a charm. All of the puppies eventually

"made" inside the car—five number ones, and two number twos. Plus, one dog produced a small amount of vomit that looked remarkably similar to my Grandma Wielgoleski's potato soup. And as an added bonus, two of the puppies started gnawing on everything in sight. The Styrofoam Sweet-and-Low bowl was the first target. It lasted only a few seconds. The next target was the fake lamb's wool cover on the driver's side seat. I was hoping that the cowboy hat adorned with a "Win in Vegas" pin on the passenger seat would be next. Not to be. Naps were now in order. One by one, the puppies snuggled into various nooks and crannies of the Impala interior, then feel asleep.

For the first time since leaving the blackjack tables, I was calm. I would have loved to stay and confront the idiot owner of the puppies, but it was time for me to mosey along. What if the owner, built like one of these WWE wrestlers, found me outside his car with the discriminating evidence of empty water bottles and puppy saliva on my face? Or worse yet, what if the owner was a burly woman packing a handgun? She might have just lost a stack of black chips too, and would be seeing things that pissed her off. Yeah, it was definitely best for me to leave the canine crime scene undetected at that time.

As I departed the parking garage in my rental car, I made a final gesture to ensure the safety of the puppies. After all, who knows how long they would still be in the overheated vehicle? I flagged down a security guard.

"Hey, you might want to check on that old Impala over there. Someone left a bunch of puppies unattended."

The guard asked, "Do you want to leave your name and make a formal complaint?"

"Nah, I just want them to be okay."

As I drove back to my hotel, I realized I hadn't named all of the puppies. Let's see, there was "Michael Phelps," "Bull," "Squatter," and "Jumper." I decided to name the last one, "Holy Shit," because I imagined that would be the first thing that the Impala owner would say when returning to the car. I laughed at my overall dog-naming abilities, nearly forgetting the evening's $1300 disaster. As far as I could recall, it was the only time I ever had fun losing all my money at the casino. When I walked into our hotel room, Lori said, "I know you won. I can tell by your expression." I didn't correct her.

THE SUPERSTITION EXPERIMENT
– INTERRUPTING THE CARDS

Raise your hand if you have heard any of the following comments around the blackjack table:

> "Cut 'em thin to win."
>
> "Let her cut—last shoe was lucky."
>
> "Oh great! He's coming in during the middle of the shoe."
>
> "I never cut. I don't want to change the cards."
>
> "I'm playing two hands to change up the game."
>
> "Why did you take a hit? You're gonna change the cards."
>
> "Not you! [comment directed to the new dealer] The last time you dealt, I lost $300."
>
> "Never cut 'em thin."
>
> "G-Krice. That was the worst goddamn cut I've seen in my whole life. I could cut better than that with my dad's old World War II machete—the one he used to hack hundreds of cod in the morning and hundreds of Krauts in the afternoon. Your cutting sucks, your blackjack skills suck, your wristwatch sucks, your eyebrows suck, your dancing probably sucks, and you suck!"

Okay. Maybe you never heard that last comment around the blackjack table. However, you hear comments like the other ones all the time. By the way, you can lower your hand. I bet you look awfully silly reading this book on a park bench or an airplane with your arm in the air. You'd really look silly reading the book on the toilet. Tons of gamblers have deep-rooted superstitions regarding the cards, and the dramatic bad fortune those cards are destined to bring any time someone tempts fate by changing the order of the cards that the blackjack gods originally intended them to be dealt. The superstitions are everywhere. Woe is you if the cards are negatively changed by your actions. If bad stuff happens when a new player enters the game, or a player leaves, or a new dealer enters and burns a card, or if the cut is three cards left of where it should have been cut, you are likely to hear someone bitch about it. The comments and superstitions never end.

Personally, I've had enough of the speculation. I know that the cards change all the time, but it is ridiculous to expect the changes to always be for the worst. Sometimes the change is for the better, or the change has no impact on the game whatsoever. Players still believe what they want to believe.

Once and for all, I decided to conduct a highly technical experiment to determine if, in fact, the fortunes of the average blackjack player significantly change after intervening events. I examined several scenarios using the exact same six-deck shoe. Being a mathematician, I know how to properly conduct an experiment. I could easily identify randomized test subjects using standard treatment nomenclature, "A," "B," "C," "D," etc. I could also demonstrate key concepts regarding hypothesis testing, control groups, variables, stratified samples, standard deviations, test design, and the Central Limit Theorem. The question is—should I explain all that boring, conceptual, mathematical crap to you? Nah. Let's do the experiment a fun way.

Here are the subjects from my blackjack superstition experiment:

Anisha'keekwa   Bobby Bob Bobby   Cheng Cheng   DeJesus

Anisha'keekwa is not African-American. She is black. Although some of you think it is politically incorrect for me to refer to Anisha'keekwa as "black" instead of "African-American," I say you are wrong for two reasons. First, the United States has run amok with political correctness. I will not be swayed by adverse public peer pressure. Second, I know that Anisha'keekwa is not African-American, because when she sat at the experimental blackjack table, she told the dealer, "I'm Anisha'keekwa, from Jamaica. Nice to meet you, mon."

Bobby Bob Bobby, was named after his father, Rusty. He is definitely from America, from the deep south. Nobody talks like that anywhere else in the world. Nobody *wants* to talk like that anywhere else in the world. Almost every word out of Bobby Bob Bobby's mouth is "NASCAR," "gimme a dip" or "y'all." He knows everything there is to know about blackjack from watching contestants playing cards before hitting the lake during ESPN bass fishing tournaments.

Cheng Cheng is from China. The name Cheng means "success" in Chinese, so his name means "twice the success." He was destined to gamble. Cheng Cheng is extremely rich and intelligent outside the casino, but highly emotional, and sometimes irrational, after losing his fortune cookie at roulette or baccarat in the casino. Even on a $5 losing bet, Cheng Cheng will throw the biggest fit if he believes the loss was due to a superstitious change of fate.

DeJesus is Hispanic. His mom once ate a pancake with the silhouette of the Son of God on it while she was pregnant, hence his name. DeJesus has a big scar on his left cheek. I will not presume how he got the scar. However, if DeJesus is married to a Mexican woman, like I am, there is a good chance the scar was given to him by his feisty wife or mother-in-law during a display of highly charged emotion.

You'll notice that I've selected quite the cultural diverse group of players. Real casinos are that way. Everyone, regardless of their cultural differences or prejudices, join together for the common goal of beating the dealer. Look at the four subjects—they're all smiling. For now. Let's see how the United Colors of Benetton behave after the cards are dealt.

While the test subjects are obviously figments of my active imagination, the following experiment was very real. To prepare for it, I thoroughly shuffled six decks of cards, then labeled the back of each card with the number "1" through "312" with a black, Sharpie marker. At the start of each of the scenarios in the experiment, the cards were arranged in the exact same order. The basic premise of the experiment was simple. The players were dealt an entire shoe of blackjack with variable conditions on how the cards were distributed. My goal was to determine if slight changes in the cards made a difference in total winnings for the players.

Scenario 1 (baseline): Anisha'keekwa, Bobby Bob Bobby and Cheng Cheng played against the dealer each betting $10 a hand. The six-deck shoe was cut exactly in the middle, and dealt to the players in a normal manner until two decks remained. All players made correct gaming decisions using Basic Strategy for blackjack.

The results for Scenario 1 are displayed on the following graph. Nineteen hands were played. Bobby Bob Bobby started with three consecutive losses, but finished strong. He was ahead $30 upon completion of the shoe. Cheng Cheng was down $40 after the eighth hand, but turned around his fortune to finish at plus $10. Anisha'keekwa started with a blackjack, but lost a double-down on the next hand. She never returned to positive earnings, and lost $35 total. See how mad she is at the end of the shoe? Do you think she expressed displeasure about the cut after getting a blackjack on the first hand? No way, mon.

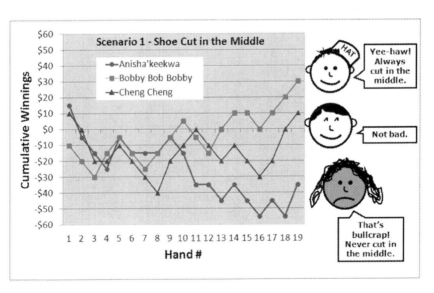

Scenario 2: Same set-up and assumptions as Scenario 1, except now, the six-deck shoe is cut "thin to win." With the exception of the starting point, the 312 cards are in the same order as Scenario 1. Obviously the cards are different. All the cards in the two decks that were not played at the end of the first shoe came into play during this scenario.

Uh oh, Anisha'keekwa is upset again. Despite the drastic change in cards, her luck was the same. She was dead even after twelve hands, but lost a total of $40 over the last eight hands. Bobby Bob Bobby surged the second half, with a net gain of $35 at the end of the shoe. In an impressive span of eight hands, Cheng Cheng had two blackjacks and a double-down winner. At one time, his cumulative winnings were off the chart. He finished the twenty-hand scenario as a big $55 winner. Perhaps he should change his name to "Cha Ching." For all three players, notice how some of the upward and downward trends are similar. For the most part, these trends are indicative of the actions of the dealer. Quite often, the dealer beats everyone at the table with a blackjack or twenty, or loses to everyone with a busted hand.

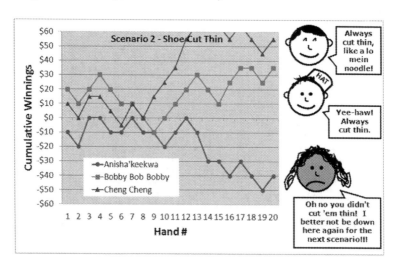

Scenario 3: Same set-up and assumptions as Scenario 1, except a new dealer came into the game after the second hand. As a general rule in every casino, when a new dealer enters the game, at least one card is burned. Do you suppose a single card out of a six-deck shoe of 312 cards can make a big difference? In this case, certainly.

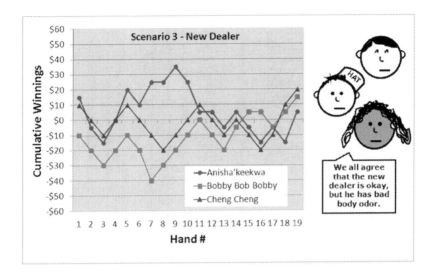

All three players ended the shoe with positive earnings. The outcomes for all players were relatively "flat" over the last half of the shoe. It is mathematically noteworthy to examine the high and low extremes between Scenario 1 and Scenario 3. In Scenario 1, the range between the final cumulative winnings of the high player and the low player was +$30 to –$35. For Scenario 3, the range was +$5 to +$20. All because of a new dealer and one single burn card.

Scenario 4: DeJesus makes his debut in this scenario. Certain blackjack players go apeshit anytime a new player enters the game in the middle of a shoe. You can sometimes hear their groans or negative comments. Someone might say, "If you're going to play, I'll drop out. I don't want to change the cards for everyone." Or they'll ask, "Can you wait a few hands? This shoe is going really well?" What pretension. The nerve these people have to think their time (and superstition) is more valuable than your time. Let's see if DeJesus affects the cards. Scenario 4 is the same as Scenario 1, except DeJesus enters the game at the beginning of the third hand, and only stays for two hands. He bets $25 a hand, instead of $10 like the others. If you think certain superstitious players belly-ache when a new player comes in, wait until you hear their reactions when the new player leaves just as quickly.

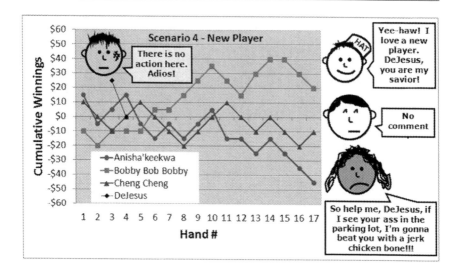

DeJesus won his first hand for $25, then lost the second. He left the table even, but his departure had quite an effect on another player. Poor Anisha'keekwa. It isn't her day. She blames all her bad luck on DeJesus, when as we all know, she has been losing most of the time no matter how the cards are dealt. All coincidence. Bobby Bob Bobby's good fortune on every scenario is also a coincidence. Data irregularities like these occur on a blackjack table.

Scenario 5: For the final scenario of the experiment, I must introduce a new player. This player is blackjackally challenged. Severely blackjackally challenged. There is *nothing* that makes some regular blackjack gamblers angrier than when a player who makes all the wrong decisions enters the game. The superstitious players at the table are convinced that bad fortune will follow. Sometimes they are right, sometimes they are wrong. Players only remember the bad occurrences.

Here is the last subject for my blackjack superstition experiment:

Egghead

Unlike the other players with distinct and diverse cultural or ethnic backgrounds, Egghead is truly from another planet. I do not want to offend any race or country by associating this dumb sunuvabitch with them. Therefore, Egghead looks like nobody else you've ever seen in the casino. Remarkably, Egghead looks more like a bluish-purple turnip instead of an egg. I'll be sure to improve the graphics in my next book.

For this scenario, Cheng Cheng left the table to make a phone call. Egghead entered the game in the exact same position vacated by Cheng Cheng. The number of players and the entire six-deck shoe are positioned in the same order as baseline Scenario 1. However, in this scenario, Egghead makes horrible decisions on his blackjack hands. He never hits a fifteen or sixteen against a dealer's seven, eight, nine, ten, or face card. Egghead never splits and never doubles-down. Worse, he hits a twelve, thirteen and fourteen when the dealer is showing a five or six. Finally, he accidentally drinks from Bobby Bob Bobby's tobacco spit-cup instead of his cup of Pepsi. After all, he is an egghead.

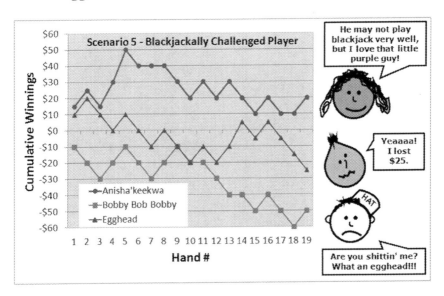

The first hand of Scenario 5 is played exactly the same as in Scenario 1. Egghead was not given the opportunity to make an egghead decision. For the second hand, however, Egghead's decision to hit a thirteen against the dealer's five changed the cards for the rest of the table, and the rest of the shoe. For the nineteen hands dealt in this scenario, Egghead made an incorrect decision six times. Two of those decisions made him and the other players win a hand they shouldn't have. Another couple decisions made the dealer bust a hand when he wouldn't have. Other incorrect decisions had mixed results. Remarkably, Egghead's egghead plays resulted in Bobby Bob Bobby losing for the first time in all of the scenarios. Conversely, Anisha'keekwa did better this shoe than any other. I wish I was making up the data.

Let's examine how bad decisions affected the individual player. If Egghead had been playing basic blackjack strategy, his cumulative winnings would have equaled Cheng Cheng's results from Scenario 1. Egghead lost $25 instead of winning $10, a difference of $35 in roughly fifteen minutes at the casino. Unlike the superstitions evaluated in the experiment, deviating from Basic Strategy is mathematically proven to affect the player negatively over the long run. While this experiment focused on a small sample of the representative population of all blackjack hands dealt from a six-deck shoe, the results should be eye-opening—especially if you are an egghead.

Maybe it wasn't the most scientific experiment, but it sure was a hoot. Here is a summary of the four main findings from the experiment:

1) The cards change for various reasons at a blackjack table.
2) Whether the change is good or bad is relatively unknown in the long run.
3) Deviating from Basic Strategy is for eggheads.
4) The countless hours of effort that the author exhausted to set-up this experiment, play the cards in identical order, tally the results for all hands, record the results in a spreadsheet, chart the results, create the imaginary test subjects, cut and paste the results into a useable report product, think of the witty responses for each player, decide on the final color for Egghead's skin, and write the report, would have been better utilized had he served soup to the homeless or performed some other type of community service. QED.

THE 800-NUMBER

There are several toll-free, 800-numbers available throughout the United States for chronic gamblers to call anytime they feel gambling has become an addiction or a source of significant stress or financial difficulty. In most states, lawmakers have mandated these 800-numbers and other state and local programs to help gamblers overcome addictions and other self-destructive actions which may stem from casino patronage or gambling lifestyles. Next time you see a billboard or a print ad for a casino, look for an 800-number for problem gamblers. It is like seeing a government warning label on a pack of cigarettes or a can of smokeless tobacco. Certainly, call the number if you suspect that you might have a gambling problem.

Personally, I've never needed to dial any of the 800-numbers. I thought about calling as research for this book. However, I decided not to fraudulently waste the time of any operator or service professional who provided much need assistance and guidance for gamblers with a serious problem just to satisfy my own curiosity. Even if I did call, what would I say? I imagine the call might go something like this:

THE 800-LADY: Good morning. Welcome to the Stop-Your-Stupid-Gambling hotline. My name is Monica. Do you have a gambling or debt problem that you'd like to discuss?
GLEN: Uh, yes, Monica. I have a problem.
THE 800-LADY: Fine, sir. We have many options to address your needs. First, may I please have your name?
GLEN: Sure, my name is Glen. Glen Wiggy.
THE 800-LADY: Did you say Wikky?
GLEN: Wiggy.
THE 800-LADY: Wiggly? Wigby?
GLEN: No, Wiggy. W - I - G - G - Y

THE 800-LADY: It is perfectly fine if you don't wish to provide your real name.

GLEN: Wiggy *is* my real name. Well, actually it was my dad's nickname, but he changed it legally fifty years ago. Have you ever heard of the Pennsylvania Dutch?

THE 800-LADY: Yes.

GLEN: My father was Pennsylvania Polack.

THE 800-LADY: Whatever, sir. I don't mind if you make up a fake last name. I'll call you "Wiggy" to move things along.

GLEN: How about you call me Glen?

THE 800-LADY: Okay, Glen. Would you like to seek assistance for a gambling-related problem?

GLEN: Yes. Yes, please. I'm beginning to feel guilty about gambling at the casinos.

THE 800-LADY: Guilt, stress and depression are commons signs of problem gambling.

GLEN: Who said anything about stress and depression? I'm not depressed or stressed.

THE 800-LADY: My mistake. Guilt then. Tell me about your guilt.

GLEN: The guilt is terrible, Monica.

THE 800-LADY: I understand. You're probably feeling guilty about losing money or control of your...

 GLEN: You're new at this, aren't you?

THE 800-LADY: Excuse me.

GLEN: You're new to this helpline thing?

THE 800-LADY: Yeah, I mean, no. Why do you ask?

GLEN: Well, I'm no Doctor Phil, but it appears to me that you jump right in with comments before you listen completely to the problem. Like a man would do.

THE 800-LADY: Is that so? Is that what you do?

[long pause]

THE 800-LADY: Glen?

GLEN: I was listening until you were done. Are you done?

THE 800-LADY: Ha, ha, you're a funny guy.

GLEN: I am? I wasn't trying to be funny. I have a problem.

THE 800-LADY: What is your problem?

GLEN: Geez, Monica, get with the program. *Guilt* is my problem.

THE 800-LADY: Sir! Please keep your voice down, or I'll have to end this call.

GLEN: And make me guiltier?

THE 800-LADY: Okay. Okay. Please, Glen, please tell me about your guilt.

GLEN: I told you. I feel guilty about gambling at casinos. I feel guilty because it isn't fair.

THE 800-LADY: Fair?

GLEN: Fair, for the house. I've been winning a lot lately.

THE 800-LADY: The overwhelming feeling of euphoria after winning is one of the symptoms of a chronic gambler. If a compulsive gambler wins in the beginning, it leads to more gaming. Self image is enhanced. You begin to have unrealistic expectations about future wins. You...

GLEN: [laughing hard] Omigosh, you are new. Is that straight from some script?

THE 800-LADY: No! No!

GLEN: Wheeeeeew. Give me a second. [chuckles] Okay, I'm back. I feel guilty, Monica, because I have an advantage over the house each and every time I gamble.

THE 800-LADY: [getting defensive] Sir, there are no games in the casino where the player has the advantage. We have brochures that will educate you on the odds of the...

GLEN: Not true. The player can have the edge in blackjack.

THE 800-LADY: That is a myth. The house always has the edge.

GLEN: Is that from the script?

THE 800-LADY: No.

GLEN: Are you a statistician?

THE 800-LADY: No, sir.

GLEN: You know what I am?

THE 800-LADY: Of course not.

GLEN: I'm a statistician. Actually, in the Air Force, they call it a "Scientific Analyst."

THE 800-LADY: [giggling] Oh, I see. I guess you're a rocket scientist.

GLEN: Don't be a wise-ass, Monica. I *was* a rocket scientist at my last assignment. But not now. Don't go assuming things again.

THE 800-LADY: Don't curse at me! You must be able to discuss your problem rationally and without swearing if you want help.

GLEN: You think the term "wise-ass" is swearing? Come on. I'm sure you've heard worse than that chatting with all those compulsive gamblers. There are a lot worse words flying around the casino on a Friday night.

THE 800-LADY: I have heard worse. However, profanity is not tolerated. This call is being monitored. If you cannot control your language, the call will be terminated.

GLEN: I thought these calls were confidential.

THE 800-LADY: Um, they are.

GLEN: You just said they're being taped.

THE 800-LADY: I didn't say you were being taped.

GLEN: Yes you did. You just said, "Profanity is not tolerated. This call is being monitored."

THE 800-LADY: I did not!

GLEN: Yeeeessss you did. Rewind the tape to see.

THE 800-LADY: [obviously angry] There is no tape!

GLEN: Calm down, Monica, it's okay. I don't mind being taped.

THE 800-LADY: Sir, you are not taking this call seriously. If you cannot abide by the rules, I'll have to...

GLEN: I'm sorry, I'm sorry. I'll be good. Where were we? Oh yeah, statistics.

THE 800-LADY: Our statistics are provided by the National Council for Gambling Research and confirmed through leading universities. It is a known fact the house [pauses slightly, while obviously reading] has a significant advantage over the best blackjack players. The odds are against you.

GLEN: Oh, Monica, you disappoint me.

THE 800-LADY: Excuse me?

GLEN: Those stats are for normal blackjack players using Basic Strategy. What does your script say about card-counting?

THE 800-LADY: About what?

GLEN: Card-counting. I count cards.

THE 800-LADY: Card-counting?

GLEN: Yeah, that's it. Have you ever seen the movie, *Rain Man?*

THE 800-LADY: No, I haven't. I was in diapers when that movie came out.

GLEN: Diapers? I don't need to hear about your personal life, Monica. If you are the freaky type who likes to wear diapers for pleasure, that is your choice.

THE 800-LADY: [angrily] I meant that I was a baby when that movie was released!

GLEN: How old are you?

THE 800-LADY: That's none of your business, sir.

GLEN: You're right. I just wanted to know if you were old enough to gamble.

THE 800-LADY: I'm old enough to gamble.

GLEN: Really? What do you play? Roulette? Slot machines? Video poker? No wait, you probably like...

THE 800-LADY: I don't gamble.

GLEN: You don't. I betcha you do.

THE 800-LADY: [angry again] I have never gambled!

GLEN: Never? In your whole life, you've never made a bet?

THE 800-LADY: [smugly] I have NOT.

GLEN: You've never played cards with your friends?

THE 800-LADY: We don't play for money. We play for fun.

GLEN: Have you ever played the lotto?

THE 800-LADY: Pardon?

GLEN: You know, Powerball? The lottery. Have you ever bought a lottery ticket?

THE 800-LADY: Um. [pauses] That is not gambling.

GLEN: Oh my god, Monica! You play the lottery?

THE 800-LADY: Not often. It isn't gambling.

GLEN: The hell it isn't. And, the lotto has worse odds than any casino game. Not only are you a gambler, Monica, you are a gambler who makes horrible choices.

THE 800-LADY: I only buy a couple tickets a month.

GLEN: Underestimating losses and downplaying expenditures are two symptoms of a chronic gambler.

THE 800-LADY: Sir, I'm going to end this call unless you have a real problem to discuss.

GLEN: I do, I do. I told you that I feel guilty because I have an edge over the casino in blackjack. I feel like I'm cheating them.

THE 800-LADY: You have an edge, huh? How much of an edge?

GLEN: Well, it depends on the type of the game—number of decks, double-down rules, whether the dealer hits on soft seventeen. Stuff like that. Besides regular counting, I keep good track of the aces separately. So, I probably have close to a 2% advantage.

THE 800-LADY: You never lose?

GLEN: Are you crazy? I've been to the casino over 800 times. Of course I lose. Nobody wins all the time. Except liars.

THE 800-LADY: It doesn't make sense. Why would you go to the casino all those times if you only win 51% of the time?

GLEN: Who said anything about 51%?

THE 800-LADY: You said you had a 2% advantage. That means you win about 51% of the time, versus losing 49%, right?

GLEN: Wow. You said you weren't a statistician, Monica. You proved it with that statement.

THE 800-LADY: What do you mean?

GLEN: I said I have a 2% edge over the house. That's only one factor. My winning percentage is actually 68%.

THE 800-LADY: Sixty-eight?

GLEN: Sure. There are normal fluctuations in the game of blackjack that make winning possible even if you don't count cards. That is why any goon can win big. In the long run, the casino makes money because of the overall advantage. They also win because a lot of players are blackjackally challenged. I use my overall advantage coupled with the normal fluctuations. In the long run, I win 68% of the time.

THE 800-LADY: Really? So how much have you won?

GLEN: That's none of your business, ma'am.

THE 800-LADY: Okay. I'm ending this call right now.

GLEN: You can't, Monica. You haven't offered me any help with my problem yet.

THE 800-LADY: All right, all right. [reading reluctantly] We have several pieces of literature to address problem gambling, or I'd be happy to refer you to a professional or support group in your area who can assist you."

GLEN: Monicaaaaaa. Why are you being that way?

THE 800-LADY: Sir, you are making a mockery of this service.

GLEN: No, I'm not. We just keep getting sidetracked. I have a serious problem. Every time I go the casino, I see people playing blackjack incorrectly, or they play correctly, but the casino slowly eats away at their chips. I see most players leave sad or angry. I want to help them.

THE 800-LADY: That's a good idea. Maybe you should help. We have openings in our company for telephone service representatives.

GLEN: Would I be able to teach callers how to count cards?

THE 800-LADY: No, no! Our mission is to educate callers on the signs and symptoms of problem gambling and the compulsions that develop when the problems grow. We help thousands of people each month.

GLEN: That's great. I think you are in a noble profession. It's just that I want to help the schmucks who never pick up a phone to call you. If they insist on gambling, they might as well increase their odds of winning.

THE 800-LADY: [angry and sarcastic again] Fine, Wiggy, I'll start telling callers, "If you really want to beat your gambling problem, I know this rocket scientist who will help you count cards and cheat at the casino."

GLEN: That's the spirit.

THE 800-LADY: I was being sarcastic.

GLEN: Me too.

THE 800-LADY: Maybe you should have your own 800-number for callers.

GLEN: Are you being sarcastic now?

THE 800-LADY: [lying] No.

GLEN: How big an office would I need for something like that?

THE 800-LADY: Well, we have ten people on the East Coast and about thirty here in Las Vegas.

GLEN: You're in Vegas?

THE 800-LADY: Yes.

GLEN: And you don't gamble in the casinos? What a waste. You should move to Utah or some other harsh environment.

THE 800-LADY: Are we almost done, Glen?

GLEN: Yes, just one more thing. You mentioned having literature about gambling.

THE 800-LADY: Yes.

GLEN: [excited] Do you have anything that discusses ace location? Somebody told me there are blackjack players who can track clumps of aces being shuffled. They wait for the groups of aces to reappear at the right time in the shoe so they can bet big. I hear they clean up. Can you send me a pamphlet that will teach me that?

THE 800-LADY: [click]

GLEN: Hello? Monica? Don't hang up on me. Tell me more about those diapers!

THE TEST

As an instructor of mathematics for the United States Air Force Academy, Embry-Riddle Aeronautical University, and a handful of other centers of higher learning, I tested students on their comprehensive knowledge of the subject material covered throughout the course. You will be treated no differently. I hope you had some fun reading this book, but it is equally important that you learned a few things about the great game of blackjack. The following ten questions will determine if you acquired any practical knowledge from my tutelage:

1. While playing a friendly game of blackjack at the local casino, an incredibly drunk and obnoxious man takes the seat to your left. He has two large handfuls of green $25 chips. He reeks of booze and barely has the manual dexterity to push chips onto the betting circle. He is loud and crude to you, the dealer and the other players. During the course of play, the drunk makes several mistakes against Basic Strategy, and appears to be on the verge of passing out in the middle of hands. You should:

A. Ignore the gentleman.
B. Notify the pit boss of the situation.
C. Calmly and silently move to another table.
D. Watch the guy like a hawk because he is likely to drop chips on the floor in the middle of his drunken stupor enabling you to have a shot at one or several of the greens chips he will mistakenly lose over the course of the evening.

Answer: D. I looooove when this happens. I've pocketed chips dropped or mishandled by a drunk three different times at the casino. I'll even follow the drunkard around from table to table.

2. Some die-hard card-counters advise that you should never tip the dealer, because the act reduces the overall expected profit gained by card-counting. This advice is:

A. Sound. You should never tip the dealer.

B. Silly. How much you tip, and how you play blackjack are independent events.

C. Solid. The dealer is already well compensated by the casino.

D. Stupid. Only a cheap prick would give that kind of advice. In fact, let's all gang up and beat the crap out of the idiot who said such a thing.

Answers: B or D. Dealers should be tipped routinely when you enjoy their company and/or service, and maybe tipped more when you are winning.

3. After years of practice and experience, you've established yourself as a relatively great card-counter, and always play according to Basic Strategy. You are also a huge fan of the Denver Broncos. One Sunday in January, you find yourself trying to simultaneously count cards and watch the playoff game between the Broncos and the Indianapolis Colts on the big-screen television on the wall over and beyond the dealer's head. You mistakenly stay on a thirteen against the dealer's ten. By the time you notice the mistake, the dealer has already taken the next card, an eight which would have given you a twenty-one. You lose $35 as a result of your inattentiveness on the hand. You should:

A. Never, ever try to count cards while pre-occupied with something else.
B. Quit playing cards, or quit watching the game, one or the other.
C. Consider killing yourself for continuing to be a Denver Bronco fan and season-ticket holder after John Elway had retired.
D. All of the above.

Answer: D. This happened to a guy who is just like me, except dumber.

4. True or false. Using Basic Strategy in the game of blackjack is guaranteed to make you a winner.

Answer: True. I absolutely, positively, guarantee that if you play one-hundred hands in blackjack using Basic Strategy, you will win at least three of those hands.

5. You are seated at a table with one other player to your right. The player is a tall, slender man approximately fifty-five years old wearing a New York Yankees baseball cap and playing $800 on the hand. You are playing the table minimum of $10. You are dealt a twelve against the dealer's two. The other player stands on his pat seventeen. Since you are playing by Basic Strategy, you signal the dealer for a hit. Before the dealer reacts, however, the other player interrupts, "I wish you wouldn't hit. I'm betting big, and I don't want you to take the dealer's bust card." You should:

A. Ignore the other player and signal for a hit.
B. Kindly inform the man, "I'll play the way I want, you can play the way you want."
C. Reply, "Fuck off, Joe DiMaggio!"
D. Tell the guy, "Okay. I'll stay, but only if you give me $10 if I lose."

Answer: D. The guy gave me two red chips even before the hand was finished. We each won our hands because the dealer busted. The dealer would have busted even if I had taken a hit. I netted $20 on the hand. Note: in this situation, if you say, "Okay. I'll stay, but only if you give me $10 if I lose," and the other player declines the offer, the correct response is then C, "Fuck Off, Joe DiMaggio!"

6. You walk up to a table and attempt to enter a six-deck game of blackjack mid-shoe while another player is head's up against the dealer. The other player kindly asks, "Can you please wait until I lose a hand? I have a good streak going." You should:

A. Wait until the player loses a hand. She did say "please" and appeared considerate with the request.
B. Reply, "I'll wait just one hand. You can't really expect me to wait much longer."
C. Ignore the player and her goofy superstitions, then continue to enter the game quietly.
D. Reply humorously, but conveying a serious message, "Okay, but then I want you to wait thirty-two hands while I play alone."

Answer: Any of the above answers are correct. A situation like this happens quite often. A player who asks you to wait is a bit selfish, but there is no reason to be mean or rude in response. We are all trying to accomplish the same goal of winning a few bucks. Actually, if you are counting cards, the answer to this question is "E. A card-counter should never blindly enter a game mid-shoe."

7. True or false. A player dealt a blackjack may double-down.

Answer: Absolutely true. Sometimes this is done during blackjack tournaments when a player needs to get more money on the table. Someone once told me that the strategy is also good in a single-deck blackjack game where the true count is extremely high and the payout for a normal blackjack is six to five. I cannot confirm or deny that is the right move, but it doesn't sound logical to me.

Do I have a blackjack?
DOUBLE-DOWN!

8. Which of the following phenomena cannot occur during a game of blackjack under the standard rules applied at most casinos:

A. A player loses or wins eight times the amount originally bet at the start of the hand.
B. A man with $500 bet on a hand of blackjack stays on a pair of aces against a dealer's four.
C. A dealer runs out of cards.
D. A player with a hard total of twenty-one asks for, and is given, another hit.

Answer: This is a trick question. All four of the answers are possible. I've never seen situation (A) occur, but it is possible. Most casinos allow a player to split pairs four times. If a double-down is made on all four split hands, the player could win or lose eight times the original bet. I witnessed situation (B). The player knew that splitting aces was the correct way to play the hand, but he did not have the money to cover the bet. I had $500, and wanted to buy one of the split aces. The player refused my offer. He also chose not to hit, fearing he would take the dealer's bust card. He stayed on a two—and lost, by the way. Situation (C) can occur in a single-deck game if the dealer inadvertently plays too many hands or there are many splits and low cards in the deck after the penetration card surfaces. Situation (D) came up in a hypothetical discussion. A guy at my table was complaining that he lost seven hands in a row. I bet him $100 that I could lose the next ten hands in a row. He didn't take the bet knowing there was a catch. There was. I told him I would simply bet $5 a hand and purposely hit until I busted every hand.

The guy replied, "What if you got a twenty-one? You couldn't take another hit."

"Yes I could."

The dealer disagreed with me. I told him and the player that they were both wrong. Most casino rules say a player can hit until the hand is busted. The pit boss settled the argument saying that I was correct.

"But, you'd be stupid to do it," the pit boss clarified.

"Not if it won me a $100 side bet."

9. Your spouse wants to spend $1000 on a new chair and ottoman for the master bedroom. The love of your life asks if you have any extra money in your secret gambling stash. You have a hair more than a thousand tucked away, but buying the furniture would deplete your gambling fund for future casino visits. You reply:

A. "Sorry, honey, I only have a few dollars left in the stash." DING.

B. "What happened to all the money you've saved over the years?"

C. "We already have a bed in the bedroom. Why do you need a chair? And, why the livin' hell does anyone *ever* need an ottoman?"

D. "I have $1083.50 in the stash. It's yours, my darling."

Answer: D. What do you think I am, crazy?

10. You are dealt a pair of eights or aces in a blackjack game that does not offer the "surrender" option. You should:

A. Always split aces and eights.

B. Always split aces and eights.

C. Always split aces and eights.

D. Always split aces and eights.

Answer: C

JUST ONE MORE HAND

"Just one more hand, honey. I'm about to leave the casino."

I've quoted that phrase to my wife many times in phone calls during the last eight years. I've also muttered "Just one more hand" to myself as a reminder that it was time to get going. Occasionally, the powerful lure of blackjack glory kept me at the table longer than expected. "Just one more hand" sometimes turned into twenty-seven more hands.

This chapter is similar. In a book of short stories and instructional lessons, there were many others shorter stories and educational tidbits not warranting an entire chapter on the subject. Please enjoy twenty-seven more anecdotes:

~ The First Lady of the American Casino Theater ~

There was a female dealer in Council Bluffs, Iowa, about fifty-five years old, with silver hair and a sweet personality. However, her personality was too sweet. She would give an over-exaggerated expression on every hand after she drew the final card. I never had to look at the dealer's cards to see if I won or lost. "Aaahhhhh, too bad," she'd say if I had nineteen and she drew a twenty. Or, "Yeahhhhh" each time she busted. Most of the time, she made the comments before showing the down card to all the players. She ruined that last-second moment of suspense. On days when I had been losing, it was unbearable to sit at her table. I wanted to reach over the chip tray and strangle her.

~ The Streaks ~

As a mathematician, I instinctively monitor and remember all trends and streaks while at the blackjack table. Nerdy, I know. The big winners and big losers are easy to remember. I once saw the dealer get five blackjacks in a row. I've never matched that feat as a player, but I have been dealt five blackjacks in a span of six hands. I've won fourteen hands in a row, but every hand was at the table minimum because the shoe had a negative running count. My personal losing streak is sixteen hands in a row spread out over two different visits. I left one evening after losing ten in a row and going broke in the process. The next day, I started with six losses in a row. *Astonishing*. I had one winning streak where I didn't bust an entire six-deck shoe playing head's up against the dealer. Conversely, I think I once busted nine hands in a row on a different table and a different day.

All seasoned players have stories about odd streaks or hands. The absolute strangest occurrence I've seen on a blackjack table involved another player who was dealt a pair of threes against the dealer's nine. I wasn't in the game at the time, but I witnessed the spectacle from the next table. The player correctly took a hit instead of splitting. It was a three. The player hit again. Another three. At this point, people started to chuckle and gasp, "Wow, look at all the threes." He couldn't possible get another. He did. The player had five threes on the table for a total of fifteen. Following Basic Strategy, he asked for another hit. The dealer proudly showed the card to everyone as it came out of the shoe. Another three, for an eighteen. *Pretty neat*. Here is where the story took a strange turn. The player now had an eighteen against the dealer's nine. He defied Basic Strategy and even basic logic by asking for another hit with a pat hand. A $50 pat hand, by the way. The player was convinced that another three was destined to give him a total of twenty-one. The next card was a six. The player busted. The dealer had an eight underneath for a total of seventeen. The ridiculous player lost $50 instead of winning $50. A $100 swing because of gross superstition.

~ The Circus Circus Chip ~

Twenty years ago, my father gave me a couple dozen chips from casinos in Las Vegas, Wendover, Elko, and a few others cities in Nevada. Dad said the chips were for my daughter to collect, but I had other plans. From that point, I expanded the collection by obtaining a $1 ceramic or coin chip from every casino that I frequented. I added chips to the collection from every casino in Atlantic City and the Mississippi Gulf Coast, plus Tunica, Shreveport, Council Bluffs, Reno, and many others including, of course, almost every available Las Vegas gaming locale. I also collected a 2£ chip from England, a $1 chip that required a 45-minute boat ride into international waters off Tampa, Florida, and a few 50¢ chips, mainly from Indian reservation casinos in Oklahoma.

My collection method was unique, because I won every chip added. I never paid for a souvenir token. For instance, when I visited Las Vegas for an entire week in 2004, I systematically visited every casino on the strip starting with Mandalay Bay and walking north. At each casino, I started with a $5 or $10 unit bet. If I won on the first hand, or accumulated winnings shortly thereafter, I'd request payout in $1 chips or coins and move on to the next casino. Sometimes, I was in the building less than a few minutes. If I started on a losing streak, I would count cards and continue until I was on the plus side.

The system worked great for over eight hours, until I visited the Circus Circus casino. I lost quickly there, and could never get back into the positives. Even with extensive fluctuations due to positive true card-counts, I couldn't leave the building a winner. Eventually, I lost all the money in my wallet, over $800. I returned to my hotel with $30-$40 in chips from other casinos, and a single, faded, white-and-pink, $1 chip from the Circus Circus. It was an expensive souvenir. I eventually ended the one-week trip to Vegas a $2200 winner. However, I can no longer say with a clear conscience that every chip in my collection had been won. To this day, I have yet to return to the big top casino.

~ The Three Stooges ~

As a reminder, always sign up for a player's club account whenever you gamble at a new casino. Usually, you'll get a free gift—buffet lunch, $5 slot voucher, T-shirt, etc.—just for opening an account. More importantly, you instantly qualify for comps or promotions like car giveaways or special drawings. Sandia Casino in New Mexico once gave away a custom built house to a lucky player's club member. While visiting my daughter in California, my son-in-law, Chris, and I played blackjack at the Chumash Casino in Santa Ynez. On the same night that I registered with the Chumash player's club, my name was randomly selected for a $300 cash drawing. Even if you don't get comped right away, you might be rewarded later by mail with free cash or special player's club drawings on specific dates.

Besides the thousands of dollars in cash comps, golf rounds, restaurant vouchers, electronics, concert tickets, small appliances, and other items, I've received some peculiar or kitschy promotional items. At Harrah's properties in 2006, there was a free giveaway for bobblehead dolls of The Three Stooges. There was one catch. You could only receive one Stooge per Sunday visit. The first bobblehead Stooge, Moe, was absolutely goofy. I gave it to my son for his bedroom. As ridiculous as the promotion was, there I was among many patrons who made repeat visits each of the following two Sundays to get all Three Stooges in the set. Mitchell reminded me all week not to miss my appointment at the casino. Marketing Department genius.

~ The Unaccounted Waters ~

I have a confession. The bottled water count in the 1536 Free Waters story is a lie. The actual water count was 1539 bottles. According to the strict accounting rules that I established early during the water scam, all the bottles that I removed from the casino should have been accounted for in the final tally. That was not the case for three of the bottles. After a visit where I won $520, I gave a homeless man loitering near the Alameda Street interstate exit two bottles of water and a twenty-dollar bill. I didn't count the $20 on the official win/loss tally, either. I treated it like a toke. On another occasion when I left the casino a $400 loser after a quick and painful losing streak, I threw a bottle of water against the wall of the underground parking garage in a fit of anger. It didn't burst open the first time, so I threw the bottle against the wall again. The contents sprayed everywhere. I felt much better. I apologize for misleading you on the official water count. I will immediately notify the publishers to change the title of the book.

~ The International Games ~

I've been fortunate enough to play blackjack in four different foreign countries. While stationed in Germany, I played in a casino which required all gentlemen to wear a coat and tie. Many of the male patrons wore tuxedos, just like in James Bond movies. I recall the German word *carten* was used to signify a hit.

During a trip to Goteburg, Sweden, to purchase a new Volvo at the factory, my family and I stayed in a hotel once frequented by President Gerald Ford. In the lobby of the hotel was a single blackjack table. I played two hands against a friendly dealer who spoke fluent English. I only played two hands, because on the second hand, I learned that the house won on pushes. Goodbye, Swedish blackjack.

After ferrying the Volvo across the sea, we stayed in a hotel in the Netherlands which had two blackjack tables in its lobby. Since the player did not lose on a push, I stayed awhile. The six-deck blackjack shoe contained three purple cards adorned with some joker-type figure. I think the locals called the cards, "bugs," but I can't remember. I do recall, however, that the three special cards were part of bonuses for the players. If the dealer had given you a purple card, you could not lose your hand regardless of the result. If you had been dealt two of the purple cards in the same hand, you automatically won the hand, no matter how the dealer fared. If all three of the purple cards had been dealt to your hand, you won some outrageous bonus prize like a thousand pounds, or franks, or guilders, or whatever currency they used in the Netherlands at the time.

Finally, I played blackjack in London once. Nothing special there. Everyone spoke English, although it was not the proper Oklahoma English that I learned as a child, or the English mixed with a spattering of Spanish words spoken in my current family household.

~ The Ripped Cards ~

While strolling through the high-dollar gaming area at a casino in Atlantic City, I noticed a Japanese man playing $25,000 a hand at baccarat. He had a visible bankroll of roughly half a million dollars in rectangular shaped chips on the table. On each deal, the man would check his two cards by holding one side face-down with the left hand, then pulling upwards sharply with his right hand. Each time, he would rip the two cards in half. As an obvious consequence, the dealer was forced to use a new deck for the next hand. An additional dealer-helper was stationed next to the normal baccarat dealer to assist with the opening and washing of the new deck.

> **washing** = the term used to describe the act of the dealer placing brand new cards on the table, checking the cards for defects, and mixing them before assembling the deck in the usual manner for a normal shuffle.

I heard the pit boss explain the ritual to an inquiring customer, "Betting that much money, a player can do whatever he wants with the cards." I asked if I could do the same thing playing $5 a hand at blackjack. The pit boss said, "You could do it once, but then you'd never play here again." What hypocrisy. I haven't tried it yet, but one day I will rip the cards just like the Japanese man.

~ The Genius ~

During a drive from Omaha to Oklahoma City to visit my parents, I stopped at a roadside casino near a small Kansas town. I wanted to play a few hands to break the monotony of driving. I sat at a blackjack table which had no posted rules. Since the dealer was in the middle of a chip exchange with the pit boss and security staff, I asked the only player at the table a couple questions. The man was diminutive, probably weighing less than a hundred pounds, and wore thick, black-framed glasses.

"What are the double-down rules? Do they offer surrender?"

Without looking in my direction, the wee man said, "Some dogs are named Talmadge."

I responded inquisitively, "Pardon."

The man repeated with a ton of attitude, "*Some dogs are named Talmadge!*"

I stood up and slowly walked from the table saying, "Oooookay then." Some dogs are named Talmadge? *What the hell does that mean?* The guy might have been mentally challenged. Or maybe he was intoxicated or under the influence of something stronger than alcohol. Either way, I determined the gentleman should remain in solitude.

I found another table where I played head's up with the dealer. A half hour later, a loud, obnoxious woman approached the game. She started blabbering even before taking a seat, and did not stop talking when the cards were dealt.

"We have been on the road all day in that blasted sun—Cousin Mary is driving me crazy in the RV—If we don't get to Yellowstone soon, I'm gonna bust—Where is the potty in this place?" She wouldn't stop yammering. Eventually, she turned my way.

"Hi, my name's Shelly, I'm from Rolla, Missouri. What's your name?"

I looked straight ahead, thought a moment, and responded, "Some dogs are named Talmadge."

"Dogs are whaaaaat?" Shelly responded with a puzzled look on her face.

I screamed in response, *"Some dogs are named Talmadge!"*

The woman quit talking for the first time and gently pulled herself away from the table, all the while giving me a strange look. The dealer, pit boss and security staff gave me puzzled looks as well, but continued their business. At that moment, I realized that the little guy with the thick, black-framed glasses was a genius.

~ The Beggars ~

Play blackjack long enough, and you'll be seated next to a person who asks for the wrong cards when taking a hit. No offense, ladies, but I've noticed that women do this far more than men. For instance, this one woman hit a hand of fourteen against the dealer's ten, "Gimme a five," she requested.

"Why don't you ask for a seven?" I pondered.

"I don't want to be greedy."

Here is superstition truly gone amok. People like this are actually afraid to beg for the right card. If you're going to engage in wishful thinking, why not wish for the best hand possible? Sometimes the player will really low ball the begging progress. "Okay, dealer, [hitting a twelve], I want a five or a six." When this happens at the table, I get miffed. I'll start begging for the wrong cards on purpose. If I'm holding a sixteen against a face card, I'll say loudly, "Give me a ten!" Or, if I split aces, I'll demand, "I want a four on this ace, and a two on this one." Or, if I get a blackjack, I'll moan, "Why? Why did you give me that hand? Damn you! I wanted a hard six. The agony!" I'll go to great lengths to show beggars how goofy they really are.

~ The Red-Chip Prostitute ~

I'm glad the red chip prostitute in Las Vegas hadn't been bothering me. She was disgusting and annoying. A woman, approximately twenty-five years old, but looking forty-five years old due to hard living, was flirting with a guy at my table who had a couple thousand dollars worth of chips. She would scoot up next to the player, chat awhile, then go to the bathroom or to the bar.

"You know, honey, we could have a lot of fun with that purple chip." By her dress and mannerisms, I gathered that the woman was a professional trying to solicit a trick. The guy flirted back, but openly told the dealer while she was gone that he would not go anywhere with the girl.

"I can't afford a purple, sweetheart. What can I get for a black chip?"

The woman didn't realize that she was being played. She whispered something in the guy's ear.

"No, no. For that, I wouldn't pay more than a green." The woman walked away.

Twenty minutes later she was back. "Okay. For two greens, I'll do it."

I shuddered in my seat thinking about "it," whatever it was. The woman smelled like a urinal.

"One green," the player countered.

"No way, pig." With that, she left. Finally. Now I could concentrate on blackjack without having to witness the freak show.

Another twenty minutes later, the prostitute was back next to the guy at my table. She acted like nothing negative had been mentioned earlier.

"Okay. One green."

"Nope. That was before you insulted me. What can I get for a red chip?"

"Fuck you, bastard!"

The women left with those words in a violent huff, never to return.

I couldn't resist offering up the obvious joke, "Was her response to the red chip offer an insult or a counteroffer?"

~ 9/12 ~

Like all Americans, I was stunned and depressed after the events of 9/11. On the afternoon of the tragedy, my unit at Kirtland Air Force Base sent everyone home early to be with family. We spent the day watching television and counting our blessings. Before dawn on 9/12, I received a phone call relating an important top-down message from our commander. All non-essential personnel at the base were ordered to stay home. As a military officer, it didn't make sense that I was directed to take the day off on the first day of the "War on Terror." Lori still had work. The kids still had school. However, I later learned that security forces on the base were able to implement higher defense posture measures on building and entry points more efficiently without thousands of ordinary staff personnel mulling around. Instead of sitting around the house alone and depressed, I played blackjack. I thought it would be a slow day at the casino on a Wednesday morning. Quite the opposite—the place was packed. Apparently many other people were told to stay home from work. Of course, the atmosphere in the casino was different. The normal anger associated with losing a few dollars on a hand of blackjack was put into proper perspective.

~ The Joke ~

I heard Larry the Cable Guy tell the following joke. It is, in my humble opinion, one of the funniest gambling jokes ever:

A homeless-looking guy is sitting outside of a casino in Las Vegas. He has torn, dirty clothes, and looks like he hadn't shaved or showered in a week. Another man, handsome and well-dressed, obviously wealthy, exits from the back of a limo and approaches the front of the casino.

"Excuse me, sir," the gruff man says, "Can you spare some cash? My wife and kids are in the car. The gas tank is empty. We haven't eaten in days."

"No, no!" the rich man replies with a ton of judgment, "You'll just use it for gambling!"

The bum retorts, "Oh, I *have* gambling money."

~ The Basketball Player ~

At Sandia Casino, for a couple months in 2007, I played a lot of blackjack with a huge six-foot-eight-inch guy named Jay. His name might have been simply "J," like the Doctor. I knew the guy well because I was forced to guard him sometimes on the basketball court during pick-up games at Kirtland Air Force Base. He was usually the best player in the gym. Initially, Jay didn't recognize me in the casino.

After sitting at the same table three or four times, he finally asked, "Where do I know you from, man?"

"I'm the guy who tries to guard you on the basketball court."

"Oh yeah, you're the colonel."

Technically, I was only a lieutenant colonel at the time, but I didn't correct Jay for promoting me. He pulled up the adjacent stool and we chatted about blackjack and basketball. After that day, Jay and I also talked frequently about blackjack between pick-up ball games in the gym. I told him about my card-counting adventures. I convinced him to shadow my bets when we were at the same table. If I doubled or tripled the unit bet, Jay doubled or tripled his. When I bet less or quit the shoe, Jay did the same. I took good care of him. He acknowledged that his casino earnings had greatly improved during the couple months of shadowing my bets. I reaped the benefits from our relationship in a different way. Jay started choosing me on his pick-up basketball team. I didn't have to guard him when I was his teammate. Jay also protected me in the paint on offense, and gave me a couple pointers to improve my lousy jump shot.

~ The Neon Chips and the Doughnuts ~

I'll never forget the time I walked past a blackjack table and noticed two new and amazing sights. A man was playing head's up against the dealer with bright, neon orange and neon yellow chips. The oranges were $10,000 chips and the yellows were $5000. I've handled a few $1000 chips in my day, but never a higher denomination. The player was surrounded by the dealer, the pit boss, the casino manager, and two security guards. If you had seen the way the man was dressed, and how his hair was combed, you'd think he was a school bus driver in a poor neighborhood. Besides having more than $300,000 in chips at the table, the man also had a dozen chocolate doughnuts on a platter along with a carafe of coffee. Apparently, it was a special VIP comp from the casino. I never got any doughnuts for playing. In fact, food was prohibited in the table games area. The pit boss and I were on a first name basis, and had been for over a year. I walked up close to the high stakes game, "Hey, Frank, I never get any doughnuts. What's up with that?" Frank sternly asked me to leave the area. The two-faced sunuvabitch acted like he didn't know me. For a second, I thought about doing a grab and dash at the table. Not for the neon-colored chips—for a doughnut.

~ The Hot Tub ~

At Harrah's in Atlantic City, I was relaxing in the indoor hotel hot tub near a poolside bar. I had a productive day at card-counting and was drinking a frozen margarita while taking a well-deserved soak. A couple joined me in the hot tub. I was forty years old at the time, and the couple looked to be about the same age. They were also drinking alcohol in the hot tub. All of us were violating one of the pool rules by doing so. The couple took turns asking me the usual hotel-like conversational questions, "Where are you from? What line of work are you in? How do you like the weather here?"

Since I won several hundred dollars that day, I didn't mind their banter. I was in a good mood. After another round of margaritas, however, the questions got personal.

"Are you married?" the woman asked.

I said "Yes." Nothing more.

The man looked around the pool area and continued, "Is your wife here? We'd like to meet her."

I started to get suspicious, but replied, "My wife is in Omaha."

"Oh," the woman said, "we were just wondering if you liked to party."

"Party?"

"You know, swing."

I fully understood what the man and woman meant, but I decided to play ignorant. "Swing? You mean like golf clubs?"

The man clarified, "No, like an open marriage. The lifestyle."

I couldn't play the game any longer. The couple freaked me out. I exited the hot tub quickly saying, "Allllrighty then. I need to be going." Just as quickly, I found a hotel towel and covered my body so as not to be ogled by either of them. I felt icky.

~ The Thursday Night Game ~

WE WILL NOT LIE, STEAL, OR CHEAT, NOR TOLERATE ANYONE AMONG US WHO DOES. These are the poignant, powerful words of the U.S. Air Force Academy honor code. While a cadet at the Academy, I lived by those words to the fullest. Fortunately, the honor code said nothing about gambling. I would have been in real trouble. During my second class and first class years (junior and senior years, for those of you who went to a normal college), a handful of us cadets in the Stalag 17 squadron (dorm) engaged in a weekly ritual that was in violation of Cadet Wing regulations (campus rules). We would play poker, three-card guts or blackjack late into the evening after 2300 hrs taps (11:00 p.m. curfew). Sometimes the game would go until 0600 hrs reveille announced with minutes by the fourth class doolies (6:00 a.m. rude wake-up call made by the freshman class which is a harmless institutionalized hazing ritual.) My roommate, Sam Powell, and a few other members of our breakfast table regulars, occasionally played in the game. Dan Tolly and I were the only seasoned gamblers who played each week, regardless of whether we had a big graded review (test) or class project (class project) due the next day. One Friday, after playing cards until 0600 hrs, I participated in a varsity golf tournament. My best friend at the Academy, Jeff Cliatt, teased me and stuck stuff in my nostrils and ears while I slept in the back of the van on the way to the golf course. I felt like crap all day, but still played a decent round without collapsing in exhaustion. When asked about my lethargy, I told my coach that I didn't get much sleep. Not a lie.

Dan and I had a mutual respect for each other at the card table in such a manner that we would never try to win big bucks off one another during the Thursday night game. Instead, we'd gang up on other players. One such victim was a guy nicknamed Twinkie. I honestly cannot remember his real name. We gave Twinkie his nickname because he looked like he ate a lot of Twinkies. The poor guy lost so much money one month, he was forced to pay off in merchandise from his room: video games, books, a $200 racquetball racquet, etc.

On March 10, 1988, Dan Tolly and I reluctantly quit playing in the weekly Thursday night game. Not because we got caught, or got in trouble, however. We quit because now if we got caught, we *could* get in big trouble. March 10th represented the last date that a cadet gambling violation and subsequent punishment would keep us from graduating. Meaning, if we were caught gambling before March 10th, we could serve our cadet-administered confinements (temporary suspension of all privileges) and still graduate on time. If caught gambling on or after March 10th, we would not be able to graduate with the rest of the Class of '88. Future leaders of the Air Force unite.

~ The VIP Invitation ~

When I first started gambling at the Sandia Casino in Albuquerque in early 2001, the facility resembled a beat up, big top circus tent just a few yards west of the frontage road off busy I-25. All the players anxiously awaited the completion date on construction of the full-service, upscale, resort casino complex and golf course located on the other side of the freeway. The new casino would be as large and amenable as anything in Las Vegas. As the Memorial Day weekend of the grand opening approached, I was tickled pink to receive a personal VIP invitation to visit the casino the day before the grand opening. Wow, it must be a special preview for forty or fifty of us preferred players.

On the day of the VIP event, I decided to dress sharply in a new pair of slacks, long-sleeve shirt, coat and tie. I wouldn't want to mingle with the small group of high rollers looking raggedy. As I approached the new casino, it was obvious that everyone in New Mexico and the adjoining states, plus many travelers from old Mexico, were invited to the special VIP preview. There were thousands and thousands of visitors. The VIP event must have been advertised to everyone and their grandmas. Most of players that night were dressed in worn-out shorts and t-shirts, just like a regular day at the casino. At the old circus tent casino, I could park and be at a nearby blackjack table within thirty seconds of leaving the car. At the new facility that first night, it took ten minutes to find a parking spot within a quarter mile of the building. They also changed their comp system in the new facility. It would now be much harder to earn a DVD player or other high-dollar comp. The good ol' days of the Shack were over for more reasons than one.

~ The Tall Stack of Chips ~

One Saturday night, I was seated at a blackjack table with two college guys and their dates. The two jocks were acting like big shots and the girls were giggling at everything the guys did. Typical casino date behavior. One of the guys had an impressive run of luck and won over $500. However, he did not have any greens chips. His entire bankroll was comprised of red, $5 chips. I know this for a fact, because the guy was piling the red chips in a single, huge stack that resembled a tower. Most players stack red piles $25, $50 or $100 at a time. This guy was showing off for his buddy and the two girls by building an obelisk all the way to the heavens with his $500+ red winnings. When he added another handful of reds to the stack, it started teetering slightly.

"You know," I remarked, "it will be really embarrassing when that stack tips over. Chips will fly off the table, some will go in the dealer's tray, others may land in ashtrays, and the game will get interrupted for several minutes."

The guy ignored my advice. Three hands later, while he attempted to add a few more chips to the tower, the stack tipped over, chips flew off the table, some went into the dealer's tray, others landed in ashtrays, and the game was interrupted for several minutes. I laughed my ass off, and unsuccessfully pleaded with the pit boss to get a copy of the eye-in-the-sky surveillance tape so we could put the video on YouTube.

~ The Paycheck ~

I've found numerous items while visually scouring casino floors:

car keys, pens, lighters, two wallets within a week of each other, a valid lotto ticket for an upcoming Powerball drawing, a $20 gift card to Bass Pro Shops, driver's licenses, other ID cards, and of course, chips, cash and coins in almost every possible denomination. I return items like wallets and ID cards. Stuff like the Bass Pro Shop card, the lottery ticket, and chips/cash became finder's keeper's. The strangest item that I found on the floor was a paycheck for one of the casino employees. The name on the check was "Joshua Owens." I knew one of the relatively new blackjack dealers was named "Josh." I reckoned that it was the same guy. Instead of simply returning the check to Josh, I decided to have some fun. I went to his table with only two red chips visibly in play. When I eventually lost all the chips, I asked if I could bet my paycheck. I unfolded the check and placed it on the betting circle. Josh said that I could not bet a personal check. I asked him to confirm with the pit boss. Josh picked up the check and called the boss over.

In the few seconds it took for the pit boss to arrive, Josh noticed the check was his and angrily exclaimed, "This guy's trying to cash my check!"

The pit boss, who had known me well, saw me smiling then smiled himself, "I think he is trying to give it back to you."

Josh looked at me red-faced and said "Thank you." His reaction was better than anything I ever expected as a result of the practical joke.

~ The Boardwalk Cats ~

The notice may no longer be posted, but at one time on the beach front in Atlantic City, there was a well-crafted sign explaining for visitors not to feed the Boardwalk cats. The minute I read the sign, I looked down and saw approximately twenty-five cats of all shapes, colors and sizes staring up at me from a dugout area beneath the Boardwalk immediately below the sign. It was like the cats purposely gathered under the sign at that moment for my benefit. It reminded me of a zoo exhibit.

This story has absolutely nothing to do with blackjack. I included it because it was fun to tell, and I have no plans to ever author a book on Atlantic City felines.

~ The Cleavage Cut Card ~

I was at a busy blackjack table on a busy Friday night at a busy casino. After waiting several minutes just to find a seat, I entered a game in which a half-drunk buxom woman and her date were having too good a time at the table. The woman was wearing a maroon cocktail dress that showed a generous amount of cleavage. All the men at the table, including the dealer and the pit boss naturally stole glances at the cleavage while the cards were played. Note to my wife: I wasn't looking—I was reading bible passages between hands.

After each new shuffle of the six-deck shoe, the dealer offered the yellow cut card to the woman. Every time she took the card, the woman would make a huge production about her "secret weapon" that would guarantee "good luck." She'd then take the cut card and rub it back and forth between her cleavage before inserting the card into the deck. All the men laughed and smirked like over-sexed idiots. Not me, honey, I was thinking of the unfinished chores on my to-do list at home.

The woman with the cleavage repeated this routine four or five times. During the course of those four or five shoes, however, I lost a couple hundred dollars. With each losing shoe, I gradually became annoyed by the cleavage cut card routine. The woman might have had nice headlights, but she slowed the game down tremendously with her half-drunken antics. Lori, I was *told* that she had nice headlights by the guy next to me. I didn't actually see 'em myself—I was busy thinking of the plight of the poor starving children in Africa. Just after the dealer shuffled another shoe, I quickly grabbed the cut card from the table before the cleavage woman could get it. I then pulled the yellow card under the table.

The dealer shouted, "What are you doing?"

I said, "I'm wiping the card on my crotch for luck. It is my secret weapon."

The pit boss intervened, "Sir, you can't do that."

"Why not? Chesty has been rubbing the card on her breasts for an hour. I believe you watched her do it three or four times." The pit boss was in a quandary. He couldn't say or do a damn thing to me for my disgusting crotch rub.

"Okay, players, let's keep the card off all body parts." Everyone at the table groaned. Then, they all gave me dirty looks. I absolutely loved it. The next shoe, coincidentally, was the best one of the night for me.

~ The Wheelchair ~

I am pleased that most casinos offer lower-than-normal blackjack tables to accommodate players in wheelchairs. The physically challenged now have the chance to lose money at the casino like the rest of us. Good for them. If no handicapped players are seated at the table, other players are usually free to occupy those seats. I like the shorter tables because they have normal chairs instead of high stools. One afternoon while I was playing blackjack at the lower table, a man in a wheelchair pulled into the spot next to mine. Shortly thereafter, there was foul odor in the air. The man in the wheelchair smelled like, well, there is no nice way to put it, he smelled like crap, literally. After a woman to the player's right complained about the smell, the man said, "That's me— I'm not in full control of my bowels." The woman and her husband couldn't take the smell. They left the table. I stayed, for two reasons. First, the guy was physically challenged. In my opinion, it would have been rude as hell to leave on account of the man's physical dysfunction, especially at a table specially designed for him. Second, the smell was not too much different than when I spent Memorial Day weekend vacations with my high school and college buddies in Fort Walton Beach, Florida, during one of the many beer-drinking, card-playing, chicken wing-eating and subsequent adolescent fart-fest marathons. The wheelchair guy and I had a lot of fun that day in between hands and shuffles. We made derogatory and judgmental comments about all the people who came to the table then quickly departed.

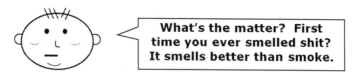

What's the matter? First time you ever smelled shit? It smells better than smoke.

~ The Case of Mistaken Identity ~

I was hanging around a casino lobby to see if I won a $1000 random drawing for that day. All the gamblers who swiped their player's club card on a machine during the last few hours were eligible for the promotion. When the casino employee drew the winner, he announced, "Let's see. Our thousand-dollar prize winner is Glen— wow, that's a unique last name." He then showed a slip of paper to a woman by his side. She chuckled considerably. It had to be me. Glen is not an ordinary first name, plus I had a really unique last name that could generate a giggle. As I started to walk to the podium to accept the prize, the announcer continued, "Glen Lamp. Our winner is Glen Lamp." *Glen Lamp?* That's not me. *What the hell?*

~ The Celebrity Sightings ~

If you are in a casino long enough, you'll invariably hear stories from the casino staff or other players regarding celebrity or famous athlete sightings. You'll hear comments like, "Tiger Woods was here last week—he tipped the dealer $100." Or, "Ben Affleck lost a bundle the other day." Or, "Paris Hilton grabbed two purple chips from the dealer's tray and nobody said a word." My personal celebrity sightings are rather tame. I spotted Larry King getting out of a Town Car on the Las Vegas strip and Marg Helgenberger in an Iowa casino near her hometown. I also spotted Daniel Stern with his kids at Disneyland, but that had nothing to do with casinos. The only famous person that I witnessed gambling was Allen Iverson when he played for the Philadelphia 76ers. Allen and a few of his friends were playing blackjack at the Trump Taj Mahal in Atlantic City. The NBA all-star was playing $50-$75 a hand. I watched for a few minutes with other gawkers. I was highly disappointed to see Allen stay on a fifteen against the dealer's nine. I lost respect for him that night. Sure, I could forgive Iverson if he missed a last-second jumper to tie a game, or if he only shot 15% from the floor during a bad game, or the fact that that Philly lost to Boston in the first round of the 2002 NBA playoffs. However, I cannot admire anyone, regardless of wealth or celebrity status, if they fail to follow Basic Strategy at blackjack.

~ The Bingo-Jack ~

Shortly after I turned twenty-one, my father took me to an Indian Reservation casino near Norman, Oklahoma which offered the game,

Bingo-Jack. At the time, card gambling was illegal in Oklahoma, but bingo gambling was not. Some entrepreneur had the brilliant idea to play blackjack using fifty-two ping-pong-like bingo balls annotated with the numbers corresponding to the values in a deck of cards. The dealer, who was not known as a "dealer," but something else like a "bingo-master" or "caller," distributed two balls to each player, and one ball for himself. Players then could ask for an additional ball or balls. The game mirrored blackjack rules and payouts perfectly, except the phrase. "Bingo Jack!" was enthusiastically announced each time a player had an ace ball and a ten ball. This happened in 1986. I don't know how long the Bingo-Jack casino was able to offer the game legally. Roughly twenty years later, a casino in the same area of Oklahoma skirted the law again by using playing cards to simulate the dice in the game of craps. Apparently, card gambling was allowed in that area, but not dice gambling. Crazy Okies.

~ The Wager with Harry Potter ~

I was once seated at third base when a new player entered the blackjack table. He looked exactly like Harry Potter—same glasses, same hair, and roughly the same age. Of course, the dealer asked for ID. After taking a driver's license from the player, the dealer placed it on the table to his right so the pit boss could verify Harry Potter's age. I glanced at the license and noticed that he was twenty-four years old. Ten minutes later, during a re-shuffle, another player commented to Harry Potter that he looked really young.

"I get that all the time. Nobody knows my real age."

I chimed in, "I bet you five dollars that I can guess your age with one try."

"You're on."

I pretended to make an educated guess, "Let's see, I won't say twenty-one. That is too obvious. Hmmm, I'm gonna guess, twenty-four."

Harry Potter responded, "Good job," and tossed me a red chip. I took the money without saying a word. All you J.K. Rowling fans probably think that I'm going to hell.

~ The $1500 Bowel Movement ~

The $1500 bowel movement can be easily explained without any messy detail. After winning exactly $1000 during a profitable morning at the blackjack table, I answered a pressing call of nature in the designated facilities of the casino hotel lobby. I didn't dare go potty in the restroom inside the riverboat casino. *Yuck*. While sitting in the confines of the men's room stall atop my porcelain perch, I happened upon a Best Buy flyer from the local Sunday newspaper. Lori and I were shopping recently for a complete home entertainment system including flat screen television, sound system and all the accessories. Best Buy had a sale on a particular home entertainment system that was $1499. Just a few days earlier, the price had been $350 greater. I decided to get the whole shebang on sale, and bring it home as a surprise for the family. I had $1000 in winnings, plus my original $500 bankroll. No other cash or credit cards. With tax, I figured the unit would cost approximately $1600. I needed another $100.

Instead of counting cards again, I contemplated winning the additional amount quickly by betting $100 on a single hand of blackjack. If I won, then I was gone. Hello Best Buy. If I lost, I would bet $200 on the next hand. Another loss, then I would bet $400. Another loss, then $800. All it would take is one win to regain all losses and get the extra $100 needed for my extravagant purchase. This system of wagering is most often called a "Martingale" strategy. I had precisely enough cash on hand to Martingale four hands with a $100 start. The chance of losing four hands in a row is roughly one in sixteen, or 6.25%. I decided to try it. Unlike my previous lack of self-discipline during the $1100 gyro and beer throw-up incident at Atlantic City, this was a calm, calculated decision to challenge the relatively low probability of losing four straight hands for a one-time benefit. As I finished my business in the men's room, and washed my hands, of course, I knew the risks of experiencing an untimely losing streak.

It happened—four quick, ugly, losing hands. And on the third hand, I had a twenty while the dealer drew to a twenty-one. Ladies and gentleman, I present to you, the $1500 Bowel Movement.

THE YEAR WITHOUT BLACKJACK

I am stuck without an ending to this book. All great books or movies have a memorable or unexpected ending. In *The Shawshank Redemption*, Andy successfully escapes from prison in an escape-from-prison movie without any of the other inmates, or even the movie audience, knowing it was an escape-from-prison movie. In *Anna Karenina*, by Tolstoy, Anna ends up throwing herself under a train. Very messy. In my favorite novel, *Catch-22*, Yossarian decides that it is impossible to run away from the bureaucratic military, so he promptly runs away from the bureaucratic military. At the end of the movie, *Citizen Kane*, everyone learns that "Rosebud" is a pair of red, Nike running shoes. Okay, I haven't actually seen that one. In *The Da Vinci Code*, you learn that the French chick is actually a descendant of Jesus Christ. Jesus Crites. How can I top that?

For this book to have a great ending, I suppose that I could exclaim that I'm rich beyond my wildest dreams because of my blackjack card-counting endeavors. Not true. I am ahead in winnings since January 2001, but definitely not rich. If you added my total winnings to the value of all comps, then divided by the sum of all the hours that I spent driving to the casino, searching for parking spots, waiting on shuffles, coloring up chips, watching the people around me, annoying the ones I didn't like, and of course, actually playing the game, then I probably made about $20 an hour. Certainly not Warren Buffet or Bill Gates money, but not minimum wage either. Plus, I earned these wages in a place where most everyone else experiences negative cash flow fluctuations.

I could also be like many other gambling book authors who teach you the basics in a game of chance, then direct you to other publications or websites promising you EXTRA-SUPER SECRETS TO WINNING YADA, YADA, YADA if you'll just pay anywhere from $19.99 to $79.99 for the next lesson. Nope. I wouldn't do that to you. If you have read this far, and have not tossed the book into a fireplace, I consider you one of my friends. Friends don't screw each other out of money. A friend might fart in a crowded room and secretly blame you to the other party guests, but a friend usually doesn't screw you out of money.

How about I end the book with an inspirational story proclaiming how I saw the light and now want to denounce the evils of gambling and preach the final message for you to avoid blackjack and all gambling in general? I can't. Some almighty entity created the person who invented the wonderful game of blackjack. That same almighty being also created a group of people who made it possible for blackjack to be played as a game of chance in casinos. Finally, he who is almighty and powerful gave humans the ability to enjoy the feeling of excitement that exists when you are sitting on the other side of the blackjack dealer. Who am I to cast stones on those divine creations? Blackjack gambling is fun as hell, especially when you have the edge over the house. I plan to play the rest of my life, plus the afterlife. My vision of heaven includes scantily clad angels shuffling the cards while Saint Peter is the pit boss keeping smokers off my table. The shoe always has a positive true count, and the dealer never gets twenty or a blackjack. There is always free water, and nobody cares if I take an extra bottle or twenty-four. My mother is winning at one of the Wheel-of-Fortune slot machines, the heavenly version, in which there is actually a reasonable chance of the wheel stopping at the top prize value. Finally, Barkley, my trusty black lab from years ago, is there guarding my mother from anyone trying to steal her slot machine.

Instead of those alternatives, I will end this book on blackjack by telling you about my life between July 2008 and June 2009, the year without blackjack.

I retired from the United States Air Force in June 2008 after twenty years of service. For my last three military assignments, approximately seven-and-a-half years worth, I was stationed at a base in relatively close proximity to a casino that offered table games—Albuquerque, then Omaha, then back to Albuquerque. As my beautiful wife, Lori, and I prepared for life after the Air Force, there was never a doubt where we would live, Colorado. The reason there had never been a doubt where we would live was simple. Lori said so. Good enough for me. Colorado it is, which meant no card-counting. Many of you may be thinking, "Wait a minute. Aren't there casinos with blackjack at Cripple Creek, Blackhawk and Central City, Colorado?" Yes there are, my astute readers, except at the time, the casinos in Colorado had a $5 limit on table games. How fruitless is that? To make money counting cards, a player must bet more when the cards are favorable. If you have not grasped this concept yet, please re-read the book starting at page one. Card-counting with a $5 limit is like going to an all-you-can eat buffet while on a strict diet. Card-counting with a $5 limit is like a blind man with no hands visiting the Playboy Mansion. Card-counting with a $5 limit is like voting for an independent political candidate in a U.S. election. Screw that. So, you probably solved the mystery: The author obviously didn't play blackjack for a year because he and his wife had moved to Colorado. End of story, end of book. Not hardly. The year without blackjack occurred while I was in Iraq.

In early summer of 2008, immediately following my retirement from active duty military, I accepted a government contractor position supporting Operation IRAQI FREEDOM at Task Force 134 Headquarters in Baghdad, Iraq. TF-134 was established to conduct detainee operations in Iraq after the Abu Ghraib incident in 2004. While there may have been a few misguided soldiers involved in the reported abuse and torture of Iraqi detainees, 99% of the soldiers involved in detainee ops at the time were doing proper work. TF-134 was established to guarantee the now high-visibility mission would be conducted by coalition forces offering the utmost amount of dignity and respect to all Iraqi and Third Country National detainees. Not coincidentally, more money and manpower went into detainee operations in Iraq after the Abu Ghraib incident. Part of the increased attention accounted for my contracted position as a research analyst tracking an enormous amount of data collected from detainees who were captured, detained or released since 2003. It was an honor and a pleasure for me to support the men and women of TF-134. The work was more challenging, more meaningful and more rewarding than anything that I had ever done in twenty years in the Air Force. Don't get me wrong, airmen, the Air Force had been great. I just never had such an important assignment in a theater of war during all my years wearing the blue uniform.

Back to the blackjack, or a lack thereof. Before arriving at Camp Victory, a few miles west of downtown Baghdad, my company briefed several important restrictions including GENERAL ORDER NUMBER ONE, signed by the Commanding General of Multi-National Corps, Iraq. In part, the general order, from the general, stated, in general, all service members, contractors and civilians were prohibited from venturing off post into the red zone without authorization. I had no problem with that. I soon learned that I would prefer to stay inside the 20-foot high concrete walls protecting Camp Victory from the local populace, some of whom were suicide bombers or other extremists placing roadside IEDs in an effort to harm or terrorize the Iraqi people and coalition forces.

The general order also prohibited the consumption of alcohol or possession of pornographic material. I had no problems with those provisions either. I figured I could always act drunk, like I did just for laughs while playing blackjack for three hours at the Borgata Casino in Atlantic City after a cocktail waitress accidentally spilled bourbon on my shirt. I acted the way that I smelled. Eventually, the pit boss asked me to leave since I had too much to drink. The no-porn clause would really be a piece of cake. I could picture my wife naked in hundreds of ways. I also had a good enough imagination to envision Scarlett Johannsson naked. Hmm, now that I think about it, I could picture my wife *and* Scarlet Johannsson together naked in the same vision.

Now for the big prohibition, the one that would be the hardest for which to comply. GENERAL ORDER NUMBER ONE prohibited any and all forms of gambling. What the—how could they? From the moment I accepted the position, I was looking forward to playing cards with the troops. In the television show, *M*A*S*H*, and during depictions of war movies throughout our nation's history, you always saw the sailors, grunts or pilots, usually bloody and dirty, playing cards when taking a break from the fighting. No blackjack? *The nerve.* What right did the federal government have to pay me gobs of money to do math in a war zone and then prohibit me from wagering it on games of chance? No blackjack for a year? I went to the casino 864 times since January 2001. I can't recall ever going a whole month without playing a few hands of my favorite game, much less an entire year. I didn't know what would happen.

Fortunately, or maybe I should say unfortunately, I had other things to worry about when my plane landed in Baghdad. The first morning in-country, I was scared shitless because I heard gunfire and explosions near my temporary quarters. The goofball from my company neglected to inform me that there was an Army firing range nearby and an area where controlled demolitions occurred periodically. Friendly coalition forces were making all the noise. That info would have been good to know before I wet my pants on day one. I was afraid to leave the confines of my trailer, because I thought Al Qaida was trying to infiltrate Camp Victory on the special occasion of my arrival.

I was also quickly educated on the 125 degree heat in the desert. You know that feeling when it is burning hot outside where you live, maybe 98 degrees in mid-July, and you enter a vehicle that has been in the sun all day? You know how the vinyl upholstery and steering wheel burn the hell out of your hand upon first touch? You know how the heat in the car interior is unbearable as you fumble for the keys and turn the air conditioner on full blast? You know how the air flows like a heater at first? You know how sweat builds up on your body from every pore while you wait for the AC to function? That is the way the summer heat in Baghdad felt all the time. And when you entered a vehicle that was in the sun all day in Baghdad—*holy shit!*

Then there was the sand and dust. Everywhere. When I checked into my permanent two-person containerized housing unit, a trailer called a "CHU" by most service members, I immediately saw a thick layer of dust, almost sand itself, on all surfaces. *My god, they haven't cleaned this trailer in months.*

"They just clean this CHU yesterday," explained the foreign billeting clerk, with less-than-perfect English.

"Where is the sink or bathroom?" I replied as I tried wiping the dust from my hand onto a clean surface. There wasn't a clean surface in sight.

"The latrine and shower stalls are one-hundred meters that way," the clerk pointed out the door and to the right, "near T-wall bunker. You want to go to bunker if you hear siren signaling incoming rocket or mortar attack."

"Thanks," I said in mock appreciation. "Where is the swimming pool?" I asked sarcastically, wondering if the clerk would get the joke.

Without the slightest inflection or smile he said, "The pool is near Al Faw Palace, but water evaporated from it a few weeks ago. It not open anymore." I hadn't expected a serious reply.

Outside the CHU, the man did more pointing. "Over there is dining hall and chapel. Laundry and linen exchange by office where you came in. Gym is down street. And, if you want to buy bootleg DVDs and CDs, bazaar is located near uniform store."

"Wait a minute," I inquired, "there is a place on post where I can buy bootleg DVDs?"

"Oh yeah," the foreign clerk stated, "They got *Batman Dark Knight*, new *Indiana Jones*, and movie where Seth Rogan and pothead is chasing all the pot."

"Isn't that illegal? *The Dark Knight* just came out last week."

"No, silly. You Uncle Sam. You the law."

So I could buy bootleg DVDs, with the government's full knowledge, but I couldn't play dollar blackjack with anyone? It didn't seem logical. I later learned there were many other illogical occurrences in the war zone, but those are stories for a more serious book.

Soon enough, I realized that playing cards in my free time would not be a huge priority while working at TF-134. What free time? Seventy- to eighty-hour work weeks with no day off were the norm. When I had downtime, I usually just wanted to eat or sleep. The first few weeks were absolutely miserable. I emailed or called Lori and the rest of my family when I could, but I was exhausted and lonely. To relieve some stress during the work day, I would sometimes feed the huge carp that swam in Lost Lake, the man-made body of water surrounding Saddam Hussein's old guest palace. I would also admire the doodling artwork of Sergeant Leif Olson, who I eventually chose to illustrate this literary masterpiece. Even with these distractions, my stressors were building each day. Things were the bleakest on the one-month anniversary of my arrival. After a 16-hour work day, and a relatively sleepless night due to a nearby rocket attack at midnight, I was greeted the following day with a mountain of work. The task given to me was almost identical to what I completed on the previous day, but the results were worthless because of the way the data collection and analysis was framed. Basically, my boss had screwed up, and directed me to repeat the 16-hour task just so he could save face.

"By the way, Wiggy, I need that brief in twelve hours."

I was peeved. I fumed all day in my cramped, dusty cubicle without a lunch break. Prior to finishing my day-long task, someone in the office noticed my sour mood and handed me a box that contained some goodies and the following letter:

> Dear Any Soldier,
>   My name is Megan. I am eleven years old. I am from Muncie, Indianna. I am very proud that you are a soldier fighting for the USA. I hope to be in the Navy one day. I want to sail around the world and see all kinds of places I have never been to. Are you afraid of getting hurt or killed? I hope you like the stuff my family bought you. My teacher Miss Grengarten said that everyone likes jellybeans! It was my idea to send the deck of cards. My dad brought them back from his trip to Las Vegas. I hope you like cards. Come home soon.
>
>   Sincerely,
>   Megan C.

The letter accompanied a care package addressed to our unit, one of a few to arrive from the states each week. As a contractor and one of the older gentlemen in the unit, I previously stepped aside and let the younger military personnel enjoy all the care packages. They deserved it. However, in my foul and cranky mood that day, I fully accepted the package because I didn't want my Army boss to have it. Since I took the goodies, I followed the rule that was established by the sergeant-major who managed the TF-134 Battledesk. I was free to enjoy the contents of the package as long as I answered any enclosed letter. I was extremely tired, but a deal was a deal. Just as I was about to compose my response to Megan, I received another ridiculous task that would keep me at work an extra three to four hours that night.

"Are you shittin' me?" I asked the corporal who handed me the assignment.

"I'm just the messenger, sir. Don't take it out on me." Ironically, he was wearing a holstered Baretta 9mm pistol with plenty of ammunition on the belt. I was an unarmed civilian barking at a soldier. A dumb move. I was way out of line, but that's how livid I was. To take a break and relieve some pent up anger and emotion, I wrote the letter. I think, maybe, perhaps, just a smidgen, I might have subconsciously taken out some of my frustrations on Megan. You decide. Here is the first draft of my response:

Dear Megan,

I received your package and letter, but I am not a soldier. I am a "government contractor." That is what the Department of Defense calls people they pay a lot of money to do things they don't want to do, like cook meals, repair roads, clean toilets, and make non-linear predictive analyses from qualitative unconstrained data. Stuff like that. Contractors are one of the reasons why the war in Iraq is so expensive. Contractors cost twice as much overseas. My company makes money on me, even though they do stupid things like neglecting to tell me that bombs and gunshots are used here for alarm clocks! Some other contractors in Iraq get paid for absolutely ridiculous jobs, like sweeping sand from sidewalks that will be sandy again the next day or raking dead palm leaves next to buildings that are partially destroyed by bombs. Do you understand? Me neither.

You want to be in the Navy? Holy crap! What the hell is wrong with you? Do you know that most of those ships in the Navy have one-hundred men for every woman on board? That is not good, Megan, unless you like that sort of thing.

I am sometimes afraid of getting hurt here, but not by the enemy. I am more afraid of all the Army guys who walk around with automatic weapons and a bad attitude. Some of them are mad at their Army sergeants or their wives and girlfriends at home. Some are mad because they have to wear god-awful helmets, flak vests and other uncomfortable equipment in the desert heat. I wear a short-sleeved golf shirt to work. Tee-hee!

I never thought I might be killed here, until you mentioned it. Why did you do that, Megan? Now I'm going to be worried for the rest of the war.

Now, I would like to comment on the things that you and your family sent. It was a nice gesture, but BEEF JERKY? Do you know that it is 125 degrees over here? Do you know anyone who wants to eat salty beef jerky when it is this hot? And the cookies, yuck! They weren't good, Megan. The fish wouldn't even eat 'em. Also, you sent jellybeans because your teacher said everyone likes them. Tell Miss Green-Goblin that jellybeans are fun when they aren't all stuck together in a hard, sticky, melted lump of colored candy. It looked like someone took a blow-torch to a beautiful glass rainbow. Heat again, Megan, think! Tell your teacher that she should give you better instruction, like how to spell "Indiana" and not to end a sentence with a preposition. Sentence structure, Megan. As for the playing cards, that was the last straw. Don't you know that I am a recovering blackjack addict who has been going through withdrawals? I can't gamble, Megan, and you just reminded me of that fact.

I will not be coming home anytime soon.
I just got here for cryin' out loud! Thanks
again, for one of your PRECIOUS reminders.
Please do not write again, Megan. You depress
me.

Signed,
Not just any soldier

P.S. Ask your dad if he brought back some
crabs from Vegas.

I did not send that version of the letter. As you may surmise from reading stories in this book, I can be mean or a jerk at times, but I'm not an uncaring idiot, especially after such a seriously thoughtful gesture. I scribbled the letter on a dusty legal pad as a joke to myself, just to relieve some stress. It worked, in a twisted, unexpected sort of way. I found a way to smile at the end of a tough day.

A few weeks later, I discovered the scribbled note to Megan along with her original letter to Any Soldier under a huge stack of papers in my office desk drawer. Providing a genuine response to her letter was a turning point for me in Iraq. After I overcame the initial shock of being in-country and working an extremely demanding job, everything in my life was put into the proper perspective. I was grateful and less selfish. I was working my ass off still, but I was well paid to support the government. Many real soldiers were working unbelievable hours and making a pittance, or were losing money because of the horrible economy at home. Living conditions were meager on Camp Victory, but the post was seen as an oasis to service members who were living in field conditions in other parts of the country. I was working in Baghdad on my own free will. Some soldiers were not. I was able to call or email my wife and kids on a regular basis. Some soldiers were unable to get close to a computer or phone for weeks at a time. Finally, and most importantly, I was healthy and secure. Some real soldiers in-country were obviously not. I was ashamed as I recalled the day that I scribbled the note.

It was many weeks overdue, but I finally provided a real response to Megan's letter:

Dear Megan,

Thank you ever so much for the letter and care package. I sincerely apologize for not writing back sooner.

All of the personnel in my unit are overjoyed anytime a person like you takes the time and effort to send something. You, Miss Grengarten, and your entire class are true patriots for thinking of us in Iraq.

It is great that you want to be in the Navy. I hope you sail all over the world. Maybe someday, you will receive goodies from a kind girl in Muncie, Indiana, or some other American town.

There are some dangers here, but all the soldiers, sailors, marines, airmen and civilians try to work together as a team to keep anyone from being harmed. With your thoughts and prayers, we will all be home soon.

Wow, the goodies you sent were great! You are extremely smart and thoughtful. When I put the cookies and jellybeans on a table near my office, you should have seen everyone try to get some! I especially loved the deck of playing cards that you sent. My all-time favorite game is blackjack. I used the cards for practice. Your gift made me realize how much fun it will be the next time I play the game. Win or lose, it will be worth the wait.

Thank you again.

Gratefully, and respectfully,
Glen W.

P.S. Always split aces and eights!

AUTHOR'S BIOGRAPHY

Glen Wiggy was born in Midwest City, Oklahoma, in 1966. His father is a retired golf professional. His mother, before her death in 2007, was a housewife and mother of six children. Glen graduated from the United States Air Force Academy—Class of '88, first class with refrigerators—and spent a 20-year career as an Air Force Officer. While on active-duty, he served as a Security Police Shift Commander, Assistant Professor of Mathematics, and Scientific Analyst. In June 2008, Glen retired from the Air Force and worked as a Department of Defense contractor at Task Force 134, Camp Victory, Baghdad, Iraq, performing research and analyses in support of Detainee Operations. In June 2009, he settled in the Colorado Springs area and currently works as a government civilian at United States Northern Command. He is also an online Statistics instructor with Embry-Riddle Aeronautical University. Glen is married with two children and three grandchildren. Besides card-counting at blackjack, his hobbies include golf and snow-skiing. He has a BS in Mathematics from the Air Force Academy, an MBA from Boston University, and an MS in Mathematics from the University of Arizona.

Glen Wiggy blogs on www.blackjackstories.com